ALSO BY JOAN DRUETT

NONFICTION

The Sailing Circle
(with Mary Anne Wallace)

Captain's Daughter, Coasterman's Wife

"She Was a Sister Sailor"
(editor)

Petticoat Whalers

Fulbright in New Zealand

Exotic Intruders

FICTION

Murder at the Brian Boru

A Promise of Gold

Abigail

Hen Frigates

WIVES OF MERCHANT CAPTAINS UNDER SAIL

Joan Druett

SIMON & SCHUSTER

SIMON & SCHUSTER
Rockefeller Center
1230 Avenue of the Americas
New York, NY 10020

Designed by Sam Potts

Manufactured in the United States of America

1   3   5   7   9   10   8   6   4   2

Library of Congress
Cataloging-in-Publication Data

Druett, Joan.
    Hen frigates : wives of merchant captains under sail /
Joan Druett.
        p.   cm.
    Includes bibliographical references (p.   –   ) and index.
    1. Ship captains' spouses. I. Title.
            VK139.D78   1998
        387.5'4044—dc21   97-37624
                                            CIP

ISBN 0-684-83968-7

ACKNOWLEDGMENTS

The compilation of a book of this scope inevitably relies on the cooperation and expertise of a great number of very helpful people. First, I must thank the Arts Council of New Zealand for a grant that allowed me to travel to New York for research; the William Steeple Davis Trust, Orient, Long Island, for a year-long Artist in Residence Grant; the Oysterponds Historical Society of Orient, which allowed me free range of their extremely rich archive over a period spanning more than three years; and the Three Village Historical Society of East Setauket, Long Island, for constant unstinting encouragement and support.

Many Long Island organizations and individuals were involved. I owe a particular debt to Michele Morrisson, and Beverly and Barbara Tyler, all three of whom amazed me constantly with their energy and enthusiasm. We owe thanks to Michele's family, too, for the many times they welcomed us into their home. Janette and Edmund Handley were gracious hosts, as were the Tylers, Frank and Fran Childs, Leighton Coleman III, Franklin Neal, Mary Coffee, and David Keegan. Ann Gill and her staff at the Cold Spring Harbor Whaling Museum provided invaluable expertise and much important material; and I must also thank Ina Katz, the Suffolk County Historical Society, Stephen and Susan Sanfilippo, the Society for Preservation of Long Island Antiquities, Cliff Benfield and the Horton Point Lighthouse Museum, Dwayne Early and the East End Maritime Museum at Greenport, the Southold Historical Society, Natalie Naylor, Margaret Olness, Alice Ross, Phyllis Dillon, and Dorothy Zaykowski, along with members and staff of the Sag Harbor Historical Society and the John Jermain Library. The Rowland Randall family have been unfailingly generous with the Mary Rowland material, while Carol Collins provided much insight into Ettabel Raynor. I am particularly grateful, too, to Thomas Kuehhas and the Oyster Bay Historical Society, for introducing me to Mrs. Dorothy Weeks Buck, the inheritor of the Alice Howland Delano journal. It was a pleasure to meet Henry Gardiner, the holder of a remarkable sampler that his ancestor, Polly Gardiner, embroidered on the way to the Pacific in 1827. One of the great pleasures of researching history is the charming descendants who so readily become friends, and in this respect Audrey and Bill Hauck deserve a special mention. I am also greatly indebted to James N. Cawse, who has been so helpful and generous with family papers. In respect to the Mary Ellen Bartlett diaries, I am indebted to Everett White. In Orient, there were too many friends to count, but I must not forget Charles and Jean Leety, Don and Mina Merle Van Cleef, Donald Boerum, Diana Latham, Anne MacKay, Freddie Wachsberger, Sylvia Newman, Elinor and Ralph Williams, Mickie McCormic, Charlotte Hanson, W. Peter Prestcott, Robert Schaefer, and last but certainly not least, John and Nene Dorman and "Sis."

In New York City, the staff of the South Street Seaport Museum and the New York Public Library were unfailingly helpful. I particularly thank Norman Brouwer, Irene Meisel, and Madeline Rogers of the South Street Seaport Museum for their support. In the Bronx, at the library of the Maritime College at Fort Schuyler, Jane Fitzpatrick and Richard Corson provided friendly support both on and off the Internet.

In Connecticut, it was the usual great pleasure to research at the G. W. Blunt White Library. I thank Paul O'Pecko, Douglas Stein and their staffs, Kelly Drake in particular, and also Joe Gribbons, Connie Stein, Andrew German, and Dede Wirth. I also owe thanks to Philip Budlong, Peggy Tate Smith, and Stuart Parnes. Bowen Briggs, Jr., has been extremely helpful in regard to his ancestor, Sarah Morgan, and in this regard I also owe thanks to Anna Peebler of the Rosenberg Library, Galveston, Texas. At the Maritime Center at Norwalk, it was a pleasure to meet J. Peter Marnane and his staff, Pat Lynch in particular. In Lebanon, Alicia Wayland has tirelessly pursued the story of

Sarah Gray of Liberty Hill, Connecticut. In this respect, I must thank Bill and Sandy Kotrba, too.

In Rhode Island, Richard Stattler, Manuscripts Curator of the Rhode Island Historical Society, was enthusiastic and helpful throughout my research into the Congdon family. Philip Weimerskirch, Special Collections Librarian at the Providence Public Library, was courteous and interested, too. As usual, I am indebted to Dr. Stuart Frank, director of The Kendall Whaling Museum. I also thank Benjamin Trask, librarian at the Mariners' Museum, Newport News, Virginia, and Peter Blodgett, curator of Western Manuscripts at the Huntington Library, San Marino, California, for his helpfulness concerning the Charlotte Babcock reminiscences. I am also indebted to Irene Stachura, reference librarian at the San Francisco Maritime National Park, for her helpfulness and efficiency in fielding my requests for illustrations.

I owe gratitude to Elizabeth Heard and her son David for their generosity with the Fidelia Heard journal, and also to Helen Sewall in regard to the Kate Thomson diary. In Edgartown, Martha's Vineyard, Catherine Mayhew and her husband, Donald, along with Art Railton and Jill Bouck, were hospitable and helpful. At the Peabody Essex Museum, John Koza, Jane Ward, and Kathy Flynne were all obliging as well as knowledgeable, and I must also thank Ann Brengle, Judith Downey, and Judith Lund of the Old Dartmouth Historical Society–New Bedford Whaling Museum, along with Susan Lamm, and Bob and Maura Saltmarsh.

In Maine, Nathan Lipfert of the Bath Maritime Museum has been unfailingly enthusiastic, knowledgeable, and supportive. Researching at the Penobscot Marine Museum in Scarsport has been the usual delight, and I thank Renny Stackpole, Sam Shogren, John Arrison, and Paige Lilly in particular. It was a pleasure to meet John Battick at last. I also thank Elsie Balano for permission to quote from Dorothea Balano's diaries, as I do Everett White, for permission to quote from Mary Ellen Bartlett's journal.

Scrimshander Robert Weiss was generous enough to allow me use of slides of his artwork. By mail and on the Internet, Mary Molloy, Klaus Barthelmess, Lisa Norling, Catherine Petroski, Joan Stoddard, Morgiana Halley, and Mary Anne Wallace have provided expertise and insight. It is a privilege to belong to the maritime history Internet list, the members of which are unfailingly helpful and knowledgeable. Special mention should be given to Stan Crapo, Edwin King, Martin Evans, Janet West, Robert Schwemmer, Dan Wilson, Honore Forster, John Harland, Trevor Kenchington, John Berg, Lars Bruzelius, Maurice Smith, Walter Lewis, and the Marine Museum of the Great Lakes at Kingston, Ontario.

ACKNOWLEDGMENTS

Further afield, I thank New Zealand seafarer Sally Fodie for introducing me to the Mary Jarvis Robinson reminiscences, and Wilfred Robinson for allowing me to use them; and yet again I thank Honore Forster, of Canberra, Australia, for her helpfulness and interest, particularly in researching medical history. I am greatly indebted to Myrtle Anderson-Smith and the Aberdeen University Library for rapid last-minute assistance with the Isabel Duncan manuscripts.

This list could not possibly be complete without acknowledgment of my great debt to my hardworking agent, Laura Langlie, and the unflagging energy and enthusiasm of my editor at Simon & Schuster, Denise Roy. And none of it would have been possible without the support and tolerance of the artist whose illustrations appear in this book: for the tenth time, I thank my husband, Ron.

EDITORIAL NOTE

When I transcribed the journals and letters that form the database for this account, my aim was to convey a general picture of the lifestyles these women and girls led at sea. Consequently, there has been some standardization applied to the words I have quoted. While most women did not underline the names of ships, and others enclosed them in quotation marks, I have italicized them all. The spelling of place names, ship names, and surnames of people has been corrected to avoid confusion, though the misspelling of ordinary words has been left uncorrected, except where it would be deceptive. Similarly, derogatory terms such as "Chinaman" have been left, as they were not politically incorrect in the women's own time. Punctuation, on the other hand, has been revised wherever the original might lead to misunderstanding, for it was common for the women to punctuate at whim, or not bother with punctuation at all. Where the women underlined for emphasis, I have retained the underlining, in preference to italics. Scholars will be interested in the comprehensive list of journals, letter collections, diaries, memoranda, and reminiscent accounts that is appended to the text.

CONTENTS

INTRODUCTION

*H*istory, I often think, is like a tap on the shoulder. This story of what it was like to be a captain's wife or daughter at sea is eloquent evidence of this, for the writing involved a whole series of nudges from the past. The research for *Hen Frigates* was an ever-evolving process, which included the discovery of a long-hidden nineteenth-century gravestone, a wedding portrait that returned home, and diaries hidden in an attic.

Like many a good yarn, this one begins with a discovery made on a tropical isle. The year was 1984. My husband, Ron, and I were cycling around the island of Rarotonga, one of the Cook Islands scattered across Polynesia in the South Pacific. Rarotonga is not a large island, as can be judged by the fact that it takes just two hours to ride completely around it, but it is definitely beautiful. In the middle is a tall, green-clothed mountain, and plantations of oranges, pawpaw, and avocado trees sweep down the slopes to the narrow, potholed road that rims the island beside the sea. On the other side of the road there is a strand of coral rubble where straggly mallows and great Wellingtonia trees

15

grow, surrounded by thick weeds. And, beyond the trees, white sand rakes down to the turquoise lagoon, the reef, and the sparkling blue sea.

We arrived at a certain place on the beach that is known as Ngatangiia at noon. It was very hot, and we expected it to be deserted, but to our surprise a young man was working away in the littoral rubble, hacking away at the weeds. It seemed such a pointless task that we became curious. Why was he working so hard to clear land that would never produce a crop? When we asked around, however, we found he did have a good reason. An ancestor ghost had come to him in a dream, and had commanded him to do this, because this bit of land was a graveyard.

Rarotonga. Photograph by Ron Druett.

This explanation was rather hard to credit, for Rarotongans do not neglect graves. As it turned out, the explanation was valid, however: this was a graveyard for outsiders. A long time ago, a sailing ship had called with a dead seaman on board, and the captain had asked the queen of the island—the *pa-ariki*—for permission to bury the boy on land, a burial at sea not being considered desirable back then.

Mission house where Mary-Ann Sherman died. Photograph by Ron Druett.

The *ariki* thought deeply about it, for the rule was that only native Rarotongans could be buried on the island, but then she relented, and had this piece of ground set aside, as a burying place for foreigners. And so it came about that more ships called, and more outsiders were buried there, and so the graveyard had been maintained. Then the sailing ships had stopped coming, and the ground had been left neglected—until this young man had his dream.

Naturally, when the job was finished, we were anxious to investigate. We found nothing in the piles of stones and weeds, however, save for a few indecipherable chunks broken from ancient gravestones. Again, it was very hot. Over to one side, a huge tree was lying where it had been felled by a recent hurricane, its dying branches dabbling in the lagoon, its tangled roots reared up against the milky blue sky. Losing interest in searching the rubble, I wandered over to rest in the shade of the roots—and, in the hole where the roots had grown, I found a grave, exposed to the light of day for the first time in 140 years.

The stone was upright, and as tall as a man. It read:

TO
the Memory of
Mary-Ann, the
beloved wife of
Captn. A. D. Sherman
of the
American Whale
Ship Harrison
WHO
departed this life
January 5, 1850
Aged 24 Years

A woman on a whaleship! It seemed incredible. Instantly fascinated, I thought I would look up a book to learn more about this young woman who had made such a strange and fatal decision to go to sea. There was no book, however. I had to write it myself. It was a quest that led me to Australia, Britain, Hong Kong, and the Hawaiian Islands—and to the museums, libraries, and historical societies of Massachusetts, Maine, Virginia, Connecticut, Rhode Island, and New York.

Grave.
Photograph by Ron Druett.

The search for Mary-Ann Sherman was by no means easy. Illegitimate by birth, dying on a far-off isle, she had left no official records. However, to my astonishment, I found that she was only one of a great host of wives who had accompanied their husbands on the long, arduous, dangerous voyages, women who called themselves "sister sailors." And so my book became a general account of their remarkable experiences, easily written because the whaling wives had virtually told their own story in the journals and letters they had left behind.

Meanwhile, a small historical society in East Setauket, Long Island, had been presented with a portrait. I remember well the day I first saw the painting, for

Detail of grave.
Photograph by Ron Druett.

I found the subject instantly intriguing, so much so that it seemed almost logical to find that she was another Mary. Her name was Mary Swift Jones, a dark-haired, pale-faced young woman who had married a scion of a local ship-owning family. In her portrait she is dressed plainly in black, her appearance relieved only by a few touches of white lace at her throat and wrists, and the small bunch of flowers in her hand. Tranquil, formal, and elegant, she seemed a most unlikely person to have lived at sea on a sailing ship, and on shore in Oriental ports. However, that is exactly what happened. In 1858 Mary boarded the China-trade bark *Mary & Louisa* with her husband, the captain, and over the next three years the port of Kanagawa (now Yokohama) became almost as familiar to her as the village at home. And while she was away she wrote letters—letters that have survived.

Here again was inspiration. Would it be possible to research and write a general account of captains' wives on merchant vessels, by allowing them to tell their own stories through their journals, reminiscences, and letters? They had traveled on all kinds of craft, ranging from the schooners and brigs that plied the coasts, to clippers, downeasters, and windjammers in the blue-water trades, so that the book would have to be as far-reaching as many of their voyages. It would have to begin with those who sailed on voyages that were much more prosaic than Mary Swift Jones's, though, for that is where women's seafaring started.

In early settlements, an extensive coastal trade grew out of necessity. Wherever roads were primitive and communication difficult, men, women, and older children loaded the produce of their orchards and farms into small sloops and schooners, and sailed off to market. When their own crops had been disposed of, they bought cargoes on speculation, or carried goods for a fee. There were thousands of these humble craft, far outnumbering the glamorous ocean-going packets, clippers, windjammers, and downeasters, like the bark that Mary Swift Jones sailed upon, that most modern people picture when they think of the Age of Sail. In effect, the little coasters were floating trucks, for they freighted necessary but prosaic cargoes such as stone, salt, coal, clay, sugar, manufactured goods, cotton, and barrel staves from producer to consumer, as well as the harvests of both sea and land. Every waterside hamlet had its pier, complete with a shed where cargoes could be stored, and most had a small shipyard as well.

And it was only logical that the wives and daughters of the men who sailed this multitude of water-borne drays should sail along with them, cooking and cleaning, dealing in butter, eggs,

Portrait of Mary Swift Jones.
Three Village Historical Society.

preserves, rendered lard, and salted meat, just as they would at home or on the farm. However, I had no luck at all in finding anything that had been written by the women who sailed along on these short journeys, not even a daybook, or financial account of goods sold and deals made, even though I knew they had done it. I could only assume that this kind of voyaging was such an everyday matter, and the accounts so brief and matter-of-fact, that no one had bothered to keep records.

And that was when history tapped me on the shoulder again. My husband, Ron, a maritime artist, was offered a long-term residency by the William Steeple Davis Trust in Orient, and so we came to Long Island to live.

William Steeple Davis, only son of a couple named Charles and Carrie Davis, and only grandson of Captain William Smith Hubbard and the village midwife, Jane Hubbard, was a noted maritime artist and pioneer photographer who bequeathed the Hubbard-Davis cottage to a trust for the use of artists, a legacy that included a stock of family papers. With this were four diaries kept by Carrie Hubbard Davis, the artist's mother. As a maritime historian, I did not expect to be more than personally interested when I started to peruse those journals. In fact, I began to read them out of idle curiosity, because I was living in the writer's house, and continued only because of the fascinating glimpse they afforded me into the life of a young woman in a rural Long Island hamlet in the period between 1870 and 1884.

And then, one day, while I was idly perusing the third of Carrie's diaries, it came as an almost unbelievable shock to read the entry for a Friday in

March, in the year 1878. There, in her small neat script, Carrie had penned the matter-of-fact message, "I started with Charlie and pa on a Trip in the vessel."

The vessel! Here, for the first time in more than a decade of researching nineteenth-century seafaring women, firsthand documentation of a woman's coasting lay before me. As an experience, it was perfectly magical.

It was like a marvelous and most unexpected gift. Not only had this intriguing young woman lived in the same house as I did, but she was a sister sailor, too. Carrie's voyages might have been short, unexciting ones, but she had a lot in common with the women who sailed on bigger ships, to much more far-off seas. Like Mary Swift Jones, she knew the slap of spray on her face, and the problems of getting around on a tossing deck. Carrie knew the problems of freights and markets, too, and had friends in another port, even if it was just Norwich, Connecticut, on the far side of Long Island Sound. The schooner she sailed upon, the *Jacob S. Ellis,* was only rated at twelve tons, more than thirty times smaller than the bark *Mary & Louisa,* but it was just as much part of the family business—more so, in fact, for the family share in the schooner had been purchased by Carrie's mother, Jane Culver Hubbard, the village midwife and layer-out of the dead. The East End of Long Island was one of the few places in the world at that time where women could not only own property, but could bequeath it to their daughters.

Carrie Davis.
William Steeple Davis Trust.

Charlie Davis.
William Steeple Davis Trust.

Jane Hubbard, shipowner and village midwife.
William Steeple Davis Trust.

Schooners at Orient Wharf.
Etching by William Steeple Davis.

Now, at last, I had to hand the whole experience of the captains' wives and daughters who went to sea, whatever the range or trade of the ships on which they sailed. Somehow, it was no surprise to find that the same society that owned Mary Swift Jones's legacy of seafaring had catalogued several lengthy, poetically written journals and many letters penned by yet another Mary—Mary Satterly, also of Setauket, who married Captain Henry Rowland in the fall of 1852 and accompanied him to sea for the whole of her twenty-four-year marriage.

Like Carrie Davis, Mary Rowland sailed in the coasting trade, sailing first in the schooner *Stephen H. Townsend.* Unlike Carrie, however, she moved on into much bigger ships, as her husband's voyages took him much farther afield in search of cargoes and profit. "Remarks On board Brig *Thomas W. Rowland,* H. L. Rowland Master," begins the first diary in the collection, which recounts Mary Rowland's fourth voyage to sea. The date of that first entry was October 16, 1855, and the brig was leaving New York for Buenos Aires, "with a full Cargo of Merchandise and Lumber." With Mary and her husband were their two-year-old daughter, Mary Emma, and an infant, Henrietta. "So ends this day and all is well," wrote Mary. "Baby is three weeks old and grows finely at sea," she serenely noted two days later.

Voyaging under these circumstances seems a most remarkable challenge, but Mary was not alone, being only one of a great multitude of women who took up the same strange existence in the blue-water trade, surviving storms, visiting exotic ports, giving birth at sea, raising children on shipboard, and socializing with other wives at scarce intervals. Yet these were ordinary, conservative, middle-class women, certainly not rebels or adventurers. Many came from coastal communities with a tradition of seafaring, which could have made the choice of sailing easier. It is striking how often the women were related to each other by birth or marriage, too. Nevertheless, seafaring was an extraordinary proposition for a nineteenth-century lady—and "lady" was the word of preference when the captains' wives were describing themselves or their friends. Even their costume was against them. For most of the century it took ten yards to make a skirt, and every decent woman wore a corset, while crinolines, hoops, and bustles came in and out of fashion, and vast amounts of time were devoted to the trimming of a bonnet.

And, just like the whaling wives, these seafarers on deepwater merchant ships liked "to scratch a few lines" when time hung heavily on their hands, so that a fund of journals, diaries, letters, and memoirs speak for the voyagers, in a testimony to endurance and courage. While the great majority of these documents have been lost, hundreds have survived, telling tales so personal and immediate that we can almost feel for ourselves the wide spectrum of emotions—fear, pain, anger, love, and heartbreak—experienced by the writers. And so their stories can be fully told, described in the words that they chose.

Mary Satterly Rowland.
Three Village Historical Society.

Captain Henry Rowland.
Three Village Historical Society.

CHAPTER ONE

The Honeymooners

As Henry says, we have only one life to live, and he cannot be at home, and it is very hard for us to be separated so much, and a very unpleasant way of spending our lives when one is thousands of miles away.

—*Mary Rowland, January 1873*

On October 3, 1906, twenty-year-old Georgia Maria Gilkey of Searsport, Maine, was married in her graduation dress. There had been no time to make a wedding gown, for the bridegroom was a seaman. Captain Phineas Banning Blanchard had proposed to her during one of his fleeting trips home, and one week later they were married. Georgia felt no doubts about the headlong courtship. As she reminisced later, when Banning had taken her out sleighing the sled had capsized, dumping them both in the snow. And that, according to a local old wives' tale, was a sure sign they were to be wed. So Georgia married her captain in her graduation gown, carrying a bouquet of pink carnations. And, after a hasty buffet luncheon, the newlyweds took the train to Philadelphia, to embark on the great square-rigger *Bangalore* for a honeymoon voyage around Cape Horn.

When the train arrived in Philadelphia the ship was ready, loaded with coal for San Francisco. Banning, a prudent and thrifty skipper, bought Georgia a sextant so she could help to navigate the 1,700-ton vessel, and then they took their departure, off on their wedding trip with twenty seamen, a carpenter, a cook, a steward, a cabin boy, two mates, and a bosun, Georgia being the only woman on board.

It was by no means unusual for a bride to be eager to try life at sea. Many, like Georgia, were adventurous, delighted with the prospect of sailing off to exotic ports. Because the captain was expected to invest a substantial sum of his own money in the ship, most young shipmasters could not afford to buy a house on land, and returning home to live with relatives might not seem a pleasant option, after the excitement of the wedding. There were graver reasons, too. Both on land and at sea, good health was a precarious blessing, and letters took so long to get about that many ships arrived home before wives found out that they were widows, or husbands learned that wives had passed away. Visiting Melbourne, Australia, in December 1853, Fidelia Heard of the *Oriental* met a "Mr. Cutler of Boston" who had just learned that one of his chil-

Georgia Gilkey Blanchard.
Penobscot Marine Museum.

Captain P. Banning Blanchard.
Penobscot Marine Museum.

Ship Bangalore.
Artist: Ron Druett.

dren had died, but his correspondent had neglected to tell him which one.

Georgia had yet another reason to sail, one which she shared with a great many other young women from the coasts of Maine. She knew exactly what lay ahead of her, for her father was a ship captain, and voyaging was a family business. "It seemed like old times being on board a vessel again," she reminisced. "I spent most of my youth at sea with my parents, brothers, and sister. Banning grew up at sea, too, and he was a captain before he was twenty."

A much less seasoned bride was twenty-year-old Alice Howland of New Bedford, who married Captain Joseph C. Delano on December 21, 1826, and went to sea with him on the Black Ball packet *Columbia* in January 1827. In contrast to Georgia's hasty and almost impromptu ceremony, Alice's wedding must have been a glittering affair, for Alice was the daughter and granddaughter of shipowners. And, by the standards of the time, Captain Joseph Delano was quite a social catch, for this was at the peak of "packet fever."

Compared to the humble, sturdy craft that carried common goods to wherever there might be a market, the packets (called thus because of the canvas or leather "packets" of mail they carried) were the "queens" of the fleets that crowded the major ports, sailing to stated destinations at stated times, carrying passengers and expensive cargoes as well as that all-important mail. The ships were designed for speed, as well as for the strength that was necessary for breasting rugged Atlantic seas, and their captains were strong, spirited, ambitious men, especially chosen for the challenge of sailing their ships to a timetable—quite a proposition in a sail-driven ship, at the mercy of the winds.

Up until January 5, 1818, when the packet *James Munroe* left the port of New York exactly as advertised despite a lashing snowstorm, ships had been unfettered by schedules, sailing only when the weather was cooperative. Unless passengers bought their tickets at the last moment, when the ships were on the verge of departure, they were given only a vague idea of when they would be expected to take over their berths. It was a case of waiting around in some hotel until the ship's agent sent a message to say that the vessel was ready. The birth of "square-riggers on schedule" was heralded in 1816, when four New York merchants, led by the Quaker Jeremiah Thompson, pooled their resources and four of their ships, and founded the Black Ball Line, promising to the public that those ships would sail to a timetable.

"LINE OF AMERICAN PACKETS BETWEEN NEW YORK AND LIVERPOOL," read a headline in the New York papers.

> *In order to furnish frequent and regular conveyance for GOODS and PASSENGERS, the subscribers have undertaken to establish a line of vessels between NEW YORK and LIVERPOOL, on a certain day of every month of the year. One shall sail from New York on the fifth and one from Liverpool on the first of every month. These ships have all been built in New York of the very best materials. They are remarkably fast sailers and their accommodations for passengers are uncommonly extensive and comfortable.*

And, what's more, speed was guaranteed. The *James Munroe* made the crossing to Liverpool in twenty-eight days, a time that was soon bettered by her sister ships. The packets sailed in fair weather or foul, with or without a full cargo, and every trip was an attempt to break a record. Between five and six weeks had been the usual time to cross the Atlantic. The packets now did the easterly trip in seventeen or eighteen days and made the difficult westerly passage in three weeks.

Legends grew of ships carrying sail until the canvas ripped to flying ribbons, of waves foaming hungrily over the leeward rail as the steeply heeled ships raced ever onward, day after day and night after night. Ralph Waldo Emerson wrote of a terrifying passage where the captain put up his cot in a locker on the quarterdeck, to make certain that the nervous first officer wouldn't order the crew to take in sail while he was asleep. The ships were manned by so-called packet rats—for the most part Liverpool Irishmen, who were magnificent seamen but among the wildest afloat. Any sign of weakness betrayed by the captain led to trouble—sometimes even murder—and so the commanders were a tough and virile breed of men, romantic enough to be beloved by the public. Traveling by packet became all the rage, and of all the packet companies the first—the Black Ball Line—was the most famous. The flamboyantly reckless captains of these ships were equally well-known, their names spoken in the same breath as the names of the legendary vessels they commanded. They were the social lions of the day, discussed in parlors and papers with the same feverish attention that film stars inspire now.

According to the journal nineteen-year-old Alice Howland Delano kept on that wedding trip, however, she felt a trifle doubtful about the "social catch" she had married. "Last eve heard a dissertation on the qualities necessary for a married lady," she noted on the first Sunday of the passage, "but did not profit much thereby." Rereading Byron's "Prisoner of Chillon" suited her mood much better, she said. "Only five hours' sleep last night," she wrote, and worried that she was turning into an owl.

Alice Howland Delano.
Oyster Bay Historical Society.

Captain Joseph Delano.
Oyster Bay Historical Society.

Like Captain Banning Blanchard eighty years later, Captain Joseph Delano had put his wife to work. Alice's job did not involve lessons in navigation, however, having much more to do with the parlor than the sea. The packet ship commanders not only had to drive the ship like the very devil, but were expected to charm gentlemen, tycoons, dowagers, and debutantes in the after cabin as well—and so, for a man like Captain Joseph Delano, a personable, fashionable wife could prove very useful.

Thus Alice found herself playing hostess to the cabin passengers, each of whom had paid about two hundred dollars for a berth in a stateroom (the shipboard name for a bedroom), inclusive of food and wine. There were hazards aplenty. On the first reasonable day she and Miss B.—"two of the most courageous ladies ever known"—led the way for a promenade on deck, "but alas although protected by our squires we fell." Miss B. and Mr. Lowe tumbled over the hen coop while Alice herself skidded under it, in what must have been a spectacular flying of skirts.

Mr. Lowe, who had "delicate health—poor appetite—can only eat one chicken for dinner," needed a great deal of soothing attention, while all the time Alice fended off the amorous advances of a lovelorn German, Mr. Shettler. Poor man, he "wanted a wife so much," and yet there were two single ladies on board. "I have not been able to decide as yet whether he is a fool or insane," mused Alice.

The accommodations, as can be expected from the cost of passage, were good. There were eight staterooms on either side of the main cabin, each with two berths, one above the other. Oddly, there was no ladder leading to the upper bunk, where it seems that Alice slept, for she wrote that she was "in nightly expectation of breaking my neck or one of my precious legs." Otherwise, each

Black Ball packet passing the Battery, 1829. From Harper's Magazine.

stateroom was supplied with a chest with two drawers and two shelves—which also served as a washstand, for it held a pitcher and washbasin—along with a looking glass and that "unmentionable" item, a commode.

The main cabin was furnished with "a table thirty feet long with seats on either side," all firmly screwed to the floor. Overhead was a skylight, from which hung an ornate glass lantern, a barometer, and two "casters"—or racks "well furnished" with decanters, bottles, and glasses. A sofa was set at the sternward end of the cabin, right under the companionway stairs, "so that one has to be very cautious how they hold their head." Otherwise, the passengers could sit in the roundhouse on the afterdeck—"but I do not know why it is called so, it is square."

The major part of the day was spent at the table, eating and drinking being the most time-consuming occupation on board. As Alice noted, it was fortunate that she had a "famous appetite," for the menu was remarkably lavish. Breakfast was at nine, and consisted of tea, coffee, bread, broiled fish, and meat. Then at noon the table was set for "tiffin," a buffet of cold beef, ship's biscuit, oysters, and cheese, all of which was washed down with copious drafts of porter. According to Alice this drink, a dark-brown bitter beer, was "a fine thing on board ship," and certainly large amounts of it were drunk by both sexes.

At four in the afternoon, when the passengers surely had not had enough time to get hungry again, the table was laid for dinner. This came in a succession of four courses. Soup arrived first, then roast meat and boiled fowl, followed by puddings, tarts, fritters, and finally apples, nuts, and raisins, all accompanied with appropriate wines. This repast could scarcely have been digested before a "tea" of fresh bread, butter, cheese, cold meat, and cake was served at half past six. "Now, I suppose all reasonable people will think we have eat & drank enough for one day," wrote Alice.

> *But no, at ten we call for our punch, biscuit, cheese and often meat. I*
> *think we are much like the old woman and what do you think*
> *She lived upon nothing but victuals and drink*
> *Victuals and drink were the chief of her diet*
> *And yet the old woman could never be quiet.*

Times were merry enough when the whiskey punch went round, for Miss B. might sing a few songs, and Mr. L. might favor them all with a tune on the flute. But passengers were a difficult lot to entertain, on the whole. "I know not a more idle set," wrote Alice. "Half the time is passed in lolling on the sofa, reading a little, looking on the chart, playing cards, &c. All of it amounts to a figure nine with a tail cut off," she decided—which of course added up to a big fat zero.

It is a pity that Cornelia Marshall Peabody, the bride of another packet ship captain, did not sail until 1855, well after Alice's time (Alice Howland Delano died in childbirth in 1834), for she and Alice would have had a great deal in common, even though they were markedly different in both temperament and character. "Connie" Marshall married Captain Enoch Wood Peabody of the packet ship *Neptune* on April 26, 1855, and sailed from New York the first week of May. Within days one of the passengers dropped dead, "poor man, died in the second cabin, left a wife and children." Then, just two days from Liverpool, the ship was overtaken by a tempest.

"Weather continues very bad. Enoch is hard at work. Scarcely had a chance to speak to me during the entire day," wrote Connie nervously on May 18. "How anxious the Captain looks, is uttered in low sad tones by the passengers." That night she sat alone and wakeful in the stateroom, listening to the roar of the sea, and heard a sudden cry of, "Breakers ahead! Hard down the helm!" from the deck.

"That fearful sound, never shall I forget it," she agitated; "and amidst the noise I heard my poor husband's voice in such tones as never before." The crisis was so immediate that Connie shifted to the present tense. "He enters the Cabin, how pale his cheek, my heart seems almost bursting. Oh, that he would but speak to me. His look is almost wild," she penned, in a style that surely reflects the kind of purple prose she must have read.

Connie had put on her wrapper (a loose dressing gown) to get ready for bed. "Why, Connie, have you taken off your dress?" he asked. "Put on all your warmest clothing." Connie complied and then lay down. "I never closed my eyes," she wrote, "but listened to the steady tread of my almost exhausted husband. How I wished for power to relieve his care." Luckily, whatever help she could have given him was unnecessary, for "about two he came to bring me the glad news that we were safe in fifty fathoms of water." The *Neptune* docked thirty-six hours later, and Connie was able to write on a much more practical and everyday note that the "passengers look so strange in their go-ashore clothes."

What with sudden death and dire storm, Connie had not been able to devote much space to her fellow travelers, apart from recording their very understandable reverence of her husband—that all-powerful lord of the quarterdeck who could hopefully bring the ship through the worst the weather could throw at them. They must have been an amiable lot, however, for she was so obviously unprepared for the veritable menagerie of cabin passengers on the return voyage to New York. One arrived in the grip of delirium tremens, another had smallpox, and—worst of all—there was a German woman and her lover traveling together openly, without even pretending to be married!

Matters did not improve. The wine was served as freely as it had been on the *Columbia* thirty years earlier, but was still not enough for one lady passenger, who hung around the table until everyone else had gone, then poured the dregs from all the wineglasses into her own, which she drained. "The steward forthwith snatched up the bottle, fearing perhaps it might go the same way," wrote Connie, sighing another time that "I am sorry we have so disagreeable a set of people in the cabin." It proved a long passage of thirty-five days, and Connie was heartily relieved when they finally dropped anchor in New York. Back in Brooklyn with her family, she went straight to the public baths, to wash every last trace of the voyage away.

Another seafaring bride from Brooklyn was Emma Browne, who in the early 1870s was courted by two young Englishmen. These men were brothers. Thomas Cawse was captain of the tea clipper *John R. Worcester*, while brother James was only first mate, but Emma chose James, corresponding with him after he left despite the somewhat casual tone of his replies. "Having nothing much to do to employ my time" would herald the start of a letter that consisted mostly of seamanlike reports of the voyage, along with an apology for not writing before he sailed, "but was very busy to the last."

Emma, however, could read between the lines, discerning a devotion that is not apparent to the modern reader, for she kept up the correspondence for two years. It was not possible to marry him, for it was unusual for first mates to be allowed to take their wives on voyage, and he did not have a home on land. But as soon as she heard the news that James had got his first command, of the same *John R. Worcester* that his brother had commanded, Emma booked passage on a packet and traveled alone and unchaperoned to Liverpool to meet him.

This was a remarkable exploit for a woman of her time, particularly when there was no guarantee that James would be delighted to see her. Emma Browne, however, was a resourceful young lady. Much later, when her youngest daughter asked her what she would have done if she had found that James was not agreeable to marriage, Emma replied, "I had my return passage right here in my purse." As it happened, the round-trip fare was not necessary. James met her in Liverpool on June 20, 1876, and they were married on the twenty-third. Then, on August 12, she boarded the ship. "I came along in a little row boat with quite a number of men, bundles, and parcels of every discription, to get on board the *John R. Worcester*, which lay out a little way in the Mersey river, at eight o'clock in the evening, and climbed up the side of the ship by a rope ladder, like any man," she wrote with palpable pride. And so Emma sailed for Sydney and the Orient, on a honeymoon voyage that spanned more than three years.

Emma arrived back in England in October 1879, with a seven-week-old daughter named Maud in her arms. The baby had been delivered by her husband on September 8, two days from St. Helena, an island he undoubtedly would have preferred to have reached before the happy event. As it happened, all went "pretty well, thank God. James," Emma decided the day after the birth, "is perfectly mag. He is exceedingly kind, no one could act nicer, or more gently. He is a good <u>old man</u>."

It was no problem at all to agree to sail again. The *John R. Worcester* was a fine, comfortable vessel, and anyway there was no home for Emma in England. She was still sailing in 1891, when James was swept overboard in a storm. He fought his way back onto the ship, but with a lungful of water that gradually

Wedding photo of Captain James Cawse and Emma.
Courtesy James N. Cawse.

Tea clipper John R. Worcester.

killed him of some pulmonary disease at the age of forty-four, though Emma nursed him devotedly. When the ship arrived in port she moved her family of five children back to America, to be with her brothers. But in the meantime she had spent fifteen happy years in the constant company of her husband.

A particularly poignant honeymoon voyage was that of Bethia Sears of Cape Cod, who wrote the journal she kept on board the clipper *Wild Ranger* especially for her sisters. When she commenced it, on October 4, 1855, Bethia was nineteen years old, a bride of just four weeks, devoted to her twenty-two-year-old husband, Captain Elisha Sears. "This book which now lies before me with its pure and unspotted pages," she wrote, "I have designed for keeping a kind of journal solely for the benefit and perusal of you my dear sisters at home, who extracted a promise from me at parting that I would daily record something until my return to my native land, should that time ever arrive— God grant that it may."

She was very happy, walking the deck with Elisha, reading in the afternoons, taking off her shoes and stockings to paddle on deck when it rained, and playing the accordion. "It is true I am leading a lazy life," she confessed. Learning how to navigate was quite a challenge, and she did "wish I had someone to sit and sew with me," but she soon learned how to box the compass, and taught her husband how to cross-stitch. "Wife gets along better than I expected her to," wrote Elisha in Bethia's journal on November 4. "She has not vomited (excuse me) but four times since leaving port & we have had considerable heavy weather. She seems happy and contented and thinks she has taken the wisest plan and followed me to sea." As for himself, he was having a slow passage, and "if it was not for Wifey I should be sick."

They arrived in San Francisco—"a very hard-looking country"—on February 15, 1856, and sailed again on the twenty-seventh, "bound for Calcutta." There was some little excitement, for Elisha was detained on shore, and the pilot took the clipper out into the stream without the captain on board. "Judge of my situation," wrote Bethia; she was alone on board, "with only the mate and a parcel of drunken sailors." Unsurprisingly, she "was frightened to death"—but then, still worse, the "Pilot appeared, wild and rattle-headed, and sat in the forward cabin all the evening drinking and telling stories."

Meantime, his ship's affairs attended to, Elisha was penning a letter "to dear sister Eunice. I have not seen Wife for 5 long hours," he related. "I heard a few moments ago from her, she was anxious for me to come off, as she was lonesome. We have not been away from each other so long since I left Boston." The spell ashore had been an enjoyable one. They had "been to one Ball, twice to the theater, and to one or two late dinners. She can carry her part well anywhere," he declared with fond pride. "She says she is going to sea with me as long as I go—What do you think of that? She is without any exception the best female sailor I ever saw, could not do better."

In April, however, Bethia started throwing up everything she ate the moment she left the table. The reason for her constant sickness is veiled in Victorian reticence, but certain entries in her journal, along with more candid mentions in letters home, make it evident that she was pregnant. Arriving in Calcutta in June, she found that a Cape Cod acquaintance, Captain Edgar Lincoln, had just sailed, along with his wife. "She will be confined on her way home," she wrote to her parents on the eleventh, but, "it was said she went off with very good courage—You need fear nothing for me."

Going on shore to board while the ship discharged her cargo and loaded another provided some relief, so that she could go shopping for "a baby dress," but by the end of July, they were on their way back down the river, and the morning sickness returned with a vengeance. "I feel miserably," Bethia wrote on September 16. "I do not take anything as I know not what to try. Am very particular about my diet. Feel down-spirited and sad at times. Beautiful weather and fair wind but little of it and a terrible sea. Sails slatting awfully. . . ."

The ellipsis is hers, and ends the last entry in Bethia's journal, as if she had a premonition of what was to come. "My poor Wifey is dead and gone," agonized Elisha ten days later—

> *She asked me a few days before she left me to note in her journal how she and the ship were getting along. I told her to let it remain and when she got well to note in it herself, not thinking but what she would do*

so in a day or two, as soon as we got into fine weather. But alas! My poor little darling Wifey has left me alone . . . Poor Wifey is dead.

When last she used pen (Sept 16th) she felt quite unwell, sat on deck with me watching the ship in company, and reading. She had my old Pea Coat on, which made us all laugh when she came up, and for the next four days she kept about the same—lost no flesh or strength . . . but [on the 24th] she seemed very restless—much pain in her chest, and towards morning was quite out of her mind. I drew a blister on her stomach and used hot baths at her feet. In the morning of 25th no better but worse. At 8 she asked me to read the Lord's Prayer. I did so and never shall I forget how pleasant and fairly she pronounced the "Amen." She then kissed me and smiled . . .

At 9½ she looked glaringly at me and said, how dark it looks. Oh, imagine my feelings. I caught her in my arms . . . she laid her head on my shoulder like a child going to sleep and Died. Oh yes, she died. I would not believe it, no, not when they took her away from me cold and stiff in death. Oh, if a mother could have been with her to close her eyes, or a sister to have wept with me—What a comfort it would have been—but no, I was all alone. She died in her husband's arms as happy and as easy as a babe going to sleep. O I would not could not believe it, I shook & spoke to her, asked her to say one more word . . . but no, she was in heaven. Oh why did she die—why has she been taken from me—oh God, have mercy.

The mates of the *Wild Ranger* took turns sitting with Elisha as he sat mourning at the side of the corpse. "I have had a coffin made tight and shall take her home to her parents, from whom she was given to me one short year before," he recorded later, but in the meantime the coffin was left open, and next morning the whole ship's company passed slowly through the cabin, "with clean shaven faces and best clothes, to take their last look of their shipmate & friend."

As they came through "one by one to look at Wifey, they (all that could speak English) would add some word of consolation for my poor breaking heart." The better educated ones produced such awkward platitudes as, "We hope and trust she is in a better world," while others, more touchingly, mumbled, "Capt, me very sorry for you." And so the sad day passed, with the first mate reading long passages from the Bible and leading prayers. "No work on board ship today," wrote Elisha in slow, heavy script. "The Ship *Wild Ranger* and her Ship's Company are in Mourning."

None of the honeymooning brides or their proud husbands could guess what tragedies or joys lay ahead, though good health was such a precarious blessing that the worst was often anticipated. Though Mary Swift Jones did not know it, there was a coffin stowed in the hold when her new husband escorted her on board the China trade bark *Mary & Louisa*. His motive was morbid but practical, for Mary was terminally ill with tuberculosis. As it happened, she survived the voyage (though she had to spend much of her time boarding on shore with missionaries in Yokohama, Japan), but died a few days after anchoring in New York, in 1861. Mary Swift Jones never saw her home village of Setauket again, but in the meantime she and Benjamin had spent thirty months together that would have been denied to them both if she had stopped at home in Long Island.

Another Mary—twenty-year-old Mary Tarbox Rairden of Woolwich, Maine—was much luckier. Mary Tarbox married Captain Bradstreet Rairden on Christmas Eve, 1850, and set sail with him on the 347-ton bark *Henry Warren* of Bath, in January 1851. It was a stormy start: "Throught [throughout] this day a gale of wind from North West attended with frequent snow squalls, under close reef'd Topsails, Foresail & reef'd Main Sail, Ship is iced much," Mary wrote on the thirty-first, but added, "Never mind, she's reeling off the leagues."

With such a robust attitude, it is little wonder that a couple of days later she was able to report, "Braddie says his Mary is a exelent little sailor." Mary escaped all but a small bout of seasickness, reporting within days that she was "quite harty and able to tweak Father Neptune's self by the Beard." Even an unexpected bath did not discourage her. "I am a cold water subject, I am," she mused on February 14. "Was on deck all the former part of the day with Braddie & best of it was Braddie and his Mary got a salt water ducking."

The *Henry Warren* dropped anchor in their destination—Havana, Cuba—that same day, just twenty-four days after leaving Bath, Maine, which, when compared to Bethia's 134-day passage from Boston to San Francisco, illustrates one of the advantages of the coasting trade. "Braddie's Mary" enjoyed the novel sights of Havana, riding out to the public gardens in a "volante," eating ice cream and drinking "lemon-ade," socializing with other Americans in port, and generally taking a view of "all that was to be seen there." There was a catch, however. Being new to the freighting trade, Mary had not realized that her husband would be so busy in port, where he had to deal with the tradespeople, the consignee, the agent, the customs officers, the shipping master, and all the other port officials.

And that was just the start of all his business. In addition to all the time-consuming chitchat that this involved, Captain Rairden had to collect money for freight, pay expenses, keep accounts, and send detailed statements of all transactions to the owners back in Maine. Mary, seemingly, felt a little provoked at all this, for on March 26, when the bark was at Matanzas loading sugar for Sweden, she wrote meaningfully, "Braddie is seated beside his Mary, singing as merrily as possible, has business on shore but the wind is blowing so hard & such a bad sea cannot think of Braddie's going in a little boat. No, no, Braddie must not think of it, he must remain with his Mary & read to her."

Thirty-one-year-old Bradstreet did not appear to be at all irritated by this possessive and naïve devotion, indulgently carrying "his Mary" onward to Sweden, Russia, and Denmark, and from thence to Cadiz, where he procured a cargo of salt for home. Finally, on Friday, September 26, 1851, Mary wrote, "My first Sea Voyage safely endid." Just two months later, on November 27, she was off on a second expedition, with Braddie "very busily engaged Joynering . . . in our own little Cabbin, think my Braddie very neat indeed."

Obviously, her honeymoon voyage had been most successful, an experiment well worth repeating. And, furthermore, it led to a seafaring tradition, for Braddie and Mary had a son, Bradstreet Junior, who eventually moved to Java in the South China Sea, and set up business there, supplying the ships and becoming the United States consul in Batavia.

Mary Tarbox Rairden.
Maine Maritime Museum.

Captain Bradstreet Rairden.
Maine Maritime Museum.

A much later seafaring wife, Emma Pray of the China trade ship *Governor Goodwin,* arrived at the Javanese port of Anjer-Lor in July 1888 to discover that the ship chandlers were Scott and Rairden, "the only English-speaking men in Anjer." When he met Emma walking in the streets of Anjer, Mr. Rairden courteously invited her to "go down to his house, and see his wife, and said we were to stop for tiffin with him. I didn't know that he had a wife," Emma commented, but went along anyway, to "a very pretty little house, and found Mrs. Rairden to be a young Englishwoman. She was quite pretty, quiet, and pleasing in her manner." Her maiden name was Frances Elizabeth Collins.

Frances had come to Java on the bark *John A. Gaunt* with her sister, her brother-in-law being the captain. Over the five weeks that the ship had lain in Anjer, Frances "met Mr. Rairden, became engaged to him, and two days before the vessel was to sail, they were married on board ship, by a minister whom they sent for, from Singapore. Her sister went on to Calcutta, and she staid here," Emma continued, obviously highly diverted by this most unusual honeymoon. The couple had been married fourteen months, and seemed "to be quite contented, and they both seem to think a great deal of each other"—which is not unexpected, when one remembers "Braddie and his Mary." Like father, like son, Emma would have thought, if she had known the whole of the story.

Braddie Jr. and Frances "had a little baby two months old, which she hardly knew what to do with. She was not used to children, and had to get most of the information from the native women," Emma related. Frances Elizabeth Collins Rairden must have learned well, for she lived to raise five children to maturity, no small feat in a place where "Java fever" carried off so many men on the visiting ships.

Rairden family at their home in Batavia, Java, where Bradstreet Jr. was the American consul. Maine Maritime Museum.

The Honeymooners

On August 13, 1853, another bride, Fidelia Heard, was almost too busy getting her quarters "systematized" at the start of her honeymoon voyage on the Boston bark *Oriental* to notice their departure. First, she "arranged all our books and movable articles so that they would not shake about by the motion of the ship," and then, "the Steward fastened our trunks to the floor by nailing a bit of wood on each side of them to the floor, quite a new sort of arrangement to me." It was a novel kind of setup for her husband, Captain John Jay Heard, as well. "The Capt. says it seems quite as strange to him to have me on board, as it is to me to be here. He having always been alone, it looks rather queer to see ladies' clothing hanging in the State Room."

Like Captain Joseph Delano more than two decades before, Captain John Jay Heard soon put his wife to work—but not with hostess-duties, as there were no passengers on board save two very young men who were headed for the Orient. Instead, like Captain Banning Blanchard, Captain Heard set to teaching his bride how to find the daily position of the ship. "I took my first lesson in navigation this afternoon, commenced learning to box the compass," Fidelia wrote on August 18, 1853, five days after departure. Next day, she "went up on deck to look about, more sails were being set, & some of the men had to go up aloft to assist. I looked with astonishment at the dexterity with which they climb," she marveled, "going out to the farther end of the yard, & reaching over until it seemed as if the ship's motion would fetch them headlong, then coming down by a single rope, letting it slip through their hands." Then, on the twentieth, Fidelia "looked through the quadrant for the first time & have been studying to find the difference of latitude and longitude. Hope to be able ere long to do it myself alone," she concluded with well-founded optimism, for on the twenty-ninth she was able to write with pride, "The Capt. paid me a great compliment today by copying my ship's reckoning into his book."

Half a century later, on her honeymoon on the *Bangalore,* Georgia Blanchard "started right off working the sights each day and marking on my chart. Usually we took them by the sun," she wrote.

Banning would be on deck looking at the sun through his sextant while I was in the cabin looking at the chronometer. When he would shout TIME I would put down on paper what it said on the chronometer. Then I would take my turn on deck and we would work out the position of the ship and place it on the chart. When the sun was not out during the day we would take the sights by the stars at night.

Then, twenty days out, when Banning was delirious with a bout of malaria, Georgia's new skill proved very useful indeed.

It was the rare bride who was not taught how to "work time" to calculate the ship's position. Some were much more adept than others, but most became capable of writing, as did Hannah Stimpson Winn, the bride of Captain Joseph Winn of the ship *St. Paul,* in 1837:

> *When the Spaniards discovered the Island of Luzon, on which Manila is, they came round Cape Horn, and by steering from east'ᵈ to west'ᵈ they lost nearly a day. We on the contrary came round Cape Good Hope steering east'ᵈ and gain'ᵈ twelve hours, as every degree of Longitude East makes ship's time four minutes faster & every degree of Longitude West makes it four minutes slower. It is thus we find our way to and from all parts of the world.*

Which meant that it was the Spaniards' fault that in Manila "their Sunday is our Monday," however! "In consequence of the Spaniards' westward steering, when they discovered Manila, they lost nearly a day," Hannah Winn wrote, "which makes their time here one day behind ours, therefore their Sunday is our Monday." If Ferdinand Magellan (who was Portuguese) had had the sense to approach the Philippines from the other direction, Sunday would have kept its proper place, and Hannah would not have been forced to "reverence the Manila Sabbath" instead of her own—or so she reckoned. It was not just the female sex that was prone to amusing errors, however. A very seasoned wife, Emma Pray, noted on the ship *Governor Goodwin,* three days after departure from New York in April 1888, that their passenger, Mr. Goodwin, had come on deck vigorously shaking his watch, "and said he didn't know what had got into it, as it had lost about twenty minutes each day for the last four days."

Fidelia Heard knew much better than that, writing on her third Sunday out of Boston, "Being over 30° east of Boston, there is consequently more than two hours difference in time, as just about the time our Boston friends were going to morning service, we were through ours, & were sitting down to dinner." This was quite a feat of intelligence, for Fidelia was a very inexperienced seafarer, finding it a challenge to walk in a "slandicular" fashion, and having more than a little trouble with sea terminology, too. "I often make most ludicrous mistakes," she confided in September, for she had just given her husband cause for some hilarity by talking breathlessly of what she had seen "while I was sitting in the yard!" Of course she meant while sitting on deck, but he was very amused, for a "yard" at sea is a spar high up on the mast, to which a sail is attached. Fidelia reported enjoying a chuckle of her own, however, when she overheard her husband call some common old ropes the "sheets!"

Fidelia wasn't the only wife to become puzzled by salty phrases. When Hannah Winn noted in January 1838, "Men employed fishing the main mast," she wondered in her journal, "What can that be?" and answered herself, "It is what *I* should call mending it." By contrast, Mrs. Follansbee, who sailed with her new husband Alonzo on the four-hundred-ton ship *Logan* in 1837, was quite lofty about her grasp of sea language. "By this time I had learned all the nautical phrases," she wrote on July 10, two months after departure from New York; "though I did not choose to use them, lest I get in the habit, and use them on shore, which would be very mortifying for a captain's wife."

A much less pretentious bride was Sarah Tucker, who married Captain Charles Low in May 1852, when she was nineteen. Two weeks later they set sail from New York on the extreme clipper *N. B. Palmer,* at the start of a remarkably eventful honeymoon voyage, throughout the whole of which Sarah behaved with astounding stoicism. Storms did not faze her, nor the mutiny that Low had to put down off the east coast of South America, in which his first mate was shot in the leg. In January 1853 the ship sailed headlong onto a reef in the South China Sea. The ship was floated off, but leaked badly, and Captain Low steered for Batavia, ninety miles away. Just as they limped into harbor, Sarah serenely gave birth to a boy. This last-minute delivery was to turn into a habit, for at the end of her second voyage, as the *N. B. Palmer* was passing Sandy Hook on her way into New York, Sarah gave birth to a second son.

An even less romantic honeymoon was that of Henrietta Elliott, who married her cousin, Captain Joshua Slocum, on February 22, 1886. Slocum was a widower with two sons, and was still mourning his first wife, Virginia, who had died at sea less than two years before. Nonetheless he took Henrietta and the two boys on a honeymoon voyage, on the *Aquidneck* of New York. The ship was wrecked on the coast of Brazil, in December 1887. The resourceful Slocum built a canoe-like craft that he christened *Liberdade,* and ferried his family home on that. And it is not surprising that Henrietta stayed home once she got there, refusing ever to try the briny again.

Another woman who learned her lesson was Elizabeth Daskett, who married Captain Otis Clark, master of the three-masted schooner *Eva L. Ferris,* in Philadelphia in December 1901. The schooner was loaded with coal and dynamite for Boston, and Otis Clark wanted her to take the train and meet him there, but no, Elizabeth insisted on her honeymoon voyage. She had never been to sea before, and wanted to find out what life on board ship was like.

And so she sailed, and enjoyed her voyage, too, until New Year's Eve, when a gale stormed onto them from the icy northwest. Captain Clark was not unduly worried at first, calculating that he could wait the storm out until it abated. Instead, the gale increased, so that vicious seas thrashed across the ice-sheathed decks. Then, in the dead of the tumultuous night, a particularly violent wave wrenched out the bowsprit stays, opening the bow to the sea.

Tons of water foamed into the forward part of the ship, and the decks bowed with the sudden release of pressure, bouncing out the mizzen boom, which crashed down through the lifeboat, so that their only chance of escape was in splinters. Below decks, it was a nightmare of smashing glass and crashing furniture. "It's bad, isn't it," said Elizabeth to her husband when he came down to carry her up to deck. "It's bad, all right," he agreed.

Captain, crew, and captain's bride huddled on the poop, the only part that was not constantly swept by the hungry seas. Because of the thick ice, it was impossible to take refuge in the rigging. All they could do was wait for rescue—and while they waited, Elizabeth sang. She sang everything and anything that came to mind, hymns and folk-songs, shanties and vaudeville, just to keep their spirits up, while all the time the sinking schooner drifted and another dreadful night loomed. Then, just before dark descended, the *Lizzie M. Stanley* materialized out of the murk. The rescue could not have been timed more closely. Moments after Elizabeth, Otis, and the shivering crew were dragged on board the *Lizzie M. Stanley,* the *Eva L. Ferris* slipped beneath the icy surf.

According to the somewhat chauvinistic stories told at the time, Elizabeth Clark then did something unusual, for a female. She turned to her husband, and allowed that he had been right. She should have gone to Boston by rail, she said. Then she most sincerely assured Otis she would go by train henceforth—and that is exactly what happened. Unlike Mary Rairden, Sarah Low, Emma Cawse, and many hundreds of other brides who continued their voyaging on all kinds of craft, from humble coasters to the grandest of downeasters and clippers, Elizabeth Clark never, ever returned to the sea.

CHAPTER TWO

At Sea

It is now nine O'clock, and I will retire to my little room. The vessel moves along at the rate of eight knots per hour, and it is light, pleasant, and clear this evening, everything is still and quiet, not a sound is heard, save now and then the jaws of the boom give an occasional squeak which sounds very unpleasant. I will ask the second mate to throw a bucket of water on it, thus give it a drink and stop its groaning.

—Mary Rowland, March 27, 1856

In August 1853, Fidelia Heard's first night at sea on the bark *Oriental* was a wakeful one, for "everything was so new & strange to me, the motion of the ship—working of ropes, rudder &c. I shall soon get accustomed to it," she penned hopefully.

On May 8, 1837, Captain Alonzo Follansbee's bride blinked awake after the first night of her honeymoon voyage on board the ship *Logan*, disturbed by equally queer noises. "The first sound I could hear, and directly over my head, was the tramping of the men getting ready to swab down the deck," she wrote. "This operation," she soon found out, "is performed every morning before breakfast," accompanied by "peculiar sea-phrases" such as "Bear a hand there!"

Mrs. Follansbee (whose Christian name is unknown) must have passed just as wakeful a night as Fidelia did in the same circumstances later, but—unlike poor Fidelia, who was "too sick to write"—she did not feel at all seasick. And, like any captain less than one day out of port, Alonzo was up on deck. So Madam (as she termed herself) scrambled out of the captain's double berth in a fever of curiosity, eager to inspect her new quarters and get acquainted with the ship. First, however, she had to get dressed—which meant that she had to decide what to wear. What would be appropriate for daily life on board?

In port it was much easier to make up one's mind, for a shipmaster's wife was a person of consequence, and dressed accordingly—though how well-dressed depended rather on the conditions on shore, as well as the state of her husband's wallet. In Callao, Peru, in September 1860, Sarah Everett found that the wisest course was to confine herself to wearing an old black suit that she quickly refurbished, for "it is so dirty on shore that one wouldn't want to wear very rich clothes even if we had them." Normally, however, dropping the anchor was the moment for a reasonably affluent captain's wife to rig herself out in the massive floor-length skirts, wincingly tight corsets, trailing shawls, mittens, tippets, fringes, beadings, and bonnets that were so beloved by Victorian and Edwardian women, enhanced by crinolines or bustles whenever the fashions of the era demanded it. "Wore my lavender silk and a Camellia in my hair," wrote Emma Gray in November 1868, after attending a philharmonic concert in Shanghai.

At sea, this kind of froufrou was clearly inappropriate. When fifteen-year-old Caroline Stoddard voyaged with her parents on the ship *Kathay* in the year 1856, she was highly amused when a Shanghai friend gave her "a flounced silk to wear on board ship. Fancy me dressed up in a flounced silk on board the ship," she wrote. "Oh, shocking. I should be afraid that the wind would get under the flounces and carry me right over the side, or else up into the mizzen top!"

The sensible thing, of course, would have been for a woman to adopt the dungaree pants and shirts that the menfolk wore about decks. Eliza ("Lizzie") Edwards of the *Black Eagle* was liberated enough to mention wearing "Bloomer dress"—a combination of waltz-length dress and baggy trousers frilled and gathered at the ankle, designed in 1850 by Libby Gerrit Smith and named after the women's rightist Amelia Bloomer. Unfortunately, while

"At Sea
and
in Port."

much more practical than floor-length skirts, the Bloomer outfit was so comical in appearance that it did the women's rightists more harm than good, being so easily lampooned. They gave up promoting the costume after a couple of years, and a respectable young matron like Mrs. Follansbee would never have dreamed of wearing one, even if it had been invented in 1837, which it had not.

Instead, like the majority of seafaring women, she would have worn at sea the same dress she would have worn at home—on Mondays, when fires were lit, water was hauled, and the laundry attacked. This was called a "wash dress," and was made of some cheap material that did not show the dirt. Captain Horace Atwood, who was a humorist, called his teenage daughter Hattie's shipboard gown her "bed-ticking dress." The alternative was an old "black bunting dress" that had belonged to Hattie's oldest sister.

The skirt of a wash dress was ankle-length, or else hiked up over an ankle-length petticoat, for the good reason that floor-length hems would drag in the mud while hanging out washing—an arrangement that was equally suitable for rough planks that were swept with spray and washed by the occasional wave. Interestingly, this was the working costume adopted by the missionary wives as well, for they lived and worked in conditions that were either dusty or muddy. Carrie Stoddard of the ship *Kathay* recorded that one missionary in Shanghai, Mrs. Nelson, wore her hems a full foot from the ground—rather excessive, in Carrie's opinion.

When she was pregnant, Emma Cawse wore "a nice short wrapper" on deck—a "wrapper" being a loose Mother Hubbard dress that opened down the front, more usually used as a dressing gown but eminently suitable for this purpose, once shortened. For the same reason, on deck the captain's wife often wore the wooden-soled overshoes called "pattens" that kept her feet out of the mud when doing outdoor work. Emma Cawse bought some "Chinese boots" in Shanghai, which fulfilled the same purpose. Coasterwoman Helen York of the schooner *Benjamin C. Cromwell* made her own, calling them "splashers." Whaling wife Lizzie Edwards noted that hers were topped with laced "gaiters," which would have protected the ankles.

And, just as on "blue Monday," the dress was covered by an apron with two ties, one around the waist and the other near the hem, to cinch in the skirts and reduce the risk of catching fire. On board the *W. F. Babcock* in 1884, Maria Murphy's seven-year-old daughter Jennie made her an apron, and gave it to her for Christmas. Another seasoned seafarer, Mary Rowland, recorded that she sewed a big pocket in her shipboard dresses—which seems very prudent, for small items rolled around and were easily lost if put down. Another adjustment Mary Rowland remarked on was wearing "wrappers for my sleeping dresses," as "ladies do in general that go to sea," these being not only "much more desireable than white nightdresses," but also more modest if called out of bed in a hurry. Headwear was equally sensible. Fancy bonnets, leghorn hats, and calashes were abandoned in favor of easily laundered gingham or calico sunbonnets, often quickly cut out and sewn on board as the novice wife realized how convenient they were.

So it is probable that when Madam Follansbee explored the after quarters of her husband's ship she was wearing a shortened dress of some easy-care fabric like calico, which would have been dark in color to hide shipboard dirt, and almost certainly protected by a natural linen apron. Later on in her journal, she revealed that her hair was short and curly, and this was probably kept tidy with a cap when she was below. This modest, milkmaid-like appearance would have been completed with a handkerchief tucked into her bosom, knitted worsted stockings, and small slippers that could be readily slid into pattens when she went upstairs to deck.

But her first priority was to find her way about the quarters. When she opened the door of the captain's stateroom, she stepped into a cabin that was

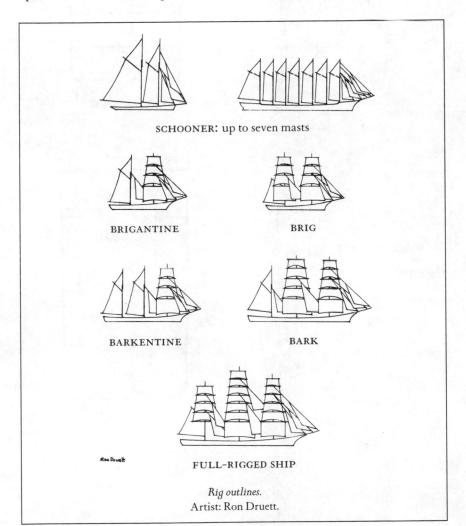

SCHOONER: up to seven masts

BRIGANTINE

BRIG

BARKENTINE

BARK

FULL-RIGGED SHIP

Rig outlines.
Artist: Ron Druett.

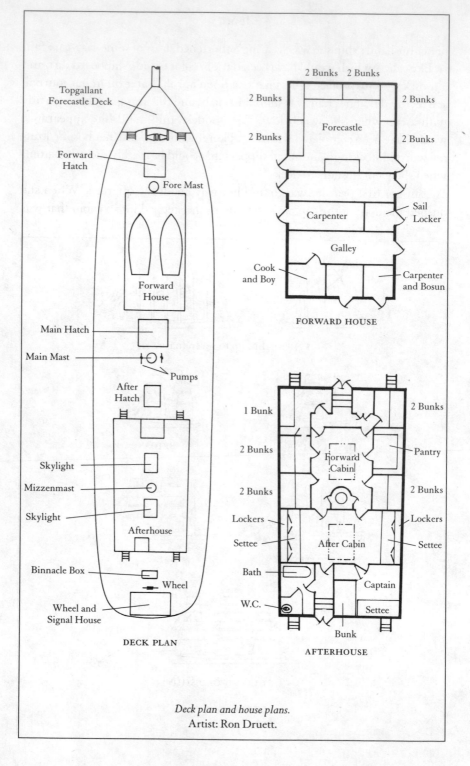

DECK PLAN

- Topgallant Forecastle Deck
- Forward Hatch
- Fore Mast
- Forward House
- Main Hatch
- Main Mast
- Pumps
- After Hatch
- Skylight
- Mizzenmast
- Skylight
- Afterhouse
- Binnacle Box
- Wheel
- Wheel and Signal House

FORWARD HOUSE

- 2 Bunks   2 Bunks
- 2 Bunks
- 2 Bunks
- 2 Bunks
- 2 Bunks
- Forecastle
- Carpenter
- Sail Locker
- Galley
- Cook and Boy
- Carpenter and Bosun

AFTERHOUSE

- 1 Bunk
- 2 Bunks
- 2 Bunks
- 2 Bunks
- 2 Bunks
- Pantry
- Forward Cabin
- Lockers
- Lockers
- Settee
- Settee
- After Cabin
- Bath
- W.C.
- Captain
- Settee
- Bunk

Deck plan and house plans.
Artist: Ron Druett.

used as both sitting room and dining room. This seagoing parlor was small—
"but handsome," wrote Madam—paneled in

> *polished mahogany with gilt, rosewood, and satin-wood trimmings, and*
> *furnished with a large mahogany center table, which could be enlarged*
> *to a dining table; bookcase with mirrors in the doors and two medicine*
> *drawers underneath, armchairs, and cushioned transom, that formed*
> *a long sofa, and Brussels carpet. And in the center overhead hung*
> *the ship's compass, and at one side hung the Capt's thermometer and*
> *barometer.*

These would have been hanging in the big skylight which helped to illumi-
nate the room, and which could be opened for ventilation in fine weather.
There was a door in the opposite bulkhead, in the port—left-hand, or lar-

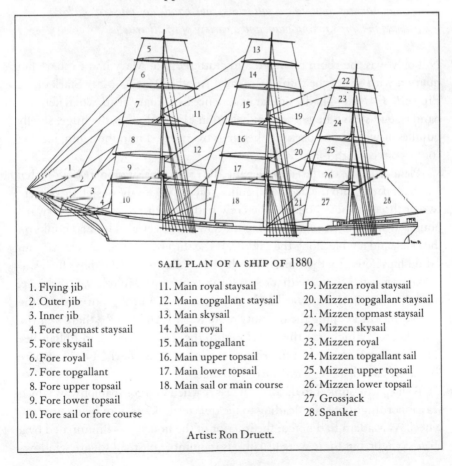

SAIL PLAN OF A SHIP OF 1880

1. Flying jib	11. Main royal staysail	19. Mizzen royal staysail
2. Outer jib	12. Main topgallant staysail	20. Mizzen topgallant staysail
3. Inner jib	13. Main skysail	21. Mizzen topmast staysail
4. Fore topmast staysail	14. Main royal	22. Mizzen skysail
5. Fore skysail	15. Main topgallant	23. Mizzen royal
6. Fore royal	16. Main upper topsail	24. Mizzen topgallant sail
7. Fore topgallant	17. Main lower topsail	25. Mizzen upper topsail
8. Fore upper topsail	18. Main sail or main course	26. Mizzen lower topsail
9. Fore lower topsail		27. Grossjack
10. Fore sail or fore course		28. Spanker

Artist: Ron Druett.

board—side, which led to the room where the first mate slept. Stateroom doors were usually slotted or latticed, to allow movement of the air. A third door, in the forward bulkhead, led to where the steward reigned in the pantry.

All in all, it was a surprisingly luxurious setup, considering that the *Logan* was rated at only four hundred tons. Conditions were much less comfortable on the small barks, brigs, and schooners that plowed the coastal routes to Charleston, New Orleans, and the West Indies, and ventured as far as the Channel, the Mediterranean, and the Baltic. Mary Dow of the 279-ton bark *Clement* described quarters that were very spartan indeed. She regularly cleaned her room herself,

> *which is something of a job I assure you. It is about eight feet long and twelve wide. One third is occupied by a bedstead, the other two-thirds is filled up with cabin furniture, such for instance as one table, one chair, one sea-chest, two small trunks, one band-box, one box of claret wine, the ship's maintopsail, and a variety of small articles.*

Not only was the room cramped and cluttered, but Mary had to share her quarters with one of the ship's spare sails! Another Mary—Mary Stark of the clipper *B. F. Hoxie*—had a similar experience in January 1856, when her husband loaded such a huge cargo of baleen in Honolulu that the huge, smelly bundles of whalebone packing the holds overflowed into the cabin, leaving "only room enough for the sofa."

Plain or fancy, cluttered or elegant, the cabin was sited in a "house" that was built partly into the deck. Depending on the size of the vessel, there were two or three of these houses. The crew had their quarters in the "forward house," which was the one closest to the bow of the vessel. This had bunks on the sides, and a table along the middle. If the ship was big enough to have an "amidships house" in the waist of the ship, the galley where the ship's food was cooked was sited there, with a room for the cook and cabin boy. Otherwise, the galley was in the forward house with the men, and the stove served the double duty of keeping the off-duty crew warm. And finally, there was the "afterhouse," which was the one closest to the stern. As Madam Follansbee found on that first day of exploring her quarters, this afterhouse was where the captain lived, along with one or two mates.

Being partly sunk into the deck, it was reached by a companionway, which was a short flight of stairs leading to the quarterdeck, its door being near the wheel. As Madam had noted, the interior of the house was illuminated by a large skylight, but there were usually also a number of small square windows set high in the walls, which opened onto the alleyways of the deck and were protected by heavy shutters—or "deadlights"—that could be closed during storms. Often there were portholes in the staterooms. The roof of the house was flat, except for the protruding skylight, and served as an open-air promenade for the captain's wife, and a playground for his children.

On small vessels like Mary Dow's *Clement* there was just one room in the house, where the captain lived in a state of almost complete lack of privacy. It was bedroom, parlor, and dining room. Here, he not only performed the normal daily functions of sleeping, dressing, washing, and shaving, but also carried out the business of the ship. Here, he kept his journals and accounts, settled disputes among the crew, worked out the ship's position, entertained officials in port, and ate his meals in company with his family and the mates. Because the galley stove was sited forward (to keep the smoke out of the helmsman's eyes), this cabin was often cold. Mary C. Bartlett described conditions so bleak on the brig *Lawrence Copeland* that her husband, Samuel, "got a piece of plank which he heats on the [galley] stove and brings into the cabin for us to put our feet on." And yet this room, small and comfortless though it might be, was the heart of the ship. Captains and wives and children died here, and many women gave birth.

On the four-hundred-ton *Logan* the plan of the afterhouse was similar to

In the saloon of the Dudhope. *Courtesy San Francisco Maritime National Historical Park.*

that on the *Clement,* being made up of just one room, but Madam Follansbee—unlike Mary Dow—had a separate stateroom for sleeping. On the 275-
ton brig *American Union* Mary Ellen Bartlett (not the Mary Bartlett of the
Lawrence Copeland, but probably a relative) also had a stateroom, which she
shared with her husband and two children, but it "smells so badly have moved
our bed into the cabin," she noted in August 1862.

On larger vessels the dimensions of the afterhouse increased in proportion
to the size of the ship, measuring forty by twenty-five feet on the eleven-hun-
dred-ton clipper *Clarissa B. Carver.* This meant it was big enough to be divided
into two cabins, the sternward half being the captain's room—or "after
cabin"—and the forward part being the dining room, usually called the "forward cabin," though at times it was known as the "messroom," or the "saloon."
On the *Clarissa B. Carver* the messroom measured ten by twelve feet. Dou-

ble-bunked staterooms
led off from either side of
this, occasionally allo-
cated to passengers, but
usually taken up by the
first and second mates,
and sometimes the stew-
ard and cabin boy. Mary
Swift Jones, who traveled
as a bride on the 497-ton
Mary & Louisa in 1858,
had her meals in a din-
ing room that was hung
with a large mirror and
"painted pure white, with
gilded moldings." A pas-

Mrs. Montgomery in the cabin of the Carrie Winslow.
Ruth Montgomery Collection, Penobscot Marine Museum.

sageway led out to the deck from the forward part of this, with a pantry, a
storeroom, and sometimes two more staterooms to the sides of it.

The bigger the afterhouse, the greater the scope for indulging in the lavish clutter that was so beloved by the Victorians. The shipbuilders furnished
and decorated the quarters with generous abandon, and because the captain
usually held a major share in the ownership of the vessel, he felt free to add
improvements, too—to gild the lily, so to speak. "Are now enlarging a stateroom so that I can have a closet," wrote Maria Murphy on the *W. F. Babcock*
in 1883. When Captain John Mathieson carried his bride, Frances, on the *Antiope* in 1905, he took down the walls between the after cabin and two state-

rooms to make a magnificent captain's room with six port-holes, a full-sized bed, a writing table, a large bookcase, and a full lounge suite of settee and arm-chairs. The saloon was even more marvelous, with a white-enameled, elaborately paneled ceiling, bulkheads of highly pol-ished teak, a grand piano, settees, chairs, tables, flowers growing in

Frances Wishar Mathieson in the cabin of the ship Antiope, *1906.*
From "Master of the Moving Sea."

boxes, and canaries in cages in the skylight—"and with gay rugs on the floor, it was very cozy indeed."

"Our suite of rooms look real comfortable," wrote Emma Cawse on the 844-ton tea clipper *John R. Worcester.* "Nice red curtains on all the windows, and a nice large one by the bed with gold borders. We have a nice private sit-ting room." The saloon on the seventeen-hundred-ton square-rigger *Banga-lore* had red cushions on the port side, and green cushions on the starboard, perhaps to prove that they were at sea. The stateroom was almost as grand as the one on the *Antiope,* with "built-in double berth, built-in couch under the porthole." Off this was "a bathroom with a tub and toilet. The toilet was right in the stern and was on a platform with an arm on each side to hold on to in bad weather," she elaborated.

Unsurprisingly, this unequal state of affairs led to some jealousy among the wives. In March 1860, Sarah Everett of the *Kineo* met a Mrs. Rich in Melbourne, Australia, whose accommodations on the ship *John A. Parks* were very superior. "They have a splendid cabin," Sarah wrote enviously, "large, painted white & gilt, varnished & landscapes painted on the panels." Similarly, in September 1853 at the Chincha Islands off Peru, Cynthia Congdon attended "a party given on board the *Tornado,* a splendid ship of eighteen hundred tons," adding, "her cabin was rosewood and Mahogany, and most elegantly furnished."

As the century wore on and timber suitable for shipbuilding became scarce, the biggest windjammers were made of iron, which led to an unex-pected problem. On the huge thirty-two-hundred-ton *Arthur Sewall* Maria Murphy found that "we have felt the cold very much." There was a deck cabin on the poop, called the "chart-room," which had an oil heater. "I have slept here on the lounge all the way round the Cape," she wrote, commenting, "Iron ships are very cold—there is no way to heat the staterooms."

Stewards and cabin boys found yet another problem—that steel doors are difficult to knock on hard enough to wake a slumbering captain or mate. The small children of one Maine captain did find a solution, when they were trying to rouse the second mate to come on deck and play. Their little fists were of no avail, so they fetched a belaying pin and delivered his stateroom door a clangorous hammering. It is doubtful, however, that they did it more than once.

"The day begins with coffee for the watch on deck between one and two bells, 4 ½ to 5 o'clock A. M.," wrote Calista Stover on the bark *Daniel Barnes,* "after which they wet and scrub down the decks and tops of the houses, both for cleanliness and to counteract the effects of the intense heat of the sun." On the *Antiope,* Captain Mathieson was awakened at 6:30 A.M. by the cabin boy, who was bearing a cup of coffee. Once shaved and dressed, he inspected the newly washed decks, took his first navigational sight of the day, and at eight ate breakfast with his wife, Frances, and whichever of the two mates was off watch.

Similarly, Madam Follansbee wrote, "At daybreak, every morning, the watch on deck turns to, to scrub and swab down the decks with sand and water." The next early morning job was to fill "the scuttle-butt" with the daily allowance of fresh water "from the big water tank," and then, "at 7 bells (half past seven)," all hands got their breakfast. And, on that first morning at sea, seven bells—breakfast—meant that Mrs. Follansbee was about to meet at least one of her husband's officers.

It was her next challenge. Alonzo Follansbee might be the king of the vessel, but like any other governor he had to have his ministers. These were his "mates," who ate at the same table as the captain and his wife.

Usually, there were two ship's officers. "The Chief Mate," described Madam, "is the superintending officer. The Captain tells him what to have done, and leaves him to see to it that all his orders are executed. He also keeps the Log Book." In port, he was in charge of the ship while the captain was dealing with shore officials, having the responsibility "of the stowage, safe-keeping, and delivery of the Cargo."

"The Second Mate's duty is to oversee and allot the sailors' work, and is responsible for its being done well," she continued. "He is expected to enforce obedience." Thus the second officer was in charge of discipline, and if he was a brute, as sometimes happened, he had the power to make the sailors' lives miserable. "He also eats in the Cabin," Madam added—which meant that the two mates had the power to make her life miserable, too, because they lived, ate, and worked in such very close proximity.

A properly prim Victorian woman was perfectly capable of reducing the toughest of fire-eating mates to mumbling, red-faced bashfulness with one thin-lipped stare, but nonetheless it is not surprising that most wives studied new officers with some anxiety as they arrived on board. "Our crew seem like good men, and I trust there will be no trouble with the officers," wrote Maria Murphy after the departure of the *W. F. Babcock* in January 1883; "I have not got used to them yet." On the *Governor Goodwin,* Emma Pray noted that they were very reliant on the officers, for out of the crew of sixteen seamen there were seven under the age of twenty-one, and none who could be trusted to steer.

Jane Barber of Westerly, Rhode Island, who sailed on the coaster *Ocean Eagle* in the early 1850s, reported in a letter to her parents that her husband had had "considerable difficulty" finding officers, "and was finally obliged to go to the shipping office and get a man whom he had never seen and of whose abilities he knew nothing at all, and whose personal appearance, to say the least, did not recommend him as anything very forcible." Twenty-five days out, this man—named Flagg—still had not shaved, and "to cap the climax, he has two large boils on one side of his face." Mr. Seymour, the second mate, on the other hand, "is a very good-looking man with broad shoulders and an arm like Hercules." Mr. Seymour's ability matched his impressive appearance, luckily, for their six seamen were not at all satisfactory. "Wm. says he never saw such a stupid sett get together," she remarked. One, a Spaniard, did not even understand English! "You will not wonder that under these circumstances," Jane concluded, "I went to sea feeling very anxious."

As the captains looked for good seamanship and leadership skills when they chose their officers, fine manners and a gentlemanly appearance being very low in their priorities, there was no guarantee that the mates would be pleasant table companions—or even, for that matter, clean. Mariners traditionally began their careers as adolescent boys, and a sour, surly nature—often the result of chronic disease, for seamen were notorious for living hard and neglecting their health—was common. "I got so mad at our cross old mate this morning that I have a real fever all the afternoon," wrote Mary Swift Jones on the China-trade bark *Mary & Louisa.* "In Benjamin's absence I stepped in to stop the noise, it was the first time I had ever said anything to him except the common civilities of the day, & the old Scratch was so surprised he went on deck & has been as good as cream all day."

Mary Rowland had the opposite problem on the brig *Thomas W. Rowland* in March 1856, for the mate, Mr. Bennett, was obstinately and sullenly silent— "will not speak if it can be prevented and does not answer when spoken to unless the fit takes him, and the spirit does not move, only occasionally." Mr. Bennett had some kind of lung disease: "he is daily wasting away and may die before we get to Europe, if our passage proves a long one," wrote Mary. As it happens, Mr. Bennett survived the passage, but there is an inescapable impression that no one on board would have been particularly sorry—except for the inconvenience of being without an officer—if the worst had occurred.

There were pleasant mates, of course, for they were often brothers, cousins, or old shipmates of the captain, the second mate of the *Logan* being Alonzo's brother Augustus, "of Pittston, Maine." Some, indeed, were too personable by far. On the clipper *Young America* in 1855, Charlotte Babcock described "an incident which caused us a great deal of trouble, and much extra care and anxiety." The first mate had begun "a flirtation with one of the lady passengers," and—still worse—this shocking dalliance happened "while he was on duty!" Captain David Babcock summoned the erring female to the after cabin for a serious chat, but though his lecture about proprieties "was said kindly," it fell on deaf ears, making "no impression on this particular lady—and that very evening when it was his watch on deck she was talking to the officer as usual!" Obviously, such a scandalous state of affairs could not be allowed to continue. "As there was no alternative, the Captain was obliged to put the officer off duty, and confine him to his room." The ship altered course to send a boat into Pernambuco, the flirtatious fellow was set ashore, "and we never afterwards heard of him."

This made it difficult for Captain David Babcock, for it meant that he himself had to take over the duties of the man he had fired. Normally, once breakfast was eaten, the captain of a large vessel merely inspected the decks with his mates beside him, and handed out directives. The only men under his direct control were the sailmaker and carpenter, as the mates supervised the sailors, and his wife was in charge of the steward.

"We have breakfast at half past seven and I sleep till nearly then, and get up in time to dress and comb my hair, which occupies about 5 minutes, as I think more of the comfort than the looks at sea," wrote Mary Rowland in 1873, after more than two decades of voyaging. Once dressed, she would wash and brush her teeth, "wind Chronometer Watch and clock," breakfast, and help her husband Henry take his first observation at half past eight.

And so the day progressed. The next observation was taken at noon, and dinner—the main meal of the day—was served at twelve-thirty. On the *Governor Goodwin,* Emma Pray wrote, "We have breakfast at half-past seven, dinner at half-past twelve, and tea at six." Captain James Cawse took a nap in the afternoon "providing there is a good breeze blowing." This was a sensible precaution, because if the weather blew up he might have to be on deck all night. Wives tended to avoid naps, for if they did sleep in the afternoon it became too difficult to sleep at nighttime. Caroline Stoddard, fifteen-year-old daughter of Captain Thomas Stoddard of the ship *Kathay,* testified that bedtimes were early, for one night after playing whist the family was "quite astonished" when they looked at the time, and found that it was after eight o'clock, for at that hour "we are generally in bed."

All in all, the ship's routine was much more reminiscent of school than home, being so regulated by bells and rosters. "The sailors are divided into two watches," wrote Madam. In her time, these were known as the "larboard" and "starboard" watches, but—as Mary Rowland pointed out in 1873—the word "larboard" was later replaced by the word "port," the words "starboard" and "larboard" being too much alike, "and mistakes occurred from that cause." On smaller vessels, like the brigs that Mary Rowland knew, the starboard watch was the captain's, and the port watch the mate's, but on bigger ships like the *Logan,* the *Bangalore,* and the *Antiope,* a second mate was shipped to look after the starboard watch, to give the captain more leisure for command. On "all ships," however, "the Capt allways occupies the Starboard or right hand side of the ship in the cabin, at table &c.," wrote Mary Rowland, "while the port watch is the 1st Mate's and he allways has his room on the left hand side, which is the Portside."

Each watch (except for the two two-hour dog watches in the late afternoon) lasted four hours, and then the men who had been on duty retired to enjoy "a watch below," and the other watch came on deck. This meant that at just about any given time of the day someone would be trying to sleep. "The bell strikes every half-hour," Mrs. Follansbee wrote. This was probably a hangover from the distant past, when ship's time was measured in half-hour sandglasses. The bell was tapped once at the first half hour of the watch, twice at the second half hour, and so on, up to eight taps at the end of the fourth hour, being the end of the watch. And then the cycle started all over again, on through the night and past the next dawn. Interestingly, in 1838 Hannah Winn described the watchman calling out "All's well" as he struck the bell at night—a very old custom indeed.

For the novice wives, this ringing of bells was confusing at first, but they soon got used to it. When Hannah Winn wrote in January 1838, on board the *Cato,* that she "slept the A.M. 'til about 4 bells," she was using seafaring language to indicate that her night's slumber had ended at six in the morning. Harder to get used to was the fact that the ship's day started at noon, not midnight, Katurah Pritchard writing on January 8, 1848, that it was Friday night by her reckoning, "but called Saturday by Mariners, the day commencing at twelve, at noon."

Getting about was yet another problem for wives who had not yet found their "sea legs." Katurah Pritchard had her first fall within moments of boarding the brig *Massachusetts* on Christmas Eve, 1847. Tumbling backwards, she knocked herself out, and came to with her husband bathing her neck and shoulders with brandy. Even on the biggest ships there was a lot of pitching, rolling, and waggling of the stern. "The ship rolls very badly," wrote Mary Henry on the ship *Cato* in December 1851, "so that my rocking chair don't make anything of rolling over." Worse still, "it took me with it once." This was a common event. "At breakfast time the ship gave a pitch," wrote Hannah Winn on the *St. Paul* in May 1837. "Poor me went one way and the chair another, broke the chair not a little. I can imagine how my Salem friends would have laughed to have seen me in that plight. I laughed myself," she confessed.

Some such accidents were too frightening for even the shakiest of laughs. One night the *Eclipse* rolled so hard that Adelaide Hamilton was thrown clear out of her berth, crashing facedown three feet away. "For a minute I thought my face and all my bones were broken, I had so much pain all over." Crying out, she woke her husband, who lifted her into her bed and had begun to fix it up "with a rope and blocks so as to let it down on one side and up on the other," when the ship gave another fearful lunge, pitching Adelaide, ropes, blocks, and bedding on top of her husband, and throwing them all in a heap on the floor. "I was terribly frightened the rest of the night and did not dare go to sleep afterward. My bed was like a steep hill and I down at the foot of it, not a very comfortable way to rest."

A sudden squall overtook the *Wild Ranger* in February 1856, when they had just come out of San Francisco and the cabin was still in its portside condition, with nothing lashed down, "and the way the chairs tables &c came tumbling down to leeward was a caution," wrote Bethia Sears. This could happen in calm seas as well as rough ones, the simple process of tacking the ship being enough to tip people and objects from one side to the other, as the ship turned her bow, caught the wind from the other quarter, and then leaned in the other direction.

Accompanying this process were the "peculiar sea-phrases" that Madam Follansbee had noted, and they were always the same ones. A wife soon recognized the cry "Stand by for stays!" as the signal to pick up her work basket and set off for the other side of the deck. The order, "Hard a-lee!" came next, prompting the helmsman to put down the wheel to turn the ship's head, followed by "Tacks and sheets!" and a grand commotion of slatting sails and banging blocks as the ship came round, following her bowsprit as it swung past the eye of the wind. Then, "Mainsail haul!" as the sails bellied out with a snap, and finally, "Board tacks and haul aft the sheets!" as all was secured, and the captain's wife could settle down again, on the other side of a deck that sloped the other way.

Susan Brock, small daughter of the captain of the *Midnight,* reminisced that the long-drawn cry "Mainsail ha-a-aul" was the signal for her and her mother to brace themselves for the lurch as the ship came round. It was not so easy at night, though, or in rough weather, or when the ship leaned a long way over, having been badly stowed. "At 4 o'clock A.M. tacking in shore," wrote Mary Rowland in May 1856. The vessel was "rolling and pitching badly, everything below is upside down and there is no rest or peace to be had." Worst of all, one could "hardly keep in bed, especially on one tack, and when I sit down must of necessity take the floor for a sofa."

In February 1855, on the coaster *J. J. Hathorn,* Susan Hathorn complained that she had slept badly, "for the ship was tacked so often." Four months later, she got out of bed and immediately took a tumble, the bark "being at an angle of full forty-five degrees." Fred Duncan, who spent his childhood on the *Florence,* reminisced that he slept in the after cabin on whichever of the two settees was on the downhill—or lee—side, for it would have been impossible to stay on the one that was on the uphill—weather—side of the ship. He became so accustomed to moving from one sofa to the other when the ship tacked, that he could do it without waking up, despite all the yells and the noise.

Being in ballast compounded the problem, and so could the cargo, Mary Rowland testifying that ships rolled a great deal with a cargo of cotton. "Oh, a ballast ship is horrible," wrote Carrie Stoddard. "Such a time as we had last night, the ship rolled so that everything in the cabin was rolling around." Books went one way, and the contents of the work basket the other, "but I suppose we shall get wed to it." Even cats lost their footing, as Mary Rowland described, when her "poor puss" was "tossed from one side of the cabin to the other."

On the *Cato* a can of lamp oil capsized "and run all over the cabin," creating a greasy mess. There was a bonus, however. Mary Henry was kept so busy cleaning up that it was "the first time that I have not been sick in a storm." Inevitably some of the saltwater crashing about the decks above overflowed into the cabins, and mopping up was the job of the steward, usually assisted by the captain's wife or daughter—though some shirked, as the Chinese steward of the *Charles Stewart* had evidently learned before the year 1883, when Hattie Atwood accompanied her father to sea. The *Charles Stewart* shipped a number of waves one night, and next day the Chinese man was overheard remarking admiringly to Captain Atwood that his daughter was "dammee smart girlie. She no go bed and cye. She bailee water like hellee."

Madam Follansbee experienced her first rough weather in June 1857. There came "a heavy lurch of the ship," she wrote, "and off the table would go soups, meats, dishes, and everything, down the other side of the cabin, all in a smash." When she "remarked that it was pretty rough," her husband and the two mates "would laugh and tell me I must not call it rough." Despite the provoking male hilarity, however, Madam was forced to take a tin pan of food "and sit on the cabin floor, and hold on with one hand and eat with the other."

On December 8, 1855, Captain Henry Rowland's small brig was "rolling too much for comfort and convenience. Thus we take our meals from the table cloth spread upon the floor and all kneel around," wrote Mary. As she noted another time, the furnishings flew about rather too readily for safety, and going to sea could "prove a lucrative business for a person whose occupation was mending broken furniture." Eating thus was rather hard on the back and knees, admittedly—but at least it gave her something to write about in her journal, which she used to help pass idle shipboard hours away.

Storm-racked whaleship.
Artist: Ron Druett.

After Emma Cawse commenced her honeymoon voyage on the big tea clipper *John R. Worcester* in 1876, she found to her surprise that despite her best efforts to be cheerful and look on the bright side of things, at times she was homesick and lonely. The crew was made up of "quite a good lot of men, are very obedient and willing so far, they are real quiet, I never hear them only when pulling the ropes. You would hardly think there was anyone on board sometimes." With no one to talk to and too much time to think, she tried to entertain herself by singing. "But failed," she wrote. "I felt rather homesick (hung my harp on the willow)."

This was the next challenge. The reason time tended to lag for the young bride was that she had very little to do, save watch the men carry out tasks that she did not understand, and yet this was an era where women were expected to be busy and productive, when a common phrase was to "improve the time" with work, and a popular proverb was "Satan makes work for idle hands." Even if the captain's wife came from an affluent family and was accustomed to

servants (which was very rare), there was nothing resembling the round of social visits and good works that made her feel useful at home. At sea on a clipper, a windjammer, or a downeaster, her only real job was to keep the captain
company and look after his children, oversee the steward's work in the pantry,
entertain passengers if there were any, and otherwise sit with folded hands.

"Do not do enough work to keep me in running order," complained Maria
Murphy in December 1883, and went on to sigh, "One gets so lonely at sea, I
almost forget how to laugh." In January 1838, everyone was busy on board the
ship *St. Paul*—everyone, that is, except Hannah Winn. "Some of the sailors
painting the house, the remainder as busy as bees at work on the Ship's rigging, and myself greatly troubled with the worst of afflictions. Well, what can
that be?" she rhetorically inquired of her journal. "Nothing more or less than
laziness," she replied. At home, she could have donned a sacking apron and
helped paint—as indeed Maria Murphy did, on the *W. F. Babcock*—but while
it was acceptable for the captain's wife to help with navigational sights and
reckoning, working with the sailors was not really a respectable option at sea.

A few wives broke with convention, but this, in a time when the roles al-
lotted to men and those assigned to women were sharply differentiated, was
considered both eccentric and amusing. At the island of Lobos de Afuera in
September 1884, Hattie Atwood noted the arrival of the *Eudora* of Nova Scotia, commanded by "Capt. Fulton, who has his wife with him. Her weight
must surely be three hundred pounds. She was dressed in a light pink wrapper and pulled lines with the sailors. It was a funny sight." Similarly, Ettabel
Raynor, daughter of the captain of the *Ruth B. Cobb,* observed with tart
amusement in January 1915 that there was another vessel in sight, the "*Man-
nie Swan,* who is known all along the coast as having two captains, Capt. Belle
and her husband." Men were even more hidebound. In Hobart, Australia, the
harbormaster came on board the *Charles Stewart* while Hattie Atwood was
at the helm, dropping the vessel astern as the sailors worked at the windlass.
"What kind of bloody vessel is this," he hollered, "to come up into a strange
port without a pilot and with a woman at the wheel?"

And so the more respectable wives had to devise other means of keeping
themselves busy. When stuck for something else to do, Lady Brassey of the
British yacht *Sunbeam* had herself hoisted up to the foretop masthead in a bosun's chair with a rope tied about her petticoats to make certain of her modesty. This kind of maritime pursuit, however, was not at all typical. The
average captain's wife filled in her sea time with feminine tasks such as sewing,
knitting, writing, and reading, certainly not in having herself hoisted into the
ship's rigging.

Of all these activities, sewing—both plain and fancy—was the most popular, for it looked productive, even if the result was frivolous in the extreme. "I was very industrious making shams," wrote Emma Cawse when one week out; "they look real pretty, with lots of tucks which cross at the corners, and wide ruffling. Mag," she added, meaning "magnificent," ignoring the fact that frilled pillowcases were not likely to be very useful at sea. Mary Rowland did not like sewing, "as it gives me a disagreeable aching between my shoulders," but nevertheless she accomplished a great deal of mending and making. In April 1855, Mary Stark wrote to her mother, "I have got over 50 yards of cloth & calico for shirts, patchwork &c; I have got calico for 6 shirts, & work enough, if I am well, to last me 6 months." As it happened, there was a great deal of sickness on board and, while Mary herself was well, she was so busy nursing a series of patients that the needlework was never done, but it was a wise precaution to take plenty along. Many wives and daughters cut out fabric before the voyage or in port, for—as Caroline Stoddard remarked—"we can do it so much better when the ship is still."

"I was very busy, trying to finish some work before I got home," wrote Madam Follansbee in April 1839, exactly two years after leaving Boston on her honeymoon voyage,

> when the captain inquired if I knew how many yards of cloth I had made up since I had been on board the ship. I answered, "No," I had no idea how many, but I had the bills of everything I had bought, and I looked and found to my own surprise that I had made up over 600 yards of different kinds of material, some for sheets and pillow cases for the ship, and some for ourselves, table cloths, towels, curtains, underwear, dresses, linen, jackets, pants, vests and shirts for the captain.

As well as all that, she had read books, practiced navigation, studied French, and walked about the decks whenever Alonzo desired her company, for her husband believed that this last was her most important job on board. "The Captain insists on my being on deck and walk with him in pleasant weather," Madam wrote much earlier in the voyage, "and if I say I want to sew, or study a little longer, down comes the steward with a broad grin, and says Massa Capt. say Madam must come on deck." Another refusal—and Follansbee's response was swift and decisive. Down came the shutters, rendering the cabin "as dark as midnight," and up on deck came Madam, having been forced to admit defeat.

When such difficulties are considered, Madam's list of accomplishments fully deserved self-congratulation. What is even more marvelous, however, is that she apparently never ran out of yarn, cotton, or fabric, for that was the bugbear of every other wife. In January 1855, Susan Hathorn of the bark *J. J. Hathorn,* who was remarkably fond of embroidering slippers, would have been delighted to finish one of the current pair, "if I only had the needful shade of worsted." In February 1838, in the middle of the Indian Ocean, Hannah Winn noted with delight, "In my Traps found a fine spool of cotton, which I was in great need of. No shops on this turnpike," she quipped. "One is obliged to use chips, blocks and all up."

Hannah Winn coped with the long ship's day by following a rigid schedule of her own. She liked to take a long walk before breakfast, evidently on the top of the house, for the men would have been busy washing the decks. Then, she "sowed most of the day," before taking another long walk by moonlight. Many women found that the evenings were often the nicest time on board ship. These were the hours when a voyaging wife and her husband walked the decks, watched the stars, read by the light of a lantern, sang, or chatted with each other and the mates. "After tea walked on deck, or stood musing over the rail, of the past, present and to come," wrote Mary Dow on the *Clement;* "at eight went below, and played three games of cards with George, then read my bible and went to bed." On board the *W. F. Babcock* in 1884, Maria Murphy recorded that she romped with the children after tea, playing a game like hide-and-seek; "afterwards we all have dominoes, then J. and I finish off with our usual game of backgammon."

In later years a piano—or parlor organ, or melodeon—was carried along, piano playing being particularly fashionable after 1850, when the great showman P. T. Barnum introduced the Swedish songstress Jenny Lind to the world. It was a fad that was helped along by the catchy tunes Stephen Foster was turning out at the time, "Oh! Susanna" in particular being roared out in ships' cabins on all the seven seas. Reading was another enduringly popular way of passing away the hours, particularly in latitudes where the evenings were light enough to read on deck. Vast numbers of books, newspapers, and magazines were taken along and exchanged with other seafarers as the voyage progressed. In New York, the Loan Library for Seamen put books on board for the sailors, and Calista Stover testified that they were read eagerly by the captain's family.

Many of the women noted the titles of the books they were reading, with well-thought-out comments about the content. Understandably, many took great interest in books written by other Victorian lady travelers, such as Abby Jane Morrell, who sailed on the exploratory schooner *Antarctic* in the early 1830s, and wrote a long dissertation about her experiences that sold better than her husband's even lengthier book. At about the same time, the English actress Fanny Kemble's highly controversial account of her travels in the Americas, published under her temporary married name of Butler, merited a lot of criticism from patriotic seafaring wives. "Began reading Fanny Kemble's journal or rather

Passing away the hours with needle and thread. From the Girl's Own Paper, *1883.*

Frances Ann Butler's," wrote Mary Dow in June 1838. "She is a curious woman I should judge from her writings, not much refinement about it." However, she added, "I do not know as we can expect much from a theatrical character. Some parts are very good, some witty, and some are very foolish."

Reading aloud was very popular, too. Maria Murphy read *David Copperfield* to her children, and seven-year-old Jennie, in particular, was "deeply interested—you would laugh to hear the indignant remarks about David's stepfather." Even more successful were "Miss Alcott's stories." Captains and wives read aloud even when there were no children on board, needing no better audience than each other. Somewhat eccentrically, George Dow chose to read out accounts

Passing away the hours with reading. From the Girl's Own Paper, *1883.*

of "distressing shipwrecks from the *Mariners Chronicle*" to his wife, Mary, on the eve of a storm in June 1838. "Oh! dear," Mary wrote, but George did not take the hint.

On July 1 the bark was beset with thick fog, so "more of his accounts of shipwrecks" were read. "I shall be glad when he gets through with it," Mary penned with a perceptible shiver. Two days later she recorded "sitting in the upper cabin on a cotton bale all day, wrapped in a blanket and cloak squaw fashion listening to hear George read more shipwreck accounts. He finished them today," adding with even more palpable sincerity, "and glad am I." It was a too-vivid reminder of the other challenges that lay in wait for unlucky lady mariners.

Abby Jane Morrell, who sailed around the world on the exploratory schooner Antarctic *in the years 1829 to 1831—and lived to write a book about her travels.*

CHAPTER THREE

Sex and the Seafaring Wife

Seasickness is no desireable thing—especially at Sea.
—*Mary Rowland, August 18, 1856*

On her first day at sea, Madam Follansbee was extremely fortunate to escape "paying homage to Neptune" (as she herself phrased it), for the typical green seafarer—and many a seasoned one, too—spent the first few hours or days of voyage groaning in her bunk. Everyone on board, not excluding the captain, was liable to a bout of motion sickness, especially if the cargo was a smelly one, or they had been several weeks in port. Fidelia Heard was laid low for seven days after leaving Boston in 1853. "It is a most indescribable sort of sickness," she wrote with the passion that was typical of sufferers. "It unfits one for every effort, entirely destroying all energy, and creating such a feeling of extreme indifference to everything."

Likewise, Mary Snell, who sailed on the ship *Victoria* from Boston to New Orleans in early 1839, described the nausea and dizziness as "a dreadful feeling indeed, did not care whether I lived or died." If she tried to sit up, she "was obliged to lie down again, with no kind Mother to call upon." Bethia Sears re-marked four weeks after departure that she still arranged her hair very hastily, as "nothing makes me so dizzy as looking in the glass."

Men and children usually got over seasickness quickly, but because of lack of fresh air and exercise, the women were prone to long bouts of this tedious complaint—though the whaling wives had it much, much worse than their sister sailors on merchant ships, probably because of the eternal stench of ran-cid oil that oozed up from the bilges. Nancy Bolles, who sailed on the *Alert* in 1850, wrote to her sister that it was lucky her baby Isabel was "a verry good child," for "although I have had to feed her ever since I left home, I have been sick so much that I haven't had scarcely any milk for her, when I was seasick I vomited till I vomited blood."

It was almost as uncomfortable for the sufferer's husband as it was for the woman herself, for he generally felt so helpless. While most seasickness passed with no lasting ill-effects, and many people "comforted" those who longed to be thrown overboard with the reminder that seasickness was never fatal, pro-longed vomiting could lead to very serious side effects, including dehydration. Adelaide Hamilton, who endured an appalling passage about Cape Horn in 1881, threw a fit that could have had terrifying consequences. Her husband had badly wrenched his neck, and she was rubbing it with petroleum jelly that she warmed at a candle, when he screamed out with pain, and the sudden fright sent her into convulsions.

Her lighted candle was still held in her hand as she threshed. "Joe was so frightened he lost all pain and jumped up and caught a hold of me," she wrote shakily later, "but it was some time before he could catch hold of my hand with

Nancy Bolles. Mystic Seaport Museum.

the candle in it, as it was first over my head and in every position imaginable, my hands and feet all going. He expected I would set fire to my hair, clothes or the room before he could take it from me." When he did grasp it, Adelaide came out of her fit, and "went off into a faint."

Captain Henry Bagley of the *Levi C. Wade* was at a loss to do anything to help his wife Laura's almost constant nausea, save note her daily progress—in the official logbook! "Laura still seasick in her Bed," he wrote on March 12, 1880, two days after taking their departure from Cardiff, and then, on the fourteenth, "Laura still sick in her bed, poor lubber." On April 6 she was "still sick and lazy," and two days later Henry, perhaps in desperation, cut her hair off. It didn't work. On the sixteenth, "Laura has been seasick all day, groaning about the strong Trades," he wrote, recording that he corrected her, for it was "not wright" to criticize "the good SE Trades." So strongly did he feel about it, that he added in red ink, "When this you see, think of your old Henry, always in his glory with a Breeze."

Other captains had pet nostrums, which they were perfectly willing to try out on their wives. On March 4, 1853, Cynthia Congdon wrote that "the motion of the Ship made me feel very uncomfortably sick, and I had to acknowledge I was seasick. They had beef steak and onions for breakfast and I do not think I shall ever forget beef steak and onions." That particular dish might have been ruined for her forever, but her husband, John, treated her by giving her saltwater to drink, "and I was quite bright again."

Kate Morse Thomson, daughter-in-law of the captain of "the good ship *J. F. Chapman*," had a much more enticing medicine—"crackers and Champaigne." On the brig *Massachusetts*, Katurah Pritchard calmed her stomach with molasses gingerbread. Jane Barber of the *Ocean Eagle* wrote that going out on deck and walking was "the best remedy—always relieving it at least in a measure." This was not as easily accomplished as it might sound, the tricky part being to get out on deck to start with, the nausea being accompanied by dizziness. "I like going to sea very much," she added; "at least if the sea would always be smooth."

Fidelia Heard found that taking a cold saltwater plunge in the sitz bath she had carried along gave her the energy to get dressed, but after that she was not fit for anything but lying on the transom sofa and wondering how she could possibly manage to get undressed again. But, she wrote, "my best of husbands assisted me in the tenderest manner"—but otherwise all he could do was sigh and say, "I pity you."

In startling contrast, twenty-eight-year-old Alonzo Follansbee (who treated his bride like a rather witless child) considered her freedom from seasickness suspiciously unnatural. A "proper" woman should be sick on setting off to sea, he decreed, and so, two days out from New York, he dosed Madam with "wine of ipecac," to make her vomit and therefore conform. "Wednesday, 2 days at sea, May 9th," she wrote. "Still refused to pay tribute to old Neptune, and the Capt. proposed a dose of 'wine of ipecac' (and not a very small one) which had but little effect," and so he gave her more, until the desired "effect" was achieved.

This extraordinary domination of a woman by her husband was by no means unusual. Captain John Remington Congdon was deeply attached to his wife, Cynthia, writing a private journal especially for her when she did not accompany him on voyage, the heading of one typical logbook reading (complete with punctuation), "Written solely, for the Amusement, Instruction, and Satisfaction, of, his Much Loved, and Dutiful Wife, Cynthia A. Congdon." That word "Dutiful" was very important to John, as Cynthia herself was very aware. On March 13, 1842, the first Sunday after their marriage, she penned a prayer in her diary which ran, "May we have the same mind in everything, but if it should so happen that we do not always think alike, let us never contend, let me always feel that I am the weaker vessel and as such yield my opinion to his."

This humble, self-deprecating stance was the recommended one for females at the time, and was so deeply ingrained that it was a kind of second nature. Maria Murphy (whose sea life spanned thirty-five years) once lightly wrote about a conversation between her husband James, and her young son Wilder. They were talking, she

Maria Murphy.
Courtesy Maine Maritime Museum.

said, "about being forgotten a hundred years from now." James "remarked that his name would be <u>handed down</u> in a book as 'The Life of Capt. Murphy,'" she recounted. "Well," said her son Wilder, "I hope they won't put into the book how much you growl in calms."

The humor of this is engaging, and the life of "Capt. Murphy" has indeed been handed down, in the form of a few chapters in books, and occasional magazine and newspaper articles. What is particularly interesting, however, is that no one present during that conversation, Maria least of all, considered her own story to be the one that was really worth recording.

Captain James "Shotgun" Murphy.
Courtesy Maine Maritime Museum.

Back then, women came in all kinds of shapes, sizes, and temperaments, just as they do today, but then, as now, one particular shape, size, and temperament was considered the ideal. The dynamic, arrow-slim businesswoman admired now would be as alien to Victorian society as the demure, hourglass-shaped creature beloved by the popular nineteenth-century press seems to us. Where some people today might consider Cynthia Congdon's docility contemptible, in the terms of her own time she was doing her best to conform to a recognized ideal.

The person probably most responsible for the popularization of the strict Victorian definition of the sexes was Sarah Josepha Hale, the editor of the best-selling periodical *Godey's Lady's Book*. Mrs. Hale theorized that the male sex was naturally aggressive, adventurous, and lusty, while the "true woman" was submissive, timid, and impregnably virtuous. Mouselike though she might seem, however, the woman Mrs. Hale described had a vital role in God's plan for mankind. Woman's "divinely appointed sphere" was to save the morals of the world and settle "the destiny of humanity." By righteous example "true women" could save carnal males from their grossness.

Many people were far too sensible to pay much attention to this high-flown proposition, one being whaling wife Lizzie Edwards of Sag Harbor, who noted ironically on passage to Honolulu that many of the passengers were sea-sick, "not only weak, feeble women, but great strong men," too. Predictably, too, Mrs. Hale's philosophy aroused a lot of ire in the women's rightists set, the thirteenth resolution in their "Declaration of Sentiments" at the 1848 Seneca Falls Convention being that the creed "has created a false public sentiment by giving to the world a different code of morals for men and women."

However, a lot of women—and men—took the theory very seriously, as evidenced by the huge success of Mrs. Hale's magazine, and the many peri-odicals that sprang up in imitation. In 1836, when Mrs. Hale moved from Boston to Philadelphia to take over the editorship, the circulation of *Godey's Lady's Book* was about ten thousand; twenty years later, the figure was a stag-gering 1.5 million—and the audience for this kind of propaganda in *Godey's* and similar magazines was certainly not confined to women. Wilder Murphy, when he was first mate of the *Shenandoah* in 1898, wrote to his mother that he had read all "the Women's Worlds and Gentlewomans" that she had given him. He had handed them on to the captain's wife, Apphia Jane Starkey, but in the meantime he had been an appreciative audience.

A side effect of this philoso-phy was that swooning became the fashionable female response to any kind of distress, Elizabeth Young Linklater observing in her memoirs that "occasional faint-ing" was considered necessary "to prove the refinement of the gen-tler sex." Once, when they were in Port Chalmers, New Zealand, an English actress came on board the *Norval* to pay a call, stopped in the middle of the short but narrow gangplank, clapped her hand to her breast, and de-claimed, "I'm going to faint, I'm sure I shall faint!"—with the re-sult that the attractive first mate was forced to assist her.

It is a wonder that the men-folk did not become impatient with this, particularly at inconve-

Downeaster Shenandoah, *the four-masted bark (the sailors called her a "shipentine") that was considered so beautiful that the federal government featured her picture on all master mariners' licenses.* Courtesy South Street Seaport Museum.

The Victorian Ideal.
From *Harper's Magazine,* 1854.

nient moments. When she heard a violent scuffle on the deck of the *Young America,* for instance, Charlotte Babcock promptly swooned, which could well have annoyed her husband, who was busy enough already. However, many men heartily concurred with Mrs. Hale's philosophy (never seeming to find it odd that they found out about it by reading women's magazines); apparently it made them feel tremendously virile, even if it did mean they had to put up with all that swooning.

Women seemed to enjoy this image of themselves, too, perhaps because it made them feel important, and many tried hard to model themselves on these stated ideals. It was a major reason so many of them wrote journals, for they were trained as girls to keep diaries as a check on their spiritual well-being. On Saturday nights they made lists of all the work they had accomplished in the week, and on Sundays they wrote down pious meditations. "Thirty-two years of my life has gone, and what account can I give of them?" demanded Mary C. Bartlett of herself, on the coasting brig *Lawrence Copeland* in 1849. "These are solemn questions, and involve my future happiness." Mary was as retiring and timid as the delicate female sex was supposed to be, hiding in her room "like a scared child" when they made port in Havana.

Shipmasters seem to have been particularly apt believers, perhaps because seamen are aggressive, adventurous, and lusty by long tradition. Like Sarah Hale, Captain John Remington Congdon definitely held that meekness was "woman's highest ornament." Another aficionado was Captain Edwin Brown of Orient, Long Island, who described the qualities of "a real fine wife" in a letter to his wife, Martha, dated June 1853. Not only was the wifely exemplar "modest & resurved," but she was also "perfectly submissive" to her husband's will: "in fact she has no will of her own, his will is hers, & tis her greatest pleasure to gratify him in all his desires."

While this may seem extreme, it must be remembered that shipmasters were accustomed to being in absolute command already, in a situation where even muttered grumbling could be regarded as mutiny. As Madam Follansbee remarked, "The Captain is often called King on board his ship," his word being "law." Oddly, this apartness from the rest of the crew was a major reason why so many wives were carried to sea. A captain had to keep a dignified distance from everyone on board, up to and including the mates—even when he was eating at the same table—and so he reigned in rank-endowed loneliness, with no one to talk to, unless his wife was aboard.

It was hard on the wife, however, for on shipboard she was doubly dominated, by her own personal domestic Jehovah as well as the master of the ship, and many wives' diaries betray some resentment of this. When Mary Rowland was writing a letter in January 1873, she noted that her husband, Henry, "comes now and then to the door, says I must have a great deal to write, as I am so long at it. Says he should think that I would like to come on deck this very pleasant evening."

Mary wanted to put off her walk until she had finished her letter. "But he is getting tired, I see, of waiting, and men in general are not overstocked with

Meditations.
From the *Girl's Own Paper,* 1884.

patience, and on shipboard here he is used to command, and I have occasionally hinted to him that my name is not down in his Ship's Articles, even if I did promise to love and obey him some 20 years ago when I engaged to be his Mate for life." Another time, she became very cross with him, for Henry decided that she was sleeping in too long in the mornings, and sent the cook to wake her up. "I do not like the joke," she wrote, for "while he can go to sleep in a moment," she spent many hours of the night listening to him "snoreing at the rate of 10 knots per hour." And she was conscious, too, of his real reason for getting her up and on deck: "He is never contented unless he sees me near him."

For these Victorian women sex was, of course, the great unmentionable, but it is possible to glean hints from letters and diaries. Some of Mary Rairden's honeymoon diary entries, while enigmatic, are revealing as well. "My Braddie kind of easy fellow," she chuckled in the port of Havana; "doesn't know but what I shall put him through shortly," and again, two days later, "Yes yes yes, we'll show the Yankees how it's done." Marian Smith, who accompanied her husband, Horace, on whaling voyages toward the end of the century, wrote to her father in May 1895, "Oh! I quite forgot to tell you that yesterday Horace took me over his knee and spanked me. Wholly without provocation too, for all I did was to flirt my mittens in his face."

Her giggle is almost audible, and at the end of the letter there is a note written by her husband. "Pop, she was so sassy I just had to take her over my knees." In 1891 on board the *J. F. Chapman*, Albert Thomson indulged in rather similar frolics with his bride of five months. "I fooled with Albert until he got me mad," wrote his wife, Kate, "tearing my hair all down & putting his feet in my face."

Sailors being traditionally lusty and so forth, the prospect of a companion in the double berth must have been a compelling reason for a captain to take his wife to sea. Whaleman Jared Jernegan of Martha's Vineyard wrote to his wife, Helen, when he was urging her to take passage to join him, "I shall let you git rite up into my lap just as you used to, then I will tell my beautiful little wife how lonely I have been." According to then-prevailing philosophy, however, when Helen obeyed Jared by undertaking a tortuous, expensive, and definitely dangerous journey south to Aspinwall, across the Isthmus of Panama, and north to San Francisco (where he failed to meet her) in 1865, her only motive was dutiful wifely devotion. This was because the female sex was supposed to be naturally frigid, woman's nature—

Helen Jernegan and her husband, Captain Jared Jernegan. Scrimshawed tusks. Courtesy of the scrimshander, Robert Weiss.

according to Sarah Hale's contemporary Elizabeth Oakes-Smith—being ideally "a tribute to the respectabilities, decorums and moralities of life, devoid of its enthusiasms."

Some wives—even remarkably liberated Dorothea Balano, who sailed with her husband, Fred, on his coaster from 1911 onward and kept a diary that included many candid accountings of their quarrelsome sex life—seemed to be in agreement with this common understanding that men and women had different carnal appetites. Dorothea grumbled in June 1911, "I had a long, hard night, and feel like hell," and followed up several similar complaints over the next three months by informing her readers that whenever her "precious, darling husband" got affectionate, it usually preceded a fight. "It's simply that the husbands are leading up to copulating and with that they'd like a bit of fellatio, lacking which they get nasty and start a battle." Well, she declared with spirit, "I shall not be a fellatrix, Captain, oh my Captain, and if that be mutiny, make the most of it."

A marriage guidance pamphlet of Dorothea's time strongly urged its female readers to "give little, give seldom, and most of all give grudgingly." Published in 1894, this advice came too late for Martha Brown of Orient, Long Island, but

Martha Brown.
Oysterponds Historical Society,
New York.

Captain Edwin Brown.
Oysterponds Historical Society,
New York.

it is doubtful that Martha would have taken any notice, even if she had read it. Martha was the wife of Captain Edwin Brown, who carried her to sea on the whaleship *Lucy Ann* of Greenport, New York, in 1847. It was entirely his own decision. Even the most casual scrutiny of Martha's diary makes it clear that she would have much preferred to stop at home with her little girl, Ella. Conditions on board might have been even grimmer than on the usual grubby whaler, too, for Captain Brown's standards of health and hygiene were low, evidenced by the pride he took in a voyage he had made in 1843, when he was in command of the bark *Washington,* also of Greenport. For some reason—perhaps because he was newly married—Edwin had sworn to get home within the year, and so he circled the world in 363 days, without ever dropping the anchor. This meant that the crew of thirty-odd men existed almost entirely on the salt provisions and freshwater that had been put on board in Greenport. It was indeed a remarkable feat, but it is even more amazing that his crew survived the ordeal. It's a medical miracle that they didn't all die of scurvy, and no doubt Martha was properly thankful that she hadn't been along on that voyage.

So Martha was risking more than shipwreck when Edwin decreed she should sail. Nevertheless, like many of her sister sailors, she made the best of it. Being with her Edwin (whom she certainly loved) made it reasonably worthwhile, for Martha had definite carnal cravings, writing once when Edwin was away, "Night succeeds night, but I am not permitted to clasp the object of my fondest affection." In October 1847, on board the *Lucy Ann* of Greenport, she wrote, "If quince groves and moonlight nights are incentives to make love, surely moonlight nights on shipboard are doubly so." Naturally enough, she became pregnant on voyage. Edwin's response was to set her ashore in Honolulu in

Pages from Martha's journal.
Oysterponds Historical
Society, New York.

April 1848, alone, friendless, and without enough money, failing to return until mid-November, when the infant was nearly three months old.

Whatever the sexual craving, opportunity for satisfaction was an uncertain matter on board. It is no coincidence that during the month that Martha Brown rhapsodized about moonlight nights and conceived her child, the weather was calm and the sea was smooth, and that Mary Rairden wrote about teasing her Braddie while at anchor, for the ship was the ultimate mistress. Storm, fogs, or proximity to shore meant that the captain had to stay on deck for days and nights at a time. Like many wives, Calista Stover often noted whether her husband, Joseph, came to bed or not, and this was much more likely to be an indication of sea conditions than a comment on their sex life. "Friday night Joe laid down on the sofa for an hour," Adelaide Hamilton recorded on the way around Cape Horn in late 1881, "the first rest he has had in eighty hours."

Adelaide, who enjoyed an affectionate relationship with her husband, Joe (though she called him "the Boss"), noted that they had separate bedrooms, presumably so that he would not disturb her when he was called up to deck, but also perhaps because she was so constantly seasick. "Took everything out of Joe's bedroom and scrubbed all the paint and drawers," she wrote in January 1882, on one of the very few days she was not ill. Then, two days later, she cleaned her own room.

Seasickness must have been a most effective contraceptive. Also, it was commonplace for babies to sleep with their mothers, and though small children usually had their own cribs—Elizabeth Marble quipping on the whaler *Kathleen* that her husband, John, had made their little boy George a swinging cot "to keep the bedbugs from carrying him off"—they were taken into the mother's bed if they were sick or frightened. Even when the captain felt easy enough to retire to the marital bunk, a rolling ship or uneasy swell would have made matters difficult. Scott Dow reminisced that the captain's double berth had a "shifting board," which divided the bed so the occupants would not roll into each other.

So it can probably be safely assumed that sex happened a lot less often at sea than it did at anchor or on shore. Cornelia Peabody started her diary the day she got married, on April 26, 1855, and recorded that she and her new husband had "naps" together in the afternoons. After May 5, when the *Neptune* sailed, she scarcely saw him. By the same logic, the children who were born on voyage had most likely been conceived either before the voyage commenced, or else in some exotic port.

✦ ✦ ✦

In view of the "refining" nature attributed to the female sex, it is interesting to speculate whether any of the seafaring wives imagined they could exert a "civilizing influence" on board ship. It would have been quite a challenge, mariners by long custom being independent both in behavior and speech. However, one very pious wife, Calista Stover of Bucksport, Maine, tried very hard indeed.

Calista was thirty-six when she married Joseph, a man twenty years her senior, in 1874. It was late to adapt to motherhood, let alone life on his sailing ship, *Daniel Barnes*. She accomplished both, however, giving birth to a daughter, Maria Calista, in October 1875, and a son, Edward, in September 1881, and sailing almost constantly from 1878 to 1890, the year that Joseph retired, at the good age of seventy-one. Calista circled the globe twice, and doubled Cape Horn four times, becoming familiar with such wide-ranging ports as Yokohama, Liverpool, Melbourne, and Hong Kong, though she never, ever lost her fear of rugged seas and storms.

And she never stopped trying to reform the men, despite constant grave disappointments. "Just as it is ashore, so it is afloat," she bitterly complained in February 1882. "Some cannot be bothered to go to Church. We have two [such] men this voyage. One replied that he is too old and has been too long at sea and over the world to be affected by religious influences. Some tell me that they have not been inside a church for more than twenty years and have not looked into their Bibles since they left home." However, Calista persisted, employing her children as acolytes when they were old enough to take part. "A good meeting tonight," her thirteen-year-old daughter Maria recorded on September 17, 1889. "Subject, Temperance. Three of the men signed tonight, and Eddie and the steward signed again. I sang, 'Have Courage My Boy To Say No.'"

Maria's little brother Eddie had only just celebrated his eighth birthday, which seems a little young to hold up as an example for toughened sailors, but by such means Calista pursued her virtuous course, at one time managing to persuade the entire crew to sign a "solemn promise to abstain from Liquors and Tobacco." Once on shore in Yokohama, this pledge was promptly broken, but nonetheless the feat of getting hardened mariners to sign at all was quite remarkable.

And so it seems very likely that any woman who tried to exert her "civilizing" influence on board ship was doomed to failure. Mary Atkins, a spinster who taught at a seminary for girls in California, took passage on the brig *Advance* during a sabbatical in 1863, and did her utmost to reform the first mate, Mr. Pendleton, en route, giving up on the second mate without trying, for he was reading a book in Swedish that he told her was a testament. Mr. Pendleton proved a lost cause, however, becoming offended when she censured him "for swearing so constantly in my presence. He seems to look upon profanity as an accomplishment," Miss Atkins added in disgust.

In a letter to her husband, Joseph, written after leaving the ship, Abbie Griffin confessed that she wished she was back at sea, even if it did mean she had to put up with his swearing. Fidelia Heard noted with perceptible satisfaction

79

shortly after embarking on the *Oriental* that when she "heard a loud oath from one of the sailors, he was immediately reproved by the mate, who told him that no profane nor vulgar language would be allowed, for there is a lady on board!" The exclamation mark indicates some surprise as well, so it seems that Fidelia was too realistic to expect this elevated state of affairs to continue.

Emma Pray of the *Governor Goodwin* was a particularly down-to-earth seafarer, greeting with outright derision a missionary's suggestion that she should try to reform the sailors. The reverend had come off to the ship in Hong Kong, and with a nod toward her parlor organ had craftily observed that "it looked as if it might be a very good-toned one." Then, having got that bit of flattery off his chest, he had gone on to suggest "that it would cheer & inspire" the sailors. "I told him," said Emma roundly, "I didn't think anything in that line <u>would</u> inspire them." Then, when he tried to convince her otherwise, she informed him that "if he only knew sailors better, he would know that there would not be one out of ten who would go to the church, if he could go ashore and get drunk instead." And anyway, if she were foolish enough to invite sailors into her cabin, she sniffed, "It would need to be scrubbed for a week."

A MISSIONARY IN A CHINESE TEMPLE.

A missionary in a Chinese temple.
From *Missionary World.*

It was particularly necessary to be pragmatic on the packets, clippers, and downeasters, where captains relied on speed and fast passages for their reputations, driving their men to the limit of endurance in a merciless effort to outrun all their competitors, often with a heavy bet on the outcome. Inevitably, discipline could be ironhanded. Captains like Joseph Delano and Enoch Peabody might be suave, civilized hosts in the after cabins of their ships, but on the quarter deck they were uncompromising taskmasters, with mates who backed up their orders with fists, boots, and belaying pins. Then, as steam began to take over from sail, and expenses had to be cut to the bone to make sailing vessels profitable, harsh treatment of the crews became so commonplace that in September 1888 the National Seamen's Union of America attempted to amend the situation by publishing a "Red Record," which reported extreme instances of brutality, along with the names of the captains and mates involved. Publication lapsed within six years, but in the meantime the "Red Record" engendered a lot of public comment.

One of the captains cited was "Shotgun" James Murphy of Bath, Maine. In October 1893 it was reported in the "Record" that a seaman on board Murphy's ship *Shenandoah* named Bahr "fell overboard from the royal yard and no effort was made to save him.

> *Capt. acknowledged this, but excused himself on the ground of rough weather. Ship had topgallant sails set on the wind. A passenger reports that the food was a revelation (to him), being meager in quantity and bad in quality. Cruelty and constant abuse charged to the officers. Capt. Murphy refused to see these goings on or to interfere when complained to.*

Shotgun's wife, Maria, never wrote a word about ill-treatment of the men, however. According to her voluminous sea letters, Shotgun was a kind father and a generous husband, and nothing of the kind ever happened on his ships. Indeed, she was terribly upset when one of the men fell from aloft in June 1884, dying later of his injuries. "He will be buried tomorrow morning and J. will read the Burial Service, so that he will not be put overboard like a dog. I trust that God will deal tenderly with his soul," she wrote.

They knew next to nothing about the poor fellow, "only that he was an Englishman—he had scarcely any clothes and no letters to tell anything about him." Interestingly, however, Maria did mention that the deceased seaman had been prone to epileptic fits. Captain Murphy had "told the mate not to send him aloft," but the first officer had ignored the command, as the seaman "was a good sailor, willing and capable," and wanted to work in the rigging. And so it seems that if anyone was at fault, it was the mate, but there is no mention of the first officer being reprimanded for the decision.

It was usual for the captain to leave the control of the crew entirely in the hands of his officers, and some of these were definitely sadists. According to some accounts, the *Shenandoah* was a so-called hell ship, but much of this could have been due to a notorious first officer, James Kelly, for Shotgun was never brought to trial. There were two suicides and a murder on one voyage of the *Gatherer* of Bath, Maine, and it was the mate, "Black" Charles Watts, who was sentenced to prison, not the captain.

Captain John Mathieson of the *Antiope* wrote that he "never interfered with the mates in their working of the crew"—and yet it was probably inevitable that the "working" should deteriorate into "working up," or "hazing." To the mates of the big square riggers, physical brutality would often seem to be the only means of keeping violent seamen under control. On the *Charlotte Reed* in August 1850, first mate Horatio Gray had a great deal of trouble with one man, who "took his knife out & swore he would rip us open." Eventually, the sailor was subdued, but it took both mates to beat him into submission, while Captain Weeks stood over them with a pistol in his hand in case things got serious, and Mrs. Weeks watched silently from a distance.

Horatio was no slacker himself, taking on the famous clipper *Flying Childers* in a race when he was master of the *Cossack* in 1859. His wife, Emma, made no comment whatsoever about the treatment of the crew in her journals, possibly because she was a seasoned sailor, having voyaged with her father, Captain Levi Hotchkiss, on the ship *Harvard* of Boston. Bel Wood, wife of Captain Aaron Wood of the *Sovereign of the Seas* and the *Sagamore,* related in a letter to friends in July 1874 that one night Aaron was dreaming of "pitching in" to one of his men, and she had to quit the bed in a hurry to evade the flying blows. However, her letters also make it obvious that she and Aaron enjoyed a most comradely relationship.

Some captains exercised a certain amount of censorship where their wives were concerned, too. When Sarah Gray objected to her husband's language on the whaleship *Hannibal* in 1849, Captain Sluman Gray merely told her to go below, where she would not hear it. In Kobe in September 1888, seven men staged a mutiny on the *Governor Goodwin,* and Captain Samuel Pray sent his wife to board ashore until the fuss was over. A ship at sea was a public place, however, and many wives must have opted to keep a diplomatic silence.

After all, attempting to moderate a "driving" captain would have been an exercise in frustration. One bride who tried was Sarah Gilkey, who married Captain John G. Pendleton and went to sea with him on the *William H. Connor.* A few days out she asked John if he would kindly shorten sail, as it was "awfully trembly in the cabin." Before he could reply providence did it for him, the maintopgallant sail bursting out of its boltropes and disappearing downwind. John Pendleton, however, simply ordered that a replacement sail be bent and set, and drove his ship on at the same pounding pace.

Another incautious soul was Margaret Fraser, who sailed with her husband, Captain George Fraser, on the famous clipper *Sea Witch* in 1852. Though they had been married four years, this was her first venture, and—as she confessed later in her journal—the friend she thought she had married turned out to be a "stranger" instead.

George Fraser was a Scotsman who first took command of the clipper in April 1850, having been mate of the same ship under Captain Waterman, a man the *California Courier* called a "vile monster," notorious for recruiting his crews from "the jail sweepings of the Atlantic ports." Fraser was a driver after his old skipper's heart, with the result that his 1850 voyage set a record—

ninety-seven days from New York to San Francisco—which remained unbroken until the following year, when Captain "Perk" Cressy did it in eighty-nine days, on the maiden voyage of the *Flying Cloud*.

Margaret Fraser, dazzled by her husband's reputation, was the most unquestioning of wives when she first boarded the *Sea Witch* in August 1852. "I have been sitting on deck this evening with George and the two passengers," she wrote on the twenty-fifth, two days after departure; "the gentleman has been playing on the flute and George has been singing and telling some of his pleasing stories, it is a most glorious night, the moon shining in all its majesty upon the calm bosom of the broad Atlantic. I am very well and O! most happy." It grieved her "to hear him swearing at the men," but she had no trouble finding "a thousand excuses" for "my dearest George, beloved husband! With you my mind is at rest," she thrilled in truly Victorian terms, "my heart's desire satisfied."

Margaret had no good reason to feel "at rest," however, for within a few days it became ominously apparent that George Fraser was not the most emotionally stable of men. "All hands have been very busy," she recorded on September 3, "some making and repairing old sails, others attending to the rigging. The carpenter is repairing one of the boats, my beloved husband superintending the whole, at one moment ordering and screaming at the men, on the next in the cabin laughing and joking with me."

Margaret Fraser was a tiny woman who had to stand on a chicken coop to see over the ship's rail; she was surely deserving of gallantry. Instead, George began to play cruel practical jokes on her, such as tricking her into taking hold of a newly tarred rope and laughing when her hands and clothes became indelibly smeared, and deliberately unfocusing a spyglass before handing it to her to look at a whale. Then, on the fifteenth: "George has been reading in my journal," she wrote with perceptible uneasiness, "and finds fault with my endearing mode of expression as regards himself. Well!" she penned, "it is better I think that he should complain of a too great fondness than not enough"—but the sugary prose evaporated, her diary-writing style becoming cautious instead.

Indeed, it becomes apparent that Margaret started using her journal to send him definite messages, some of which can be interpreted as outright pleas for moderation. On September 19 she wondered in script why she had left her happy home "to roam the trackless waste of waters, with whom?—One who is comparatively a stranger to me; for although we have been married better than four years, still his constant absence from home has left me no opportunity of studying his disposition. . . .

"I know he holds it in his power to make me very happy and contented, or on the contrary, most miserable," she continued, and added deliberately, "I have not the least fear of the result"—when it is obvious that she meant the complete opposite.

There is little doubt that George read this, but his choice was to make her miserable. For instance, he always insisted that she play "a few games at backgammon in the evening," even though he was unbearably irritated by her "want of comprehension." Understandably, Margaret often felt "as though I cannot play again, [but] still I dislike to refuse him any request, or make an objection to anything that tends to amuse him." His behavior was evidently childishly cruel, for he reminded her so of her brother William, petulantly "annoyed with me when I make a wrong move, and so out of patience with my stupidity and want of attention."

Other people were paying attention, however. "It has turned out that we have a poet on board," she wrote glumly one month after the voyage had begun. This was Mr. Benman, the passenger, who had "written a most satirical production" that had fallen into Captain George Fraser's hands. In no way was it flattering to the captain, "comparing him" to that well-known tyrant "Nicholas of Russia." Mr. Benman, a shrewd observer, "says my face is shadowed with gloom, in consequence of the ill-treatment of my husband." Instead of offering sympathy, however, he cast aspersions in the lowest manner possible—"judges my age to be 43, notwithstanding people say I am young, thinks that I may drink." In view of George Fraser's propensity for violence, this composition was most ill-judged. In the face of his rage, Mr. Benman fled to his room, kept thereafter in seclusion, and quit the ship as soon as they dropped anchor in San Francisco.

As her confidence drained away in the face of this constant contempt, Margaret became sickly and very prone to tears. And then, on October 6, her husband became furious when he missed two cases of liquor (which turned out afterward to have been packed in the wrong room), and somehow Margaret's foot became lamed.

In her words, "In some way or other I have sprained the chords on the instep of my left foot, which is very much swollen and inflamed." It could have been an accident, but when more unpleasantness occurred, Margaret feared suffering further injury. She experienced violent dreams, detailing one in which her brother William (with whom she had already identified her husband) was beating her, and her father was slashing him with a knife so that "the blood flowed in a stream." Not surprisingly, Margaret woke up "crying like a child."

Meantime, George was becoming more irrational than ever. Going about the Horn, his customary dress was "old dressing-gown and pyjamas," in which he superintended the work, while "all hands watch him as narrowly as possible, and I am grieved to suppose that he is more feared than loved by them." The implicit messages in her journal continued, perhaps because they were her only safe means of communicating her hopes and fears. "I am highly gratified," she wrote on November 16; "for these two days past I have not heard my husband use any bad language; would that he could have resolution enough to quit it altogether, I am sure he would get along quite as well."

That entry has the word "Humbug" scrawled across it—but still Margaret Fraser persisted. She made him a more respectable dressing gown, and George refused to wear it. Then, figuring that he might exert some self-control if she was about decks more often, she learned to assist in cutting and sewing sails. "I know George will not be able to get along without me after this," she wrote hopefully after helping him splice warps on November 19, but these deck activities soon came to a halt. Going ashore in San Francisco gave her a respite, but when she reembarked she was miserably seasick, and "wretchedly lonely." Then, in February, he got into a violent scuffle with one of the men.

"George had left me but a moment to go on deck," she wrote, "when I heard such screaming.

> *I raised up to see what caused it, and the first thing that met my view was George, his face one mass of blood, grapling with one of the men. My first impression was that the man had stabbed him, such was not the case, however. It appears that George hit him and turned to go away when the fellow tripped him up, and struck him over the head, cutting three frightful wounds.*

As it turned out, George was not badly hurt, though three days later his eyes were black and swollen—which could have been the result of another brawl. One unpleasantness succeeded another: he accused her of extravagance; her cabin boy was "severely" punished by him for pilfering tidbits from the storeroom; the water tank was sabotaged, and the leakage not discovered until it was nearly empty. Then, at long last, the *Sea Witch* arrived back in New York, June 27, 1853, five days after a sadder, wiser Margaret had written, "It is ten months today since we left home; it is years to me."

It is difficult to tell how typical Margaret Fraser's awful voyage might have been. Certainly, many captains were so desperate to achieve record passages in the face of uncooperative weather and clumsy or unwilling seamen, that—

justly or unjustly—they were cited in the "Red Record" for cruelty. Shotgun Murphy was renowned as a flamboyant master who raced other downeasters, usually after placing a large bet on himself. In 1892, when he was master of the famous *Shenandoah,* he lost three thousand dollars—an immense sum at the time—in a contest with Captain Peabody of the *Tam O'Shanter* (another man cited in the "Red Record"). Undeterred, Murphy raced against Captain Duncan of the *Florence* the following year, taunting the captain's wife with the boast that he would be waiting in San Francisco with a buoy to help them moor. Kate Duncan said nothing, but spent a few days while going about Cape Horn making a miniature cork buoy, which she then dipped in gold. Sure enough, the *Florence* arrived ahead of the *Shenandoah,* and when Captain Jim finally reached the dock, Kate stepped forward and demurely handed him the toy.

The clipper Swordfish. *Launched in New York in 1851, the* Swordfish, *commanded by Captain David Babcock and with Charlotte Babcock on board, competed in a famous race to San Francisco, making a record passage of 90 days, 16 hours.*
Artist: Ron Druett.

Even Captain Duncan resorted to his fists at times, once felling a knife-wielding seaman with one pop to the jaw—though when his son Fred sailed on another ship at the age of twelve, he was horrified by the brutality of the mates. Burgess Sorensen Coghill, who was raised on her father's ship *Snow & Burgess* (having been named after the vessel, in time-honored fashion), described her father's alarm when a drunken seaman almost beat him in a fight. Without physical superiority, it seems, he was not qualified to do his job.

Maria Murphy's seagoing career spanned thirty-five years, which surely indicates that her daily life with Shotgun was not all that unpleasant. Picturesquely named Captain Horatio Nelson Gray was a devoted and generous husband, showering Emma with diamonds in Oriental ports. Captain Thomas Pritchard, Jr., who carried his wife, Katurah, on the brig *Massachusetts,* was extremely solicitous of her well-being, and became so concerned when she persisted in hating the sea and anything to do with it that he interrupted the normal course of the voyage to take her sightseeing. He wanted to show her Paris, but a revolution got in the way (it was April 1848), so he took her by steamer to London, instead. When, in March 1849, she left the ship in Charleston to take passage home, he was so disconsolate that Katurah felt extremely guilty, writing him a letter in which she repeatedly assured him, "When you are far away on the blue sea, I shall daily think of you, yes, hourly."

Mary Snell regarded her husband, Nicholas, so lightly that her diary of the 1839 voyage of the ship *Victoria* sounds remarkably like one kept on a cruise liner today, her days an enjoyable mix of walking the deck, watching other ships and scenery through a spyglass, and eating lots of good food that had been cooked by someone else—all with never a mention of Nicholas and the responsibility of the ship, even when the sails caught fire while being towed up the Mississippi River. "I am getting quite fleshy," she meditated after sixteen days of this self-indulgent existence.

Even the toughest of mariners could meet his match in a scrappy, spirited spouse—such as the wife of Captain "Wildcat" Anderson, who was known throughout the Pacific as "Slippery Kate." According to Captain John Mathieson of the *Antiope,* one night the people on the ships that were taking on coal at Newcastle, Australia, were entertained by a loud-voiced row echoing from the Andersons' vessel, the *J. H. Lunsman.* Next morning, when Kate flounced off ashore to buy fruit for the passage to San Francisco, Wildcat saw his chance, and raised anchor and sneaked away. To his profound disgust, however, she was waiting on the wharf when he arrived in San Francisco, having talked the ship's agent into giving her money—Wildcat's own money—to buy steamer passage to California.

This was the turn of the century, however, when women had gained the confidence of moving into the white-collar workforce, having seized that invention, the Remington typewriter, and made it peculiarly their own   an impressive piece of opportunism, when it is considered that up until the 1880s all clerks had been men. For earlier wives, their era was definitely against them. Many of them were on the defensive before they even set foot on the ship, for at home it was often not considered appropriate for a woman to accompany her husband to sea. "Surely if I did wrong in leaving home, that sin has been atoned for," wrote Margaret Fraser at the end of her dreadful voyage. "How did Betsy Ann's mother get along with her going away?" asked Sarah Morgan about another seafaring wife in a letter home, dated December 1880. "Did she make just as much fuss as before? If so, I pity Betsy Ann from the bottom of my heart." Mary-Ann Sherman of New Bedford was declared dead when she went off with her new husband on the whaleship *Harrison* in 1845, the family putting up a gravestone as evidence. Unfortunately, she did not return home to prove them wrong, as she died before the voyage was over; her true grave was the one we discovered on the South Pacific island of Rarotonga.

On the 1852 voyage of the *Hannah Thornton* that ultra-patriarch, Captain John Remington Congdon, became displeased with his wife, Cynthia, when "one of the passengers taught me how to play chess. Perhaps I have done wrong in learning," she humbly confessed. "My time, I think, might have been better employed." This meekness was an attitude of the time, greatly intensified by being the lone female on board ship—a mind-set that must have contributed at least in part to Margaret Fraser's humiliation on the *Sea Witch*.

Margaret's journal ends on June 27, 1853, the day they arrived in port. "Took a pilot at about 5 o'clock last evening," Margaret wrote with tremulous excitement at dawn on the day of arrival; "and with a fine breeze in our favor throughout the night passed Barnegat at 4 o'clock this morning, and at night will be at home, sweet home!"

It is impossible to tell if she was foolish enough to accompany George when he departed from New York again in August. One certainly hopes not, for on that voyage of the *Sea Witch* one of the seamen became so desperate that he tried to sink the ship by boring holes in her bottom. And then, in early 1855, George Fraser was murdered by his first mate.

Somehow, the violent manner of his death does not seem surprising.

CHAPTER FOUR

Children at Sea

*The sea is high and the vessel rolling badly, I have just been taking
a nap as I could not sleep last night and seldom get a chance to get
a nap through the day on account of the Children. As soon as I get
one asleep then the other awakes. It is two O'clock. The man has
just been relieved at the wheel. The mate is giving some orders to
the men, I believe to make more sail, for the wind is abating. I can
not hardly stand at the desk to write, for the motion of the vessel. I
must go now and regulate the crockery ware in the pantry for they
are making a clattering, have got into a frolic regardless of the
Sabbath Day. For dinner had Beef, Pork, Cabbage and potatoes, a
pudding &c. Thus ends this day.*

—Mary Rowland, Sunday, March 2, 1856

On July 30, 1879, to the astonishment of a large crowd of spectators,
the ship *Templar* sailed into San Francisco. She had not been heard
of for more than three hundred days, and had long since been given up for lost.

Even more amazingly, the person in command of her was a fifteen-year-old girl, the captain's daughter, Emma Armstrong.

Eight days from New York, the *Templar* had been caught in a heavy gale, emerging so badly damaged that Captain George N. Armstrong made a run to Rio de Janeiro for repairs. Unfortunately, a plague of yellow fever was raging through the port, and nine of the seamen died before the vessel weighed anchor again. Rashly, Armstrong decided to press on with the voyage, shipping more men and gambling that none of them was harboring the plague. He lost his bet with fate. Within days his wife Andelusia expired, along with two of the seamen, and Armstrong himself was prostrate and delirious in his berth.

This left the ship without a navigator, for the surviving mate knew little about taking bearings. Fortunately, however, Captain Armstrong had taught Emma how to navigate, and so she assumed charge, finding their position every noon, and directing the few fit seamen in the setting of the sails. Because the ship was so light-handed, progress was slow, but in the end Emma Armstrong did it: she brought the *Templar* safely into port, along with a cargo worth $200,000. It was an astonishing feat for a fifteen-year-old girl, particularly as Emma herself was so ill that she had to be carried up on deck in a litter to take her sights and issue directions.

Emma's presence on board her father's ship was by no means unusual. Throughout the nineteenth century and on into the twentieth, hundreds of children were raised on board ship, and many of these were born at sea, so that large numbers of shipmasters were faced with the intimidating task of delivering their own children. This was definitely one of the disadvantages of carrying a wife. However, though some tragedies happened, most women (and captains) came through the ordeal unharmed. According to Joanna Colcord, who spent her childhood on her father's ships, more than seventy citizens of the small Maine town of Searsport were born at sea, with only one fatality in childbirth. Captain William Blanchard delivered all six of his children, and on one occasion when their ship, the *Wealthy Pendleton,* dropped anchor in Kobe,

Two girls on the wharf at New Bedford.
Courtesy Joseph D. Thomas.

Japan, he found the *Willard Mudgett* there, flying a signal for a doctor. Captain Blanchard and his wife went immediately on board, found the captain's young wife in labor, and delivered the baby with the matter-of-fact expertise of long practice.

It was a tradition that carried on to the next generation. On June 13, 1907, the *Bangalore* was twenty-nine days out of Kahului, Hawaiian Islands, and Georgia Blanchard remarked that they were in the same latitude "that the *Bangalore* was on September 11th, 1902 when, at 10.00 P.M., Eleanora (Rosebud) Blanchard was born to Mary and Albert in the Captain's cabin"—also twenty-nine days out of the Hawaiian Islands. In October 1883 Maria Murphy recorded that her daughter Jennie (who had been born on the bark *Alexander*) "asked me whether Wilder was born in the morning or night—when I said morning, she remarked, 'How surprised you must have been when you woke up and found him in the bed with you!' "

"The Capt Wif gave birth to a child," runs the logbook entry of the brig *Thomas W. Rowland* for October 21, 1857. This was in "Latitude 25.50 North, Long by D Re 75.45W," near the Island of Abaco, where earlier that morning the brig had spoken a ship from Bremen. Mary Rowland's two little daughters, Henrietta and Mary Emma, were sent between decks with their dolls to play while Henry Rowland delivered the baby boy, who was christened Woodhull. "When the new Baby was first exhibited" to the little girls, Henrietta asked in great puzzlement, "But where did you find it?" Mary Rowland reminisced later that she was hard pushed for an answer, "not being prepared," but Mary Emma answered quite readily for her, "Oh, I know—he came from the Bremen ship"—presumably in a boat.

If the women were nervous about having their husbands deliver their babies, they certainly did not betray it. It seems likely, however, that they felt a few inner pangs—or that their friends felt it for them, on their behalf. "Capt. Henry Green's wife is going to have a baby & she has gone north with him to have it on board the ship, for she says she isn't a bit affraid to trust herself to her husband's care," wrote Eliza ("Lizzie") Edwards to her Wheeler family at home in Sag Harbor, adding on a candid note, "She has more confidence in him than I'd have in mine." Luckily, however, all turned out well, Mrs. Green arriving back in Honolulu with "a beautiful girl babe," looking perfectly hale and hearty, "& all of one third larger than when I saw her last."

If the ship was in company with a fleet of other vessels, the wives assembled for the birth, for at home it was a group event, sisters, mothers, cousins, and even neighbors being called, along with the midwife or doctor. When Mrs. Whitman went into labor at the Chincha Islands, Peru, on New Year's Eve,

1859, all the wives from the other ships gathered on the *Moses Wheeler,* thus creating a workable facsimile of the supporting domestic circle of home. This was very important to the woman who was giving birth. When Martha Brown was alone and friendless in Honolulu in 1848, she was very worried about how she would cope when her labor pains started. "Must I be confined without my husband, or one that I can call my friend?" she demanded of her journal. Another seafaring wife came to her rescue, however. This was Sarah Gray, who "was with me dureing my confinement and did for me and my child, as an own sister would have done."

"There is a captain's wife boarding here by the name of Mrs. Childs," wrote Lizzie Edwards to her mother from Honolulu, in October 1858. "Well," she went on, "last evening she concluded to have a little <u>party</u> & it resulted in

Mary Rowland's shipboard family: Woodhull, Mary Emma, and Henrietta. Three Village Historical Society.

a nice little girl baby weighing 7 lbs." Mrs. Damon, who was the wife of one of the missionaries, presided, and Lizzie "officiated," along with the doctor and the lodging-house keeper's wife, Eliza Cartwright. Lizzie (who was childless) filled the humble station of holder of the bowl and napkins. Then, once everything was tidied up, Lizzie slept with Cordelia Childs, "with the baby on my arm."

In Macao in July 1838, Madam Follansbee was offered a Chinese baby for fifteen dollars but turned this remarkable bargain down, for she was creating a child of her own. After passage up the pirate-infested River Pearl to Canton, she made herself comfortable while the cargo was being unloaded. Awnings were put up over the afterdeck, which was covered with straw matting and furnished with settees, chairs, and a table covered with a cloth of red damask. And, just like home, part of this deck parlor was partitioned off and equipped with a lying-in couch, for a sick room. A doctor and a midwife were engaged, both European. Dr. Holgate had been practicing in Canton for a year, and his assistant was a captain's wife, an Englishwoman by the name of Stevenson, who had six children of her own and a female servant. Then, having bought a milch-goat, Mrs. Follansbee sat back and awaited the happy event.

It did not take long. Two days later, a Captain Rogers called on board, and he, being the father of six, measured her up with a knowing eye and advised Alonzo not to go far from the ship, for "he might be needed at home." Sure enough, at ten the next morning one boat was sent off for Dr. Holgate, and another for Mrs. Stevenson, and at eleven an eight-pound boy was born.

"Well, there never was such a proud father," wrote Madam. "The first thing he laid him on a pillow, and took him up into the reception room, to show to the Mates and all hands." Some of the parental pride rested on debatable grounds, Alonzo declaring that "he was the first white boy ever born within the Celestial Regions of China," but no one in Canton was quibbling. Captain Stevenson proved a disappointment. Being drunk, he would not allow his wife to lend Madam Follansbee her servant, and was forthwith shunned by the people on the other ships of the fleet. However, this made little difference to Madam, who got out of bed three days after the birth, took a bath, and received a constant stream of visitors, all of them bearing gifts.

A less happy story is that of Sarah Todd of the clipper *Revely,* who was on shore at Singapore on October 21, 1857, when she was "taken sick and our baby was born.... An interesting little babe weighing about 4 lbs." When the ship left Penang on December 13 Sarah wrote that she was frail, "and have been failing since. My cough never was worse, my side is very bad and my stomach also. I am weak and sick. I greatly fear I can never reach

New York, yet it is my constant prayer that I might be able to, on account of my darling babe, who is a weakly little thing and must suffer greatly if left to the mercy of strangers."

Caring for a new baby was difficult enough on shore, particularly for a novice parent, but on shipboard the problems must have seemed insurmountable at times. First and foremost, it was crucial that the mother should have a plentiful milk supply, for when it was lacking there was no alternative, unless a good nanny goat was carried. Sarah Todd's sister, whaling wife Lucy Ann Crapo, wrote on Wednesday, April 24, 1867, "At quarter past six, our little babe was born, a daughter, and tremblingly amid our hopes we took her to our arms, scarcely daring to say ours," and noted two weeks later that the baby was being fed on "rice water sweetened with sugar, with what milk I can give her." Scanty milk production must have been a family failing, for Sarah Todd was unable to nurse more than once a day. The tiny baby, named

Family life on board the St. James, *about 1900.*
Courtesy San Francisco
Maritime National Historical Park.

Agnes Tapley and her daughter Adelaide.
Courtesy San Francisco
Maritime National Historical Park.

Ida Revely, was fed on crushed ship's biscuit in water, and must have suffered a great deal, for she was constantly covered with boils. "Our goat is dead. My preserves are good for nothing," Sarah wrote in despair. Madam Follansbee's goat proved useless as well, for the kid got into a tub of molasses, and Alonzo was so angry that he gave it away to the washerwoman. The nanny goat promptly dried up, but luckily Madam was producing enough milk of her own.

The St. James, *on which the Tapley family sailed.*
Courtesy San Francisco Maritime National Historical Park.

Perhaps worst of all for Sarah Todd, however, was that the maid who had been shipped to help care for the baby had been found in compromising circumstances with one of the men. "Fanny we have found guilty of so many things that I dare not trust my little one with her," Sarah vowed, though too feeble to pick the infant up herself. It was a remarkable demonstration of the inflexibility of Victorian morals, for Captain Edward Todd was too ill to be of assistance, being shockingly swelled up with scurvy.

Diaper cleaning was another problem, and the mother's sanitary napkins had to be washed as well. At sea, menstruation was usually taken care of by the use of a finger-shaped sea sponge, which was inserted like a tampon. This was encased in a silken net with a tassel for easy withdrawal, and had the great advantage of needing only a little fresh water to be rinsed clean. Indeed, the

Cassady family on board the Greta, *c. 1885. Surprisingly few women died in childbirth, but Margaret Cassady was one of the unfortunate ones. Pregnant when this picture was taken in Port Pirie, Australia, she died shortly after giving birth to a second daughter.*

more sophisticated women used "the sponge" as a contraceptive device, soaking it beforehand in vinegar or sour milk.

Women who bled copiously needed something more than a sponge tampon, however, and so napkins—usually soft cloths familiarly known as "grandy rags"—were used. These were held in place by a napkin strap, which was attached to a band that went about the waist. "Commenced to work napkin strap," wrote Mary Stickney on the whaler *Cicero* on Saturday, June 11, 1881, and Monday noted "Finished napkin strap"—not having been able to sew on the intervening Sabbath. And, when the rags were washed, they were hung out inside something like a pillow case, to save the sailors any embarrassment.

In Victorian times babies' napkins were made of red flannel, and stitched onto the baby with needle and thread—very useful tools, for in rough weather babies were often sewn into their cribs as well, with stitches attaching the swaddling blanket to the mattress. Washing diapers was a bigger problem, though Elizabeth Linklater recorded a young father tying napkins to a rope and towing them behind the ship. This seems a very efficient way of laundering them (provided they did not attract sharks), but unless they were very thoroughly rinsed in freshwater, a residue of salt would remain behind that would not be ideal for baby skins.

Even if the diapers were washed much more conventionally, in a tub, saltwater was often the only kind available. Rinsing in freshwater might not make any difference, either, for they would be encrusted with salt while hung out to dry, because of the spray flying up into the rigging. One solution was simply to scrape solid matter off the diaper, and then hang it up in the cabin for the urine to dry out before putting it back on the baby. Lining the napkin with rags, soft paper, or even dried mosses was another. Once the baby was old enough to crawl—or "creep"—about the deck, there was the Oriental alternative of dressing the lower half in open-bottomed drawers, or even leaving the baby's bottom half naked.

The barefooted sailors could not have liked this very much, and the screaming of a teething or colicky infant was hard on the nerves of everyone on board, particularly the mates. Worst of all, however, was the heart-wrenching whine of a very sick child, for this was a time of high infant mortality, and it was a very rare mother who did not write—as Nantucketer Azubah Cash wrote about her little son William—"He is a pet, and I hope he will be spared us." Virginia Albertina Walker, who married Captain Joshua Slocum (the man who became the first to circumnavigate the world solo) in January 1871, bore three children at sea, and sat by the deathbed of one of them before dying herself, aboard ship in Buenos Aires at the age of thirty-four, on July 25,

1884. Virginia, a natural seafarer, could navigate and handle a gun, but when she wrote to her mother in 1879, her hand shook so much she could scarcely write. "Dear Mother, my dear little baby died the other day," she painfully penned. To all appearances, the infant girl had died of teething. "Every time her teeth would start to come she would cry all night. If I would cut them through, the gum would grow together again. The night she died she had one convulsion after another." Virginia, doing everything she could think of to save her little daughter, had thought for a moment that she was going to succeed, but "she gave a quiet sigh and was gone. . . . She did look so pretty after she died. Dearest Mother, I cannot write any more."

Some days after the birth of Alonzo Follansbee, Jr., when Mrs. Follansbee was on shore in Macao, a blackbird flew through her bedroom, and her hosts warned her darkly that this was an omen that the baby would die. Madam most certainly "did not believe in such signs," but, sadly, the prediction came true. On October 27 the baby very suddenly became ill. The family was in Manila, at the house of Mr. Sturgis, the American consul. Madam had bathed and fed him and put him in his crib to sleep, before going to the drawing room. Later, when Mr. Sturgis was passing the open door, he heard the baby's labored breathing.

Madam rushed in when the consul called out, to find "our precious baby in the greatest agony, his little hands clenched and his eyes set." She snatched him up in horror and tried to nurse him, while Mr. Sturgis sent for a doctor. A physician named Bonsell came, but a healthy adult could not have withstood the ferocious regime of castor oil, enemas, and bleeding that he commenced, let alone a sick infant. The little boy "continued in the most excruciating agony till 3 A. M., when he passed away. Dr. Bonsell pronounced it croup."

During the American Civil War, Captain Henry Rowland's bark *Glenwood* sailed under sealed orders, her destination (Pensacola, to deliver supplies to the troops) unknown until those orders were opened. The voyage south was traumatic, the vessel being struck twice by lightning, resulting in the death of one man. Then Mary's youngest child, Willie, fell ill of yellow fever as they neared Pensacola Bay. All night long as they lay hove to at Santa Rosa Island she was fighting for her son's life, while cannonballs from Confederate and Union gunships screamed above. When the battle was over the *Glenwood* had survived unscathed, but the little boy was dead.

Like Madam Follansbee, Charlotte Babcock lost a tiny baby in the Orient. The little girl was born in Shanghai, sickened in Hong Kong, got a little better in Manila, and died in the Indian Ocean. "Ah, what grief is this," mourned Charlotte, "to bury our precious babe in the fathomless ocean." This was the second little girl she had lost, for another baby, born on an earlier voyage, on the famous clipper *Swordfish,* had died just a few weeks after arriving home.

This last was a surprisingly common story. Little children who had been perfectly healthy on shipboard seemed more vulnerable than shore-raised children to whatever epidemic was prevailing at home. Whaleman John Beckerman of Pocasset, Massachusetts, took his wife, Ann, and their eight-week-old son to sea on the *Othello* in August 1853, and two more babies were born before they got home in June 1858. Within two years all three children were dead, two dying on the same day. Another whaling wife, Sarah Gray, bore three children at sea, and two of these died of unstated causes soon after arriving home. This led to scurrilous gossip in her hometown of Liberty Hill, Connecticut, that Sarah Gray was an infanticide, having engineered the premature deaths herself—which helps to explain why the old Gray house is rumored to be haunted.

A much more rational explanation of the deaths is that children who spent their infancy at sea did not develop immunity to germs that were common on land. Kate Duncan believed so, anyway, for every time the family came home from a voyage on the *Florence,* she "watched the children very carefully for two weeks to see if any contagious disease had been contracted on shore." As she remarked further, her children never had any of the common childhood diseases while at sea, so "they were all waiting for them after we left the sea and they went to school."

By contrast, Sarah Todd's tiny, sickly daughter Ida Revely not only survived the nightmare passage home on the *Revely* but survived eight months on shore as well, to be taken along on Captain Todd's next command, the *Comet*—a foolhardy undertaking that was immortalized by a poem in the *New York Leader:*

> *. . . Now softly, fair Comet—*
> *Thy salon below,*
> *Thy Brussels, thy sofas,*
> *Thy linen let show . . .*
> *I'll whisper, D'ye know*
> *The babe Ida Revely*
> *There with thee shall go?*

The *Comet* left port on December 12, 1858, and within eight months Sarah Todd was dead of tuberculosis, leaving a heartbroken letter for her parents, with instructions for little Ida's care and upbringing. "Who will love her and watch over her, if you give her not a place in your hearts?" Sarah entreated. She asked for gentleness, that no hand "be laid on her to strike her soft and precious flesh. Make her loving and lovable. Mother, I would have her learn to use a napkin," she wrote. "Let her eat with a clean knife neatly." Edward had told his dying wife that he intended to take the child on voyage sometimes, "and it will mortify him if she has bad manners." It seems that her family did their best to "grant my dying wish in regard to my precious child." At the age of twelve, however, Ida Revely Todd expired of some childhood disease.

If children did get sick at sea, it was far from any hospital or doctor. Understandably, Calista Stover became greatly agitated when her baby son Edward caught cold on passage to Japan in 1882, for she was too seasick to care for him. "Why did I come again to endure so much and with a helpless baby too?" she despaired. And it is little wonder that Maria Murphy complained in May 1886, when her children were six and eight, "It makes me very anxious to have children sick at sea when we have to depend upon our own medical knowledge."

Elizabeth, second wife of Captain Benjamin Jones of Setauket, Long Island, found herself coping alone with sick children within days of departing from New York on the *Tri-Mountain* in 1875. The first, Bessie, "all broke out, afraid she has scarlet fever," wrote Elizabeth. Then, two days later, she changed her mind, for "the flush has proved to be a rash, and we have decided it is measles." Measles, if not quite so terrifying, was even more infectious than scarlet fever, so she must have guessed what was coming next. And, sure enough, the five children were laid low, one by one. "Carrie is vomiting," Elizabeth recorded a week after the first outbreak, and added on a note of tired resignation, "And I presume she is coming down with measles." It must have been an uncommonly exhausting experience, considering that she was so far from the supporting domestic circle of home, but all the children recovered.

Tending to fractious toddlers was taxing for even the healthiest mothers when the weather was rough. "Such rolling I do not want to see every night," wrote Jemima Horton to the folks at home in Patchogue, Long Island, in September 1876. "It was lucky for Gracie and me we had a board in front of our bed." Charlotte Babcock sat "<u>crosswise</u>" in her berth with her feet braced against the side-plank, enduring rough weather for "many, many hours," with her little girl beside her and her baby in her lap.

In March 1856, on the brig *Thomas W. Rowland,* Mary Rowland also somehow coped with a two-year-old and an infant. "The vessel is rolling and I can scarcely write for the motion," she complained, "while to help the matter one of my imps is standing by me crying to help me write in my book, as she says.

I might as well try to write in bedlam, if there is such a place in existence. There always is a noise and confusion where Mary Emma is. I am well pleased when I see them in bed and asleep," she added, and no doubt the eleven men who lived and worked on the 366-ton brig felt very much the same.

A pitching ship being not the most stable of playgrounds, accidents were common. Mrs. Harkness of the *Raphael* had a five-year-old child with her in 1888, and according to Emma Pray "was in constant terror all the day for fear he would tumble in the water, or break his neck. She is a very nervous woman," Emma (who was childless) went on with scant sympathy; "was constantly uttering little shrieks of surprise or fear." This nervousness was understandable, however. Three-year-old Mary Hall fell overboard from the *Natchez* in November 1851, and her father dived in to save her, even though he could not swim—as was common with sailors, who believed that being able to swim merely prolonged the agony of drowning. Captain Hall reached his little girl and set her on his shoulders, and both were going under for the third time when the boat that had been lowered arrived. In 1865 the Australian ship *Aladdin* arrived in Hobart with the flag at half-mast, for Captain McArthur's six-year-old son had been killed when he fell through an open hatch into the hold. Mary Jarvis, who spent her early childhood on the Scottish ship *Duntrune,* reminisced that when the hatches were opened to air the cargo of wheat, she was lowered into the hold with some playthings, for her father thought she would be safer down there than racing about the deck.

Learning to walk was particularly nerve-racking—for the mother, if not the toddler. During rough weather, Mary Rowland wrote, "I have to keep the children in close confinement below, and they are very troublesome in such times. The youngest requires constant watching to save her from broken limbs, as she has such a bad habit of climbing, regardless of the consequences." Henrietta was trying to learn to walk in total disregard of the heavy motion of the ship, and so Mary was forced to "go creeping or walking around her all the time"—which was very hard on the knees and back.

Laura Bagley was just as anxious about her toddler, Hilda, writing in 1880, "I am in constant fear when it is rough of her getting hurt, for she seems possessed to walk & run by herself all the time . . . amuses us very much by bracing up when she finds the motion too much for her." Then Laura added on a distinctly weary note, "I am going to try to wean her now, before we get to Java." It must have been both frustrating and boring for the children to be so confined, and it is probably little wonder that Jemima Horton's three-year-old daughter Gracie informed her mother that she was "going home tomorrow" every day of a passage to Rio.

It was not so bad in fine weather, for Captain William Horton put up a swing on deck for Gracie, "and she runs about the deck busy about something all day"—but this meant noise, when off-watch crew were in their berths trying to catch up on sleep. "I have to devise all sorts of plans of amusement to keep peace and quietness when the mates are below," wrote Mary Rowland, "and who ever heard of keeping children quiet?" Three-year-old Muriel Jarvis was given "a musical toy that played a tune when she pulled it along the deck"—a tune that must have grown very tiresome indeed, though perhaps not as wearying as the rumbling wheels of the little cart that was made for Mary, Muriel's older sister, and harnessed to the ship's billy goat. When the carpenter of the *Clarissa B. Carver* made Scott Dow a wooden horse on wheels, his tactful parents secretly consigned it to the deep.

And yet, despite the noise and nuisance, the men seemed to derive enormous pleasure from having children on board, for captains took little sons and daughters on voyage despite grave difficulties. Five-year-old Mary was left alone with her father, the famous Captain "Bracewinch" J. C. B. Jarvis, when her mother gathered up little sister Muriel and left the *Duntrune* in Portland, Oregon, to take the train to New York and from thence a steamer to Scotland, "as she was going to have another baby." Mary was quite unmoved by the prospect of voyaging alone with her Pa—until the Portland police came along and arrested him, and took him off to jail. The crime was that of mooring the ship where it impeded the ferry. Captain Jarvis was released on bail, and ordered to appear before the court a week later. Before the week was out, however, it was an expeditious "up anchor and away."

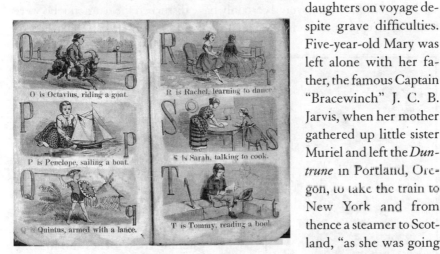

Child's book, as used to teach small children on board.

In Java in July 1888, Emma Pray met Captain Corning of the *Monrovia,* "who had with him two children, a little boy of four, and a little girl of twelve. His wife did not come this voyage," she added. Somewhat to Emma's surprise, "They were bright, interesting children, & seemed to enjoy themselves very much." Susan McKenzie noted in 1870 that Captain Cooty of the *Massachusetts* of San Francisco carried his little boy on voyage after the child's mother died, and "liked the appearance of the boy very much," though she was very disapproving of Captain Cogen of the *Josephine,* who had a seven-year-old child on board, commenting, "I pity the poor little friendless boy."

Like Captain Jarvis, these men might have taken eccentric steps to maintain a semblance of family life at sea, but many captains felt that they missed out on the rewards as well as the problems of fatherhood if they left their children at home. Maria Murphy remarked in 1883 that her husband James was so fond of their four-year-old son, Wilder, that she doubted he "could go to sea without him, so think I will have to go a while longer." In 1880, on the *Levi C. Wade,* Captain Henry Bagley devoted space in his logbook to fondly note the progress of their baby. "Hilda not very well," he wrote on June 5. "Cutting 2 more lower teeth."

Little Hilda's crying would certainly have disturbed the seamen who were trying to sleep, but it seems likely that they did not mind too much. "Sailors like to see a ship [children] are on," remarked a *New York Times* writer on December 22, 1889, in an item about families at sea, though admitting at the same time that the "sea is a queer place to bring up a child—The ship's deck is a strange playground and the rough sailor is a strange companion." The crew of the *Duntrune* certainly seem to have accepted Bracewinch's solo parenthood with good humor. One of the apprentices got a lot of fun out of "catching cockroaches and making them dance on the hot galley stove" for Mary's entertainment, and the carpenter treated her to the honor of witnessing the gory slaughter of a pig. When Bracewinch missed his daughter late one evening, he found her on the foredeck in her nightgown, being taught "to dance the sailors' hornpipe."

Sailors being traditionally generous, captains' children were showered with handsome, handmade gifts. "It don't seem

Mary Jarvis in later life.
Courtesy Wilfred Robinson.

a dog-watch since you & I were sailing boats together without a thought of wives or children, does it?" wrote Captain Aaron Wood to his brother in February 1882. Both Bel, Aaron's wife, and Oscar, their small son, were on board the *Sovereign of the Seas* with him. "Speaking of sailing boats," he went on, "Oscar owns a fleet now, he has got a sloop yacht that the Carpenter made for him, a full-rigged four-master ship that the second mate made him. I made

Ralph Starrett on the yard of his boat.
Penobscot Marine Museum.

him a ship about 30 inches long that he can tow on the stern when not going too fast, & now the Carpenter has given him a full-rigged model of a ship about 3 feet long."

Hard-nosed skippers could be amazingly indulgent fathers, Mary Jarvis reminiscing that Bracewinch used to peel oranges for her to eat, "not only peel but take off the wee inner skins." Burgess Coghill recorded that her father—the mighty Captain Sorensen, whose fast passages were so legendary that people laid large bets on them—could discipline everyone on board except herself and her sister.

This was one of the several reasons why shipboard children—boys in particular—tended to get out of hand. Another was that captains' children—just like those on shore—imitated what they saw and heard around them. When Elizabeth Stetson of the whaler *Elizabeth Corning* whipped her six-year-old son Charlie, "he turned upon me and nearly broke my wrist. Oh dear," she despaired, "will he ever leave off these lying deceitful ways? But how can I blame him? He has patterns before him that he follows to perfection."

In 1881 Adelaide Hamilton kept a journal on the *Eclipse* for her family at home to read, writing mostly about her very small son Harry's doings. "Joe heard him teaching the [cabin] boy how to haul the ropes and clew up the main royal," she recorded on September 19; "and because the boy would not run around lively, gave him a push and said—jam you, run." Then he "put one of the kittens in a pail of dirty dishwater," while the previous day he had "tried to hang one of them." Like most small ship children, he was obsessed with the ship. "Harry has been amusing himself hauling ropes and giving the sailors orders to haul the different ropes, then to belay," Adelaide wrote in October, conveying a particularly vivid picture of this child at sea, "and telling the man at the wheel to shake her a little so they can haul the sheets home, and with his hands behind his back, resting on his heels looking aloft (his favorite attitude)."

"Harry is out on deck bullying everyone as usual," wrote Adelaide another day, making it obvious that Harry much preferred imitating the mates to imitating the ordinary sailors. The cabin boy was supposed to keep young Harry under control, but all he succeeded in doing was giving him head lice. "This morning while combing Harry's hair to my fright and horror found livestock in it," recorded his mother. Harry's hair was cut and washed and inspected

"Mamie" Morgan of the bark Bridgeport.
Courtesy Rosenberg Library,
Galveston, Texas.

minutely from then on. The unfortunate cabin boy, by contrast, merely had his head forcibly shaved by the captain.

In August 1863 Mary Ellen Bartlett recorded that her three-year-old son, Willie, "came down and says, 'I want to go to bed ma.' I asked him what for and he says, 'so pa needn't whip me.' I asked him what he had done and he says, 'boke pa's pipe'—it was an accident so pa didn't whip him." She added, "He is mischievous and throws things overboard sometimes, then pa has to whip him." Willie was mischievous indeed, one of the items he tossed so blithely overboard being the rudder of the ship's lifeboat.

As we have seen, a lot of this mischief was blamed on the poor example set by sailors. Mary Rowland noted in 1867 that nine-year-old Woodhull desired only "to be on deck and with the men forward," which Mary firmly believed was "not the most propper place for him at all." Captain Jonathan Dow and his wife, Annie, were wiser, when their seven-year-old son, Scott, decided he wanted to be a seaman, picked up his toys and his blanket, and moved into the forecastle. Instead of getting upset they said nothing, but waited to see what would happen. The sailors thought it a huge joke, and gave Scott unpleasant tasks to do, and woke him up when he fell asleep on watch. Scott did not like the food much, either, and when bedtime came he wanted his mother, so before twenty-four hours were out he was tapping on the cabin door, inquiring whether he could please come back. Forbidding boys to associate with the sailors made no difference anyway, for once they were brave and agile enough to flee into the rigging, it was all too easy to escape infuriated mothers and socialize with the forbidden company aloft. This happened remarkably early. In 1884 four-year-old Wilder Murphy could race from one end of the rigging to the other "like a spider."

Many shipboard children acquired an impressive vocabulary, perhaps because hardened sailors enjoyed teaching innocent infants how to swear. In Honolulu in November 1857, the whaling wife Mary Lawrence met Captain and Mrs. Homer of the merchant ship *Messenger-Bird,* who had two children with them, "one little boy four years of age who swears equal to any man that I ever heard in my life. He made nothing of repeating an oath to his mother," Mrs. Lawrence expostulated with open horror. "How she could bear it I cannot tell, but it made the tears start to my eyes."

In her memoirs, Burgess Coghill related an amusing anecdote about her little sister, who jumped into the harbor in her starched Sunday best when she thought she was jumping into a boat. The dear little girl surged to the surface with a string of blue oaths sizzling out of her rosebud mouth, and the mate at the rail convulsed with helpless hilarity, catching just enough breath every now and then to guffaw, "Atta gal, Princess, give 'em hell." Irrepressible Harry Hamilton stole his father's eyeglasses, and then "forgot where he had stowed them, so he looked around for them for a while, then stood looking at the floor for a minute as if he was thinking,

Woodhull Rowland. Born and raised on shipboard, Woodhull became a farmer and never, ever went back to sea.
Three Village Historical Society.

then put his foot down and said—damn it." Both Adelaide and Joe had trouble keeping straight faces, particularly as Harry immediately shot behind her chair and very politely refused to come out—which is not surprising. What is remarkable is that Adelaide's sea letter was addressed to her parents, which indicates that she was not just physically a long way from home.

Many of the wives forgot their proper Victorian upbringing as the voyages mounted up, and sunnily reported mischievous sayings that could well have sent their correspondents into fits of scandalized muttering. "Last night as Wilder was going to bed," confided Maria Murphy in a letter dated January 4, 1884, "J. said, 'I think you better use the pot by the smell.'—'Well,' said Wilder, 'I 'spose I'd better get the cargo out of my rump.' Did you ever hear anything so original?" Maria blithely inquired, and went on to quote a question that was probably received with even greater tut-tutting at home: "One day he asked me what I would do if he did not believe in the Bible!"

"Wilder is a funny child," she remarked three months later. "One day last week he got offended with me for something and told me I was only his stepmother." It was difficult for a mother to have the full responsibility of a child, being nanny, nurse, teacher, and companion all at once, though Calista Stover, predictably, had her children thoroughly organized, according to a strict regime. "The children, Maria and Edward, are perfectly at home on shipboard, and enjoy sea-life thoroughly," she recorded in February 1888. Calista had been a schoolteacher though, which gave her the confidence that less well-qualified sea mothers lacked.

"Their studies commence on the first Monday at sea," she wrote, "our stay in port being their vacation. During each passage they apply themselves quite diligently to their studies, and thus keep up with their classes in the school at home." However, she did admit that they were "always glad to get into port again." Similarly, on the way into Melbourne in 1870, Anne Brown of the *Agate* wryly noted that her children were "longing to see the Pilot," who would meet the ship to guide them into port. "You'd think to hear them talk that he was some very dear friend."

Many parents shared the teaching duties. On the *Florence* Captain Duncan taught the children when they were small, and Kate, a graduate of a Brooklyn college, took over teaching duties as the studies became more advanced. On the *Midnight,* Susan Brock's mother taught her to read and sew in the mornings, while in the afternoons her father "took pains to teach me the names of masts, sails and ropes." Captain Colby, who carried his family on the *H. G. Johnson* in 1888, applied himself very seriously to coaching his two sons and two daughters in Latin, French, Greek, Spanish, algebra, and chemistry,

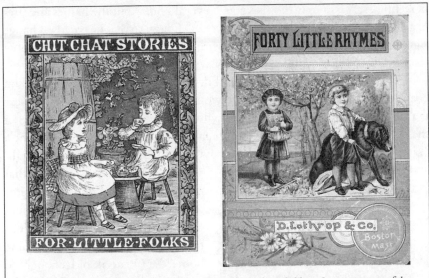

Children's books, used by shipboard mothers for teaching their children. So many copies of these were carried around the world that children in far-flung ports became familiar with them. Lulu Mair of Russell, the Bay of Islands, New Zealand, wrote, "American children's books were the first I ever had to read—I have always loved the memory of their Little Folks."

his wife having taught them the basic skills of reading, writing, and arithmetic when small.

Other women had sole charge of lessons, Helen Jernegan reminiscing that she taught her little son Prescott his alphabet from the letters painted on a rubber ball. Anna Stott of the *Northern Light* had her lessons on a transparent slate. Illustrated sheets of numbers and letters were slipped into the frame behind the slate, and she traced them. On the whaler *Kathleen* Elizabeth Marble taught her little boy, George, how to read, and he in turn taught one of the men the same skill. Maria Murphy supervised her children's schoolwork every day except Sunday, "but they can't do as well as in school," she sighed in 1883. Six-year-old Jennie was a bright scholar, which did not help, as "everything is 'Miss Ring didn't do that or this.' " When Maria read her stories, Jennie asked "more questions, it seems, than any two children. I suppose it is because she has so little to take up her mind," Maria sighed. Little wonder, then, that she recorded a few days later, "The children are racing from morning till night barefooted half the time—they are as wild and brown as Indians."

In 1886, when Wilder was not yet seven years old, Maria wrote, "He is all ship, can't sing a note but knows considerable about a ship." Wilder had his own miniature sail strung up on deck, "and goes through all the ship forms of reefing etc." Not only did he know "several knots" but the names and uses of all the ropes, as well as having his own set of flags, so that he could exchange signals with his father as they stood at either end of the deck. "I hardly know what he would do on land," worried Maria.

This was indeed a problem, for all the time a captain's son remained on board he was learning very little that would serve him well on shore. "Oscar is a real sailor now, and good friends with all on board," wrote Bel Wood of the clipper *Sovereign of the Seas* on September 14, 1879, but he had become a "kind of a little old man in his ways, having no children to play with or talk with." So it is understandable that Captain Aaron Wood wrote later to his brother, saying "if the ship does not come to New York from here, Bel will most likely come home.... Oscar is old enough to need school & more to do than he has now, so if the ship does not come home they will leave me. I shall be a poor homesick critter for a while but we think it best for her & Oscar." Like many parents, the Woods had accepted the reality—that proper schooling and a more conventional home would be a better preparation for life. They were right, for Oscar eventually graduated from a business college in California.

Wilder Murphy.
Courtesy Maine Maritime Museum.

It was a hard decision to make. When Mary Stark had left home in 1855 to sail on the *B. F. Hoxie,* her little boy Charlie had been "so sick he could hardly hold up his head, & I longed to see him, & all the rest," she confessed in a letter to her mother; "but it is no use indulging such thoughts, it only makes me sad, & does no good at all." Still worse, perhaps, was the feeling of being set apart from the important details of her children's daily life. "I think perhaps school commences today," she added; "how glad I should be to know who are the teachers—but of course I cannot hear very soon."

However, if a captain's son remained on board, by the time he reached his late teens often the only recourse was to put him to work under the guidance of one of the mates. This arrangement caused a certain amount of ill-feeling among the crew, though most would have admitted that it was only to be expected. When the *Governor Goodwin* beat the *Governor Robie* in a race on the way to China in May 1888, Emma Pray recorded that their mate, Mr. Oakes, was "much pleased, as he says the mate of the *'Robie* is Capt. Blanchard's son, a youth of nineteen whom his father has packed along, and who thinks he knows all there is to know."

It was natural for a captain's son to gain early promotion because of his father's influence. When Shotgun left to take over the *Arthur Sewall* in 1899, Wilder stayed on as mate of the *Shenandoah* under Captain William Starkey, taking command when Starkey retired later that same year. He lied about his age to get the job, saying his birth year was 1877, when in fact it was 1879. The Sewalls, who owned the *Shenandoah,* had only just learned this when they also found out that $3,235.78 of the ship's money had gone missing while the *Shenandoah* was in Sydney, Australia.

"Somebody forged his name," Maria wrote in distress after hearing the news from Wilder himself, when he came on board the *Arthur Sewall* in London in April 1900. "The poor boy was crushed when he went to the bank and found it out—he put a detective to work, but thinks he was no good." That doting father, Captain Jim Murphy, "feels terribly about it, but he knows Wilder has done the best he could."

The Sewalls held Wilder's father directly responsible, and so Shotgun was forced to pay the money back. Much worse was to come, however. Wilder went to Baltimore, where he shipped on the *John McDonald* as mate for a voyage to San Francisco. The cargo was coal, and presumably caught fire, for the ship was lost with all hands.

Though Shotgun lived for eleven more years, everyone remarked that he was a different man, and when he died from "a complication of diseases" at the age of sixty-two, people said that in truth he had expired from the lingering effects of a broken heart.

CHAPTER FIVE

Small Ladies

Where the Treasure is, there will the Heart be, yet my mind cannot be at rest in one respect, for on the land are my Children, that need a Mother's constant care, and in the Sea and often thousands of miles from home is my Husband toiling for us all, and whose constant wish is for me to go with him, so I divide my time with them and do the best I can for them all.
—Mary Rowland, January 1, 1873

In July 1850 the ship *Rainbow* arrived in Aden, North Africa, from Southampton, England, with the second mate nominally in command. In reality the crew, having mutinied, was in charge, their leader being the captain's sixteen-year-old daughter, "Miss Arnold."

It was a most unusual situation, as all the newspaper writers agreed. Captain Arnold had died ten days previously, and as the first mate was a habitual drunk, the second mate had taken over the ship. Unfortunately, he turned out to be a cad, according to the write-up in the *Sailor's Magazine,* for instead of behaving like a responsible seaman and gentleman, he "made a daring and in-sidious attempt to entice the young lady and run away with the ship." Very naturally, she "indignantly and successfully repelled all his base and dastardly attempts"—but with more spirit than most, for she took to the quarter deck, "and made a public appeal to the crew, as British seamen, and threw herself on their protection."

It was the purest Victorian melodrama, worthy of a gaslit stage. Miss Arnold's action was more "well-judged" than the cynical modern reader might imagine, however. Except for two seamen "who had been led away by the second mate," the British tars, "with that manly feeling which sailors so often display," took charge of the ship. They allowed the dastardly second mate to keep command, but in name only, informing him that if he "gave the slightest molestation to their late commander's daughter, they would pitch him overboard, and anyone else who dared to follow his example should share the same fate." Then, striking while the iron was hot, Miss Arnold begged them to perfect their pitching by "throwing overboard that instant every drop of spirits in the ship"—and in the euphoria of the heroic moment the seamen complied. Without the slightest argument they roused up the ship's store of spirits and emptied it over the rail—all except one caskful, which was used to preserve her father's remains.

While *Sailor's Magazine* (being a promoter of the temperance cause) did not mention it, the seamen probably regretted this reckless waste once their manly pride had lost its initial fervor. Deprived of access to alcohol, the chief mate fell into some kind of coma, too. However, it was a very shrewd move, for while Miss Arnold had done very well indeed thus far, there was no chance at all that she could keep control of a drunken crew. In the same spirit of cir-cumspect distrust, she decided against sleeping in her stateroom, no doubt fig-uring it was asking for trouble to be alone behind a door that was easily broken. Instead, she "had her screened cot secured near the wheel, and slept alongside the binnacle, and three of the crew kept a faithful watch around her during the remainder of the voyage."

And so Miss Arnold survived unmolested, her sturdy seamen having "pre-served the most rigid decorum, honorable in every point of view to themselves, and to that charge which they had pledged themselves to undertake." The sec-ond mate navigated, but many of the crew knew the course to Aden well, and so "all his proceedings were narrowly watched." Immediately on arrival, Miss Arnold sent a detailed written report to the authorities, and the second mate and his two comrades were arrested and thrown into prison.

This feat of keeping control of the crew and the ship "excited admiration on all sides," unsurprisingly, for such self-possession was certainly remarkable, and particularly so in such a young woman. It seems likely, in fact, that her dying father had coached her, for this was the kind of appalling possibility that must have haunted the bad dreams of many of the men and women who took their adolescent daughters along on voyage.

With very young children, little differentiation was made between girls and their brothers on board ship. On the *Levi C. Wade* in 1880, Laura Bagley's fourteen-month-old daughter Hilda ran about freely, and as a result "can pull on the ropes, and sing out like any old sailor—she learned that nearly two weeks ago, and she pulls on every string or anything else she can get hold of." It was not unknown for girls who were a little older than Hilda to run wild, too. According to Alexander Bone's book *Bowsprit Ashore,* Mary and Jane, the small daughters of Captain Hall of the Welsh four-master *Ben na Caillich,* were so "black with sin" that they were known as Pot and Kettle. One used to boast that she had been born "near the chops of the Channel during a moderate south-west gale," and both could run the rigging like sailors. Captain Hall did little to restrain them, for he thought it all a huge joke, even when he had to send a sailor aloft to bring the girls down when they had fled there to escape the consequences of the latest piece of mischief. "It was a job to keep them from going aloft with the crew to furl sail," Bone reminisced, and recorded, too, that "they occasionally used adjectives that didn't sound well from small ladies."

The isolation of the shipboard environment meant that the children grew up without more conventional role models, though most did have the chance of meeting other boys and girls when the ships were gathered in port, particularly when the other ship families hailed from the same community back home. Annie Dow of the *Clarissa B. Carver* wrote to her daughter Kate from Yokohama in 1878, saying that the *Wealthy Pendleton,* Captain William Blanchard, had been in company with them. "Their vessel laid quite near us and Allie pulled over in his little boat for Scott"—her eight-year-old son. "They were together all the time, day and night." Clytie, who was Annie's eleven-year-old daughter, "had such nice times" with the Blanchards' Nora too, "playing with paper dolls, etc., and their little Fred is such a nice little boy."

However, as always happened, the *Wealthy Pendleton* sailed away (for Hakodate in this instance), and the Dow children, just like the Blanchard children, were left without any playmates other than themselves and the sailors. Observers often remarked how immature ship children seemed, slow to learn to walk and talk, and yet strangely elderly in their manner of speech, because they lacked the constant companionship and example of playmates.

In Genoa, in August 1856, Mary Rowland disliked taking her three-year-old daughter Mary Emma on shore, as "she is indeed very troublesome when in the streets. It is most impossible to keep her with me, for she wants to run away to play with all the dirty ragged children that the streets are filled with." However, as Mary admitted, it was only natural for the little girl to want the company of children her own age, because on board there was just her baby sister. Thus when girls like Mary Emma Rowland tried to behave like females should, their chief model was their mother.

This was particularly true when the girls became old enough to be taught how to ply a needle. While boys like Wilder Murphy remained free to run around barefooted, girls like his sister Jennie found themselves increasingly restricted as birthday succeeded birthday. Anna Stott, who sailed on the *Northern Light* in the 1850s, noted in retrospect that while she was one of the first of the greenhands to know all the ropes, and sat down with the sailmaker to help sew sails, she first realized that girls were supposed to behave differently when the sailors reported to the captain that she had been trying to climb the rigging.

When Laura Mellen was a small girl on the *Europa,* her father drew a chalk line across the deck amidships, forbidding her to cross it or to have anything to do with any of the crew. Later, on the *Splendid,* however, her brother Archie crossed the line constantly, and associated freely with the men. Nellie Allen, who sailed as a child on the whaling bark *Merlin* in the 1860s, reminisced that there were times when it was hard to bear the injustice of her brother Henry being allowed to "roam the decks at will" while she had to sit and sew, "just because I was a girl." It seems odd that Nellie's mother Harriet required this, for she was a liberal thinker who contributed to the women's rights paper *The Lily;* however, the Victorian emphasis on separate roles for the sexes meant that a different kind of attitude toward raising daughters was probably inevitable.

Carrie Hubbard Davis.
William Steeple Davis Trust.

Nellie did have the privilege of helping out in the galley, along with reading stories to the men, but these were exactly the kind of feminine skills that she would have learned at home. And this was the common situation. Once they were old enough, most sea-raised daughters spent their time sewing, playing the piano, making scrapbooks, writing letters, and reading, just as their mothers did. "I have been writing and ciphering and getting my lessons," wrote eleven-year-old Asenath Taber on the *Alice Frazier* in December 1854. "I tried to sew, but I skinned my thumb last night in trying to pull the trundle bed out, and so did not succeed." It was just like school, but without the fun of friends, gossip, games, and following the latest fads. "A very un-

Her photograph album.
William Steeple Davis Trust.

The scrapbook that filled recreational hours on board her father's schooner.
William Steeple Davis Trust.

happy Christmas," Asenath brooded on the twenty-fifth. "I suppose the girls on shore are having very good times."

Girls were usually more timid than boys. A captain who was interviewed by the *New York Times* in December 1889 boasted that his son Joe was "never satisfied when it's good weather. What pleases him most is a gale," he said. "And what makes him most cheerful is a hurricane. I believe that boy would like to see us wrecked—that's about the only thing that would make him really happy." He then went on to admit that his twelve-year-old daughter, by contrast, "gets a little bit frightened when it first begins to blow." This seems to have been typical, perhaps because girls were expected to be timid, or perhaps because they were confined in the cabin during storms, often with very frightened mothers. It was not just storms which made them afraid. The *Midnight* leaked badly on the homeward voyage, so the pumps had to be manned day and night, and when Susan Brock woke up to the unusual silence of her first night on shore she cried out in terror, "Oh father, wake up—the pumps have stopped!" Five-year-old Nanny Waldron was afraid to go on the deck of the *Bowditch,* saying that one of the men stared at her with his mouth open.

Because they were more easily frightened, girls were more easily disciplined than boys, too. Preadolescent girls might be very envious of their brothers' freedom to go forward and climb the rigging, but they did not openly rebel against this discrimination. Yet girls were more likely than boys to be left behind at home, sent to live with aunts and grandmothers while their school-aged brothers were still taken to sea. For instance, Sarah and Timothy Everett left their two girls with her sister Hattie, even though it meant that Hattie had to delay her marriage, while their son Eddie was taken along. Mary Rowland, too, took nine-year-old Woodhull to sea while thirteen-year-old Mary Emma and eleven-year-old Henrietta were left behind on the small family farm, in the care of a hired housekeeper. The reason, not openly stated, was a powerful one. To put it baldly, parents of adolescent daughters were afraid that if they stayed on board they would be vulnerable to sexual advances from the men.

When Mary Congdon was on the *Caroline Tucker* at the age of seventeen, her mother became very uneasy when the mate loaned her a copy of Byron's poetry, and she would not allow her to read it. Cynthia Congdon would have been in an even bigger dither if she had known that Mary and Mr. McCrary were laying bets with each other on the speed of the ship, the forfeit being a kiss. However, Mary confided this only to her diary—which has so many erasures and pages torn out, that it must have recorded indiscretions that were even more daring than this.

Ironically enough, when John and Cynthia Congdon had decided to take Mary along on voyage, their intention had been to pry her away from an undesirable alliance. Not only had she become infatuated with a budding naval officer from her home village of East Greenwich, Rhode Island, but she had written indiscreet love letters to this unsuitable suitor, Gardiner Cottrell (whom she called "Gardie"), as well—letters which he refused to return when asked, offering instead "my word as a Gentleman that no living soul shall have the pleasure of their perusal," along with the assurance that "my word of honor will be an equivalent to sending the letters," adding coyly, "If you can with propriety, please extend my kind regards to your family."

Poor Mary. Her dalliance with the mate was probably inevitable but turned out to be equally ill-fated. "You speak of receiving a letter from Mr. McCrary," Captain Congdon wrote coldly to her on September 5, 1862, a few days after the end of the voyage. Mr. McCrary had "told me of the affairs between himself & you. I told him plainly my ideas: I respected him only as my mate, no further; in future I could not employ him. . . . I am sorry he has presumed as much as he has with you . . . [and that] you stoop lower than I ever wished for you to do."

Then Mary's father concluded the letter by writing, "I wish you would not correspond with Mr. McCrary. This is a request," he added, presumably meaning it was not an outright order, but Mary complied, and William McCrary married another woman. Like many another husband and father, Captain John Remington Congdon was a domestic Jehovah, and his slightest wish was his womenfolks' command. Mary did eventually fall in love, marrying a seaman named Ferdinand Carstein on December 22, 1870, two days before her twenty-eighth birthday. Her luck was still terrible, however; Ferdinand died not quite four years later, leaving her with two small daughters, one aged two and the other just four months.

It was not at all uncommon for the parents of adolescent seafaring daughters to worry about their relations with the mates, propinquity being so unavoidable in the cramped after quarters of a ship. In *Child Under Sail,* Elizabeth Linklater recalled that while she was allowed to talk with the officers during dog watch, her parents being in full view on the poop, if she happened to be conversing with a young unmarried one, her mother would materialize beside her, prompting, "Don't you think it is time we went below?" Elizabeth obeyed, there being "no appeal against the edict," but sighed, "I was eighteen now, and I longed for childhood and freedom again."

As it happens, eighteen was rather late for a mother to start keeping a watchful eye out. When Burgess Sorensen Coghill was a small girl on the *Snow & Burgess,* the mate approached her with a toy piano under his arm, and the proposition that she could have it if she gave him a kiss. This was definitely against her mother's rules, but when he threatened to give the toy to her sister instead, Burgess kissed him softly on the cheek, grabbed the piano, and fled. Nothing more came of it. The mate was a quiet man, and probably very lonely, but still, she said many years later, she wondered.

Thus it is most understandable that Mary Rowland should leave Mary Emma and Henrietta at home in Long Island in 1867, writing to them, "I am going with your Father because he wants me to, and so I must leave you at home with other people, but I know you have got good friends there, and you are both old enough now to know right from wrong, and I beg of you to behave in a propper manner at all times and in all places. Remember that girls cannot be too careful of their conduct, especially when their Mother is absent, do nothing that you would be ashamed for your parents to know."

Similarly, Mary Stark of the medium clipper *B. F. Hoxie* was very conscious of a mother's duty when she wrote letters of good advice to her eleven-year-old daughter, Elizabeth, in 1855. "Lizzie," she wrote on April 10, "I hope you will be one of the pleasantest little girls in Mystic, always be kind to the little boys, & do all you can to help grandmother."

"I sometimes think it was wrong for me to leave you," she wrote in September 1855, "but I thought it was best—& I know you were left in kind hands, & all will be done for you, & more perhaps, than I should do—but I fear that father or mother may get sick—or that some of you may be sick." There were so many awful possibilities "that I do not like to think about—but I will try & hope for the best, until I know the worst." As she openly admitted, if she had stayed at home, she would have been equally anxious about her husband, Captain Henry Stark—who was indeed very ill, for he died of tuberculosis almost exactly two years later, at the age of thirty-seven. And so it seems that Mary Stark had made the right choice.

Mary Rowland found a distinct advantage in having her daughters at home, for she had inherited a small family farm in Setauket, which needed managing from afar. Running a farm on land from a ship at sea was quite a problem in administration, but through her correspondence with her daughters Mary found a means of dealing with the difficulty. "I hope the Goslings will live and that Watson [the farmhand] will raise a good many chickens with you all to help," she penned in London on June 17, 1866, in a typical piece of advice.

> *I expect Mrs Hopkins [the housekeeper] makes a good deal of butter now will make considerable to sell sometime later when all the cows have calves. . . . Pa says tell Watson he wants him to keep 8 pigs and Grand Pa can do what he thinks best with the others keep the best ones ourselves to keep over so we will not have to buy Pork next year and lard. . . . I would like very much to have some of our good cherries hope there will be a good many Watson will pick them and Granma said she would come over and help Mrs Hopkins if she wanted her to, to fill up the empty jars. Don't let them be forgotten—and those pears are very nice if she will please to preserve some. . . .*

"You can read this to Mrs. H.," Mary Rowland added, probably unnecessarily, for it is obvious for whom the stream of instructions was really intended. Perhaps, however, when the girls received a directive penned in a later letter, which ran "don't let a lot of kittens live to make trouble—drown them at once, then you wont mind it," they neglected to pass it on to Mrs. Hopkins.

Sometimes the decision to leave a daughter at home had unexpected consequences. Captain Jonathan Dow and his wife, Annie, arrived back in Searsport, Maine, in January 1878, to find that their eighteen-year-old daughter, Kate, had married a clerk in the agent's office where she had called for her monthly check. Sometimes, too, the decision was regretted. In 1878, Sarah Morgan left her eleven-year-old daughter Han-

Mary Hannah Morgan.
Courtesy Rosenberg Library,
Galveston, Texas.

nah—nicknamed "Mamie"—at home with a grandmother, and missed her terribly. "It seems sometimes as though I could not stay away from her," Sarah wrote. "I get so homesick, but have to get over it." However, it is no surprise that "Mamie" went back to sea less than a year later. At the end of that voyage she went back to school, but in 1881 Sarah went home to Mystic, Connecticut, to fetch her, and they both traveled by railroad to New Orleans, to join Captain Morgan on the bark *Bridgeport*.

Captain Morgan gave Mamie a melodeon for her fourteenth birthday. Her mother gave her a black silk dress, which seems such a strange choice for a fourteen-year-old girl that it surely indicates that Sarah felt a strong need to treat Mamie as a fellow adult. Like her mother, Mamie kept a journal, recording the same matronly activities. In port she visited art galleries and walked in garden parks with Sarah, and on board ship they sat together sewing. Yet she did not seem unhappy, or even aware that in the course of her seesaw existence she had missed out on most of her youth.

Joanna Colcord, who was born on board the *Charlotte A. Littlefield* in 1882, reminisced how "out of it" she had felt when first on land, for she knew none of the "passwords" and games. It is striking what strangely shadowy figures these sea-raised daughters were, not quite part of the ship and yet ill-prepared for life on shore, enduring the same privations as their mothers but without the spur of romantic love. Born on the *Alexander* in 1877, Jane Murphy (known as "Jennie" when she was small) sailed every voyage with her mother, but her name crops up surprisingly seldom in Maria's voluminous sea letters. "Jane and I try to keep occupied so the time will go faster," Maria noted in August 1896 when Jane was nineteen; "she does very nice embroidery." And thus the slow days, weeks, months, and years trudged by, confined to the cabin and the needle.

Spending her nineteenth birthday on the *Caroline Tucker* in 1861, Mary Congdon bitterly wrote that she was not a person of any consequence, "here

Joanna Colcord and her brother Lincoln.
Courtesy Penobscot Marine Museum, Maine.

Captain James "Shotgun" Murphy
with his dog Jim and a young friend of Jane's.
Maine Maritime Museum.

or anywhere else." Marietta Pendleton, daughter of Captain Andrew Pendleton, was known at home in Searsport, Maine, to be very quiet, "not prone to saying much about herself." Even if she did talk, her conversation was about cargoes and ports, as she saw herself as being uninteresting, for on voyage she merely "sewed, read, and took care of my young brother." Her shore life was equally unremarkable, as unexciting as Jane Murphy's was, in the end. Marietta became secretary of the Kyvetta Sewing Club in Searsport, and Jane Murphy busied herself as president of the Fortnightly Club of Bath.

Somehow, the fact that many of these sea daughters remained unmarried does not seem surprising, for they were as unsuited to be the wives of shore-based businessmen as they were for shore-based careers of their own. Life at sea might have been monotonous, but they were accustomed to talk of exotic ports and strange sights, and a boy who had never ventured farther than Bath or Boston would not have appealed. It would have been different, though, if they had had the chance to marry a ship captain, for they were remarkably well-qualified to be the wives of skippers.

One of those to find this special niche was Emma Hotchkiss, who traveled with her father, Captain Levi Hotchkiss, on the bark *Harvard* of Boston. Arriving in Calcutta in late 1855, Emma met Horatio Nelson Gray. Horatio was twenty-six at the time, but courted and won her despite her extreme youth—for Emma was only fourteen. Then, when she married him, she accompanied him on voyage for the rest of his seafaring life.

The story of a Captain King, as recorded by Carrie Stoddard, is similar. Carrie met him in Shanghai in August 1856, with his new bride, a nineteen-year-old captain's daughter, on his arm. This young woman "saw Captain King on a Sunday, he proposed on Monday, she accepted on Tuesday, and they were married soon after. And he is old enough to be her father." Carrie decided that the bride, who was young and pretty, "puts on airs and dresses to death," must have married him for his money. In fact, it is likely that she married him because she saw the union as an opportunity to follow the only kind of lifestyle for which she had been trained.

And so, withal, it was more sensible to leave school-aged children at home, even if it meant that the wife and mother was wrenched between two loyalties. If the wife left the sea at the same time as the children, as Bel Wood did, it was very tough on a captain who had grown accustomed to company in the afterhouse—though Ettabel Raynor of Setauket, Long Island, reminisced that her mother rented a house in Brooklyn when her father's schooner was due in port so that the family could have as much time as possible together. Captain Eugene Raynor still hankered after companionship, however, so when Ettabel was nineteen she returned to the sea, keeping her father company on a voyage to Florida while her mother and sisters stopped at home.

When it is considered that so many captains' daughters were left at home to protect their virtue, this may seem somewhat odd, but it was quite common for older girls to return to the sea for a voyage or two. The fact that Ettabel was engaged to be married might have had some influence, but it is more likely that it was assumed she had learned how to take care of herself in the meantime, and had earned herself—as they put it in those days—"a good name." And it was easy to take a girl to sea once she had graduated—for girls, unlike boys, were not expected to prepare themselves for any career other than marriage.

And so Captain Eugene Raynor, a flamboyant fellow, bought a merry-go-round as an investment, gave his future son-in-law the job of touring it around Connecticut with a carnival

Schooner Ruth B. Cobb.
Three Village Historical Society.

One of the Raynor sisters at the helm.
Three Village Historical Society.

show, and carried Ettabel off on the *Ruth B. Cobb* for a voyage to San Fernandino. The year was 1915, toward the end of the sailing ship era, when women were becoming both independent and liberated, and so shipboard life was very much easier for Ettabel than it had been for her mother two decades earlier, and with fewer restrictions. For a start, Ettabel felt no overwhelming need to sew, much preferring to read popular fiction; Ralph Connor was a favorite author. She also loved to zoom around in the ship's motor launch, cruise

*Ettabel Raynor
and one of her sisters.*
Three Village
Historical Society.

about in motor cars in port, chat freely with captains and dock officials, and copy out racy limericks like the following on a typewriter:

> *There was a monk of Siberia*
> *Whose life grew wearier and drearier*
> *Till he broke from his cell*
> *With a deuce of a yell*
> *And eloped with a Mother Superior!*

None of this fun would have been available to her seafaring mother twenty years earlier. Bubbly, extroverted Ettabel Raynor was just as much a product of her era as prematurely adult Hannah Morgan, shadowy Jane Murphy, or reticent Marietta Pendleton had been of hers. Not only did Ettabel live at a time when women were exuberantly invading the white-collar workforce, taking over offices that had been the realm of men, but her role models were entirely different. Where the exemplars of her mother's generation were the sedate domestic goddesses of *Godey's Lady's Book,* the role models of Ettabel's girlhood were colorful, occasionally scandalous figures. One was Alice, daughter of President Theodore Roosevelt. "I can do one of two things. I can be President of the United States, or I can control Alice," Miss Roosevelt's father observed once. "I cannot possibly do both." Alice was renowned for risking notoriety, smoking in public, dancing till dawn, and pushing dignified and fully dressed congressmen into swimming pools. All of America and Europe adored her for it. Every girl had her "Alice-blue gown," and "Alice" as a name became fashionable.

Fashions in clothes were so much more suitable for shipboard life, too. No "wash-dress" for Ettabel, for her "Gibson-girl" outfits of gored skirts and loose blouses were perfectly appropriate for roaming the decks. Like all her generation, she was fascinated by the new contraptions that were appearing day by day; a few examples that she herself mentioned were the telegraph, the telephone, the typewriter, the phonograph, the camera, the automobile, and the "wheel," or bicycle, which she loved so much she borrowed one in Port Royal. For Ettabel, going to sea in a sailing vessel was an adventure, while for women of her mother's and grandmother's generations, it had been more in the nature of an ordeal, undertaken as an affirmation of love, devotion, and duty.

"The Catalogue Cover"— young women in 1911.

Ettabel might have been one of the last grown daughters to go on voyage to keep the captain company, but she was certainly not the first. Other, much earlier, girls had done it, despite the restrictions of the Victorian age. One, Charlotte Augusta Page, was not even all that closely related to the captain. In 1852, at the age of sixteen, Charlotte sailed on the great eighteen-hundred-ton ship *George Washington,* commanded by her mother's distant cousin, Captain Josiah Cummings. Mrs. Cummings was not on board, for she was tied down at home by the responsibilities of six small children, and neither were Charlotte's parents.

Obviously, then, a girl of sixteen was considered mature enough to observe the strict proprieties of the era. Captain Cummings's thirteen-year-old daughter, Mary, sailed too, and a maidservant (often called a "stewardess") was employed on board—Ann Anderson, the wife of the steward.

Charlotte was definitely demure—though it must be kept in mind that she knew her journal would be read by her mother. She filled in her time on board ship with "sewing, reading, practicing my music, and in fishing. In the evening we walked the deck about two hours." In Mobile Bay there were porpoises playing about the ship, but Charlotte scarcely varied her routine, reading and practicing, and taking "my usual walk on deck" in the evening. Then, when a party of visitors from shore came onto the ship, Charlotte played the part of hostess without any qualms, or even comment.

On passage to Liverpool, she played the piano, embroidered, wrote letters home, and despaired over long calms, just as Mrs. Cummings would have done. Luckily, hints of girlishness do crop up every now and then,

Charlotte Page.
Alvin Page Johnson.

for otherwise it would be hard to distinguish Charlotte's journal from one kept by a seafaring matron. On the day after the Fourth of July, "Mary and I went up on the mizzenmast as high as the mizzen-top," she wrote—but all in all, she behaved with remarkable discretion, and it is little wonder that on the next voyage of the *George Washington,* Charlotte's brother, who was serving as a seaman, reported that "Capt. Cummings says that he wishes Charlotte was here."

When Captain Horace Atwood took his seventeen-year-old daughter Hattie along on the bark *Charles Stewart* in 1883, he informed everyone that "he had four daughters and the fellows swung on the front gate so much it broke the hinges and he had to take it off." He had chosen Hattie to come along on voyage because she was the only one not to have a "fellow" at the time. And Hattie was happy to go along with this carefree explanation, for she wanted to see the sights and—what's more—there was bound to be a "fellow" in every port.

Captain Atwood was so sociable, and Hattie so vivacious, that one tends to suspect that he carried her along to keep the voyage lively. In any case, he was remarkably well-braced for the swarm of suitors that surged on board every time they dropped anchor. Hattie, though she "nearly collapsed" the first time an Italian kissed her hand, was equally robust in her attitude, once "pitching" four large bunches of flowers onto the deck of the ship that was moored alongside of them, when she had thirteen bouquets too many.

Entering the ship in any of a dozen ports that spanned the globe from Australia to the Mediterranean was the signal for a social whirl to commence. Hattie recorded that her father's best parlor act was to employ "the edge of the dining table for a piano," while he sang a nonsense song along the lines of "Said the young Obediah, to the old Obediah, Diah, Diah, Obediah." He put on a command performance of this in the saloon of the *Innerwick,* where Captain and Mrs. Waters were hosting a large party of captains and wives of the fleet. "Most of the folks had a good laugh," Hattie reported, though one or two of the English wives "had that expression on their face, of pity for one so gone as father appeared." However, "it was a performance I had seen since childhood," and so Hattie was undisturbed.

Horace Atwood's sense of humor got the better of any sense of discretion

Hattie Atwood.

he might have owned in Sicily, too, when a pompous little port official asked him very seriously what was it that caused an explosion, meaning when the boiler of a steamboat burst. "Sometimes wind, and sometimes beans," said Captain Atwood without a quiver, and Hattie and one of the other captains had to go up on deck "to rest our faces. Mine was actually in pain, trying to keep sober."

Hattie also flirted with handsome skippers, a certain Captain Romus (or Remus) in particular. Hattie and Captain Romus were with a party that went to a hotel for dinner in Trapani, and both ordered the same dish, "macarroni and boneless chicken." Hattie declared she could find no chicken on her plate, just a bag of skin that was filled with fat, so she reached over and helped herself to the captain's. He objected, and they ended up chasing each other all around the dining room with drawn forks, until four gallant Italians joined in, under the impression that it was a battle. So Hattie got to eat the chicken, "but was sorry afterwards." All in all, it was first-rate fun, and, as Hattie remarked with her tongue in her cheek, "If you cannot see why I did not turn the heads of all eligible young men and crowned heads of foreign climes, you must indeed be dead to all sense of attraction."

Carrie Stoddard was fifteen years old when she sailed on the ship *Kathay* to Sydney and the Orient in 1856, and, while her mother was on board as well, she was such an accomplished flirt that it seems remarkable that her father allowed her to come on voyage. Perhaps, like Captain Atwood, Captain Thomas

Stoddard enjoyed his daughter's high spirits. In the end, however, he must have deeply regretted the decision.

The Stoddards were a very close family, the oldest son Thomas, a caulker, being four years Carrie's senior, and Lyman, a clerk, two years older, while her little sister, Louisa, was only fourteen. Carrie missed them, and often wished "I could peep in on them all to see how they are getting along without us." Nevertheless, she managed to scrape every ounce of enjoyment out of her voyage, helped along by the fact that her father, though pompous in the true mold of a Victorian shipmaster, father, and husband, was remarkably indulgent.

In Sydney, just before the *Kathay* left port, a Captain Nye brought a Mr. Cook to meet the family, and Carrie gaily decided that "Mr. Cook is real handsome," and informed Captain Nye that she was "real vexed" with him for not bringing him along earlier. Then, when they got to Shanghai, a whole procession of dashing young bloods paid court, officers from the men-of-war in port included. Although she flirted with all the young men, Carrie seemed to prefer one by the name of Albert Heard. He gave her a ruby ring, and after due consideration of the proprieties, her father allowed her to keep it.

Albert, being an entrepreneur in the Orient, would have made a good match for a sea captain's daughter, but tragedy intervened. On October 16, 1856, the *Kathay* sailed from Shanghai for home, ten days before Carrie's birthday, when she turned "sixteen years old, I feel quite aged." Captain Stoddard made her a present of a gold and ivory bracelet—an expensive gift, and the last he was ever to give her.

Rebecca, Carrie's mother, was incapable of noting her daughter's birthday. She was extremely ill with some kind of tropical fever, screaming with agony whenever she was moved. Somehow, Rebecca survived. Carrie, who must have caught the disease while nursing her mother, did not.

A death notice in the *Brooklyn Eagle* read, "DIED at sea board Ship *Kathay* Nov. 17 1856 Caroline dau Thos and Rebecca Stoddard 16Y."

CHAPTER SIX

Ship Kitchens

I have finished a shirt, commenced a frock for Baby and made cake and bread, besides doing numerous other little jobs through the day, such as nursing the Children &c, and so passes my time, and I generally find plenty to do.

—Mary Rowland, February 1, 1856

On Independence Day, 1896, the giant nineteen-hundred-ton full-rigged windjammer *T. F. Oakes* sailed from the port of Hong Kong, under the command of Captain E. W. Reed. The Cape of Good Hope passage he shaped on his charts should have seen the ship safe home in the port of New York within 120 days. One hundred sixty-one days later, however, they were staggering about in turbulent seas off Cape Horn, with most of the crew too sick and starved to work the ship.

Beset by head winds within days of leaving Hong Kong, Captain Reed had decided to abandon his Cape of Good Hope course, and try for the Cape Horn route instead. Unfortunately, this involved an extra five thousand miles, on a vessel that had been provisioned for the shortest passage possible. Reed's first precaution was to put the crew on short rations. For men who were being mercilessly worked in appalling conditions this was bad enough, but worse still, the hand in charge of rationing out the food was Hannah Reed, the captain's wife.

According to newspaper reports, Hannah, a sturdy, square-jawed woman of New Hampshire stock, was fifty at the time, and had been voyaging with her husband for fourteen years. The sailors called her "a savage hellcat of a woman, heartily hated and feared." They were indubitably a rough lot, many of them deserters from the *A. J. Fuller* who had been shipped in a body when the *T. F. Oakes* was in Shanghai. What they had not realized when they signed Ship's Articles was that Reed needed new men because the American consul had made him pay off his previous crew, who were all sick with scurvy; one of them had actually died as he was hoisted into the shore-going sampan—or so the gossip went.

While the stories of the dreadful voyage are all sensational, some of them conflict with one another. According to Hannah Reed, the men were impossible to please. When she handed out apples, they declared the preserved fruit made them worse. When she gave them lime juice, they said it was nothing better than vinegar and water. When she sent them gruel and poultices the scurvy ones sent them back, with the message that she did not know a single damn thing about making a mustard plaster.

On the other hand, one of the survivors, Hans Arno, described men who wolfed their food and then licked their plates, while others got down on hands and knees searching the floor for crumbs. He accused Hannah Reed of feasting on chicken and asparagus while the men were forced to chew morsels of salt meat and hard biscuit with teeth that were falling out. One man was saving his teeth as they dropped from his gums, rolling over in his berth every time another one came out and putting it away in his chest. Some miserable soul stole those teeth, however, before their erstwhile owner was eventually carried ashore, for he was one of the lucky ones who survived the nightmare voyage.

"Starving, slowly starving, we became gaunt skeletons," Hans Arno related, "dreadful to look at, and ill-tempered too, for that horrible aching pain of hunger drove us almost mad." The first man died on November 11. Ironically, it was the cook. The next—Thomas King—died on December 26, but not before he'd had the satisfaction of attacking the captain with his flailing fists, until Reed was rescued by his hardy wife. The third—Thomas Judge— died on January 17 after scribbling a curse on Hannah Reed in the pages of his

Bible, to be closely followed by the fourth casualty, another King, named George. The first mate, Stephen Bunker, died in February, while a sixth man, Olsen, swelled up so much he could not sit down. The survivors reminisced that it "was funny watching him try." Then Olsen, too, passed away.

By the beginning of March only three men and Hannah Reed were still on their feet. She took over the helm, leaving it only to go below to prepare food for the sick—or so she said. Then—according to the stories the Reeds told later—Captain Reed was felled by a paralytic attack, and Hannah took over command as well. It was impossible to make or shorten sail, so all she could do was keep before the wind. And the wind became a horrible succession of nor'west gales, so that for hours on end Hannah was forced to lash herself to the helm.

The *T. F. Oakes* blundered on endlessly, until one night her distress signals were raised by the steamer *Kasbek*, which took her in tow. At last, on March 20, 1897, the battered, weary downeaster dropped anchor in New York. The instant the quarantine officer realized the shocking condition of the remaining crew, he ordered their removal to the hospital. The news blazed about the port, and the *Kasbek* was quickly overrun with reporters avid to gather details of what became the most infamous voyage in the annals of American shipping.

Mrs. Reed told the reporters she felt a little tired. She had stayed in the same clothes for months, she said, while she gave herself over to the needs of the ship and the sick. Many people accepted her version of the story, including the men at Lloyd's, who awarded her a silver medal for the feat of saving the ship and cargo, despite starvation, scurvy, and a seaman's dying curse.

Hannah Reed at the helm of the T. F. Oakes.
Artist: Ron Druett.

One man who did not believe her was the mate of the *Kasbek*, the vessel that had towed the *T. F. Oakes* to New York. This man, Mr. Helsham, declared that when he had arrived on the ship to attach the towline, there was a coop of twelve live and healthy chickens on the poop. When the boatload of relief supplies from the *Kasbek* came on board, Hannah Reed demanded that he put all the provisions in the cabin. "It might be some time yet before we make New York," she reportedly observed.

The case went to court, as well as being thoroughly debated in the papers, but while Captain Reed was censured, he was not punished in any way. And so perhaps it is not surprising that his house in Haverhill, Massachusetts, mysteriously burned down. Captain Reed escaped in his nightshirt, but caught pneumonia and died shortly afterwards. Hannah Reed—that consummate survivor—survived this, too, but what happened to her after that is unknown.

A complete contrast was life on board a certain Long Island Sound schooner, which set sail from the small hamlet of Orient with a cargo of carrots and turnips on a wickedly cold morning in December 1878. This was the twelve-ton *Jacob S. Ellis,* bound for the Christmas market at Norwich, Connecticut. A thick snowstorm set in as they entered Long Island Sound, and by the time they had unloaded at Norwich Wharf, the Thames River was frozen over. A grim Christmas should have loomed ahead, but instead there was an abundance of warmth and good food.

This Christmas magic was worked by the third member of the crew, Carrie Hubbard Davis, daughter of the captain and wife of the mate. The domestic work that women like Carrie Davis accomplished was formidable. "I have baked two pans of sweet Indian meal bread, a pan of sugar cake and two pans of nice wheat bread," wrote Carrie on board the schooner in March 1878. "Cooked steak and potatoes for breakfast, made Oyster pie for dinner."

And so it is easy to understand why Captain Hubbard and his mate Charlie Davis took Carrie along. Life on board, obviously, was much more comfortable than it would have been if they'd fended for themselves. The casual observer would imagine, however, that the captains and mates of oceangoing craft would not have had the same problem, for a regular sea cook was shipped.

The duties of the cook, as Emma Pray of the *Governor Goodwin* explained in 1888, were "to prepare & cook the food for the sailors, and to keep his department, which is called the galley, clean, and the coppers polished." Oddly enough, by long tradition he was stationed at the foresheet when the vessel went round in stays, perhaps because the leads for the foresheet were outside the galley doors. An old sailor's saw runs, "Shipshape and Bristol fashion, the captain on the poop, and the cook to the foresheet," and certainly in small vessels it was usual for the cook to let go one sheet, run through the galley, and haul away on the other as the foreyards came round.

His main job, however, was to cook food for the men. Back in the eighteenth century the prime qualification for a cook was the loss of a hand or foot, which meant that a seaman could no longer work aloft and had to be found another job. On the whole this did not matter, as all he really needed to know was how to boil water, for his main business was to haul a ration of salt beef or salt pork out of the "harness" cask, soak it for a while in seawater to remove the crust of dried brine, and then boil it in a caldron, to be served with a ration of hard bread ("ship's biscuit"). This, along with making a pot of tea or coffee so strong the bottom of the mug could not be glimpsed through the brew, hashing chopped meat with potatoes and onions, and boiling flour-and-water puddings—called "duff" and occasionally enlivened with a few raisins—was the extent of his duties.

Nineteenth-century sea cooks, while usually in possession of all their limbs, were not much better, indicated by the fact that if the cook got sick, he was almost always replaced by the youngest apprentice or the clumsiest greenhand in the forecastle. In contrast to the lavish meals Alice Delano and Connie Marshall described on the packets, the ingredients on freight-carrying merchant ships were most unpromising, being based on salt pork, salt beef (which the seamen, with grim humor, called "salt horse"), dried beans, dried peas, and hard ship's biscuit, together with whatever else could be picked up along the way.

The ship's "kitchen," called the galley.

The meat was coarse, fat, and extremely salty, and the dried goods harbored pests in abundance. Weevils lurked in ship's biscuits. According to Elizabeth Young Linklater, they were easily tapped out on the edge of the table, "and maggot races enlivened many a meal." Pea soup was generally hated because of the maggots that floated to the top, and rice—another staple—was "the happy hunting ground" of small black bugs. Scotch vessels were more likely than most to carry porridge oats, but these traveled no better than the rice. Elizabeth reminisced that she once "spied a little pink spot" in her breakfast porridge, which turned out to be a maggot, with a lot of maggot companions. "When I had picked most of them out, my plate was entirely surrounded by them." And everyone gave up eating porridge. Tripe came aboard Captain Young's vessels in big stone jars, and everyone in the ship was instantly aware when one was opened. Cooked properly with vinegar and mustard, tripe was considered a delicacy—but there was no certainty whatsoever that the cook was actually capable of cooking anything at all in proper style, let alone something so exotic.

"Oh! that I were home there to enjoy the real blessings of Life," wrote Thomas Benedict III (who described himself on the flyleaf of his journal as

Table set in the saloon of a small ship.

"a poor seasick boy") on the merchantman *Houqua,* bound for Canton on September 20, 1846. At home, he could "sit at my father's table of luxuries, for truly they are so, whereas here I must take my Kid of Hard Bread & Salt Beef & sit on a Hen Coop or some similar place & devour enough to keep soul & Body together." Once his seasickness was behind him, Tom had no trouble in polishing off his allowance, for youth, fresh air, and hard work all combined to give him an avid appetite, but his journal—like hundreds of similar seaman accounts—is characterized by constant complaints about the style and content of the "grub."

Many of the wives knew exactly how the seamen felt, for they were served exactly the same fare. On the little bark *Clement* in 1838, Mary Dow complained that she had taken over the cooking, for the food produced by the ship's cook was inedible. "Made some biscuit for tea," she wrote in July; "scolded to George for not scolding to the cook, he is so dirty. I think I shall have to eat my peck of dirt if I have not already. Any one that goes to sea," she vowed, "ought to have a stomach as strong as a horse."

Truthfully, however, she did not mind taking over the stove, for as well as ensuring decently prepared provender on the table, she gained a gratifying sense of accomplishment. Recording that she had "made some hop beer, kneaded up some dough-nuts, soused some pigs feet . . . made some short biscuit for tea, mended two pairs of drawers besides," she added with perceptible complacency, "Take it all together, I have had quite a day's work. Very pleasant." It was common on these smaller vessels for the captain's wife to be put in charge of the pantry, and, occasionally, oversee the cook as well, perhaps because of the captain's lively sense of self-preservation.

In 1872, when Mary Rowland was sailing on the 263-ton brig *Mary E. Rowland,* the ship was in need of a new cook, the old one "leaving to go home to New Orleans to get married." A certain Mr. Jeffrey Rivers applied for the job—though under false pretenses. "On being asked what he could cook," she narrated, "he answered, 'I can cook everything, sir,' when he should have truthfully answered, 'I cannot cook anything,' for in fact he could not."

Unfortunately, this lapse in veracity was not recognized until the brig was well out to sea, so the only remedy was for Mary to teach the man his job. "But he was willingly taught," she allowed. "And honest when given no chance to steal." Furthermore, he was "not at all wasteful, as is generally the trouble with inexperienced cooks. For the sea tells no tales, and many a spoilt loaf is secretly committed to that mighty large hiding place." Henry, Mary's husband, "calls him my apprentice," she went on. "I tell him not to, as it may give offense to one that could 'cook everything,' and receives wages, $35 a month."

It seems that the unlikely pair of captain's wife and "apprentice" cook got along in comradely fashion. "Christmas Day we dined upon roast turkey and apple sauce, mince pie &c," wrote Mary. "The aforesaid turkey stuffed and prepared for the oven by the Capt.'s wife, who, fearing it might not be done to her satisfaction, chose to do it herself. That was, by having the Cook's assistance, for it required both of them to detain the turkey on the table while the oper-

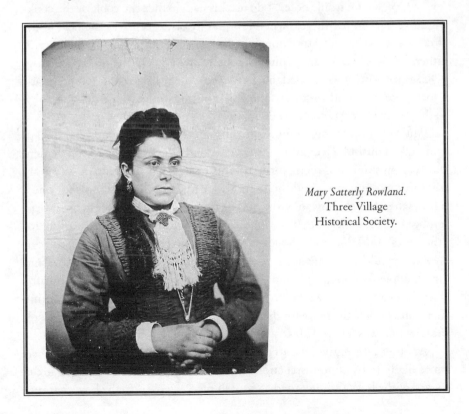

Mary Satterly Rowland.
Three Village
Historical Society.

ation of stuffing and sewing was duly performed." Mary was remarkable for more than her tact, however. Not only did she teach Mr. Rivers how to do his job, but she managed it all without ever venturing her female self into the sacred male bounds of the ship's kitchen.

There were several good reasons for this strange segregation. First, the galley was usually sited forward. On the single-decked schooners, in fact, it was often found right within the crew's accommodations, where the stove did double duty, heating their quarters as well as cooking their food. Obviously, it would have been imprudent for the captain's wife to venture there, for reasons of common decency as well as the exaggerated modesty of the time. Even if it did happen to be set amidships—which was often the case with the big square-riggers—it was in the same deckhouse where the cook and the cabin boy slept. In addition, the galley was very much the cook's kingdom. It was often the warmest place on board, where he could invite close cronies to smoke a pipe and share a yarn in a companionable—and very masculine—fug.

There were a very few exceptions, such as Mary Dow, who became so cold in Skagerrak Bay in July 1838 that she spent the day "setting in the cook's galley," adding on an ironic note, "I do not know whether the cook or the cooking stove enticed me there," when it is plainly obvious it was the heat of the stove that was the only attraction. The ban did not quite apply to small girls, either, perhaps because they could be coerced to help. On the *W. F. Babcock* in 1884, Maria Murphy recorded that her seven-year-old daughter Jennie "made a loaf of gingerbread yesterday and a loaf of cake today—she delights to go to the galley to peel potatoes and onions."

And yet, despite this strange difficulty, an imponderable number of captains talked dutiful wives into baking bread and other dainties, to supplement the Spartan shipboard diet. Normally, this meant that the women stirred up mixtures in the pantry, and then sent the readied pans and basins forward. Thus, when Isabel Duncan wrote of "baking" scones in a diary entry for September 1878, she meant that she made up the mixture ready for the oven, for "the steward fired them." However, there was no guarantee that the cook or steward would treat the stuff with due reverence. When Mary Rowland "made apple dumplings for dinner, an ample supply for both forward and aft," she felt most relieved when "the Cook done justice in the way of steaming them, and I made the sauce for them and they were as light as a puff, and Cook said not one was left and all satisfied."

Another alternative was to give the mixture to the cabin boy, who was more likely to listen to instructions. On Tuesday, October 10, 1854, Fidelia Heard of the bark *Oriental* made a squash pie, "& gave it to the boy, charging him to place it in the oven so that when the ship jumped about it would not spill over. He took it forward & put it in the stove & all went on nicely for a while." But then "the vessel gave a sudden lurch & threw the pie out of his hands upside down on the galley floor, he ran to tell me of the awful fate of my pie, looking as wild as a hawk; I could not help laughing for I had taken much pains & we were all anticipating quite a Yankee treat."

The other recourse was to do the best she could on the small stove that heated the after cabin, and many women recorded making candy this way. On a pitching ship, it was not at all easy. In 1906 Georgia Blanchard described holding the stove between her legs to keep it still while she stirred her mixtures—quite a feat in voluminous skirts. This was a testament to marital devotion, for the big windjammers and clippers included a steward in the crew, shipped to do this kind of extra cooking. As Emma Pray described it, the steward "does the pastry cooking for the cabin, waits on the table, looks after the stores, and keeps the cabins, staterooms, pantry and store room always clean, and the brasses shining." As with the cook, though, there was no guarantee that the steward could do his job. Back in 1837 Captain Alonzo Follansbee shipped a steward who had been "recommended as first class," wrote Madam. "And the Capt. expected him to prove such, but instead the Capt. found him incompetent in every way." Worse still, they couldn't get rid of the dirty fellow "till we could get to Havana and discharge him."

Annie Dow had the opposite problem on the *Clarissa B. Carver,* for the steward decided he did not like the job, and handed in his notice in the middle of the Atlantic. Captain Jonathan Dow called his first mate, and they put the fellow in irons and told him he could "live on bread and water until we arrived in Yokohama," Annie related. "He still refused to go steward but would go in any other capacity." In the end Captain Dow was forced to concede victory to the stubborn chap, and so he "put him in the forecastle" and took "the [Chinese] cook for steward. Excitement enough for one day," Annie concluded.

More excitement lay ahead, however. The Chinese did well as steward, except for the fact that he could not get along with the sailor they put in as cook, and after two months of "spatting," according to Annie's fifteen-year-old daughter, Sara, they "commenced in earnest, so the mate and carpenter had to separate them." The cook was armed with a cleaver, but the little Chinese beat him nevertheless, "so he looked as if he was nearly murdered, blood all over his face. He threatened to shoot Chinaman and would not give up his pistol," so the steward rushed down into the pantry to grab a carving knife. His excuse was that he did not have a pistol of his own to even up the fight, Captain

Dow having taken it off him a few days earlier after some wildly erratic target practice on deck.

In the meantime, however, the cook had been restrained and the pistol taken away. Captain Dow returned the cook to the forecastle, put the Chinese back in the galley, and took a stowaway they found in the cabin as steward, in a series of King Solomon–like decisions. A whaling wife once wrote, "Life at sea has its servant troubles and vexations as well as life on land," but servant troubles on shore could surely never have been as exciting as this.

Stewards were often Chinese, particularly on the tea clippers. In 1876 Emma Cawse was delighted with the Chinese steward of the *John R. Worcester.* Not only was he "very clean & particular," but "he makes beautiful bread every day & quite often makes me tarts & sweet biscuit." Peter—as she called him, for she could not "make out" his real name—"glides around like an eel, so noiselessly and quickly." He was leaving to get married when they got to Sydney, much to her regret, and she hoped very much that her husband, James, would replace him with another Chinese, because "they are so clever and quick about everything." Emma Pray had a Chinese steward who called her "Sir," which amused her greatly, though the fact that he could not cook was somewhat tiresome. Kate Duncan had fond memories of Charley Ah Hee, who was her steward on her first voyage on the *Florence,* and who not only looked after her three young children when she was horribly seasick, but tactfully coached her in the ways of life in the after cabin.

Throughout the nineteenth century, it was common to assign "women's work" on board ship to nonwhites. While Chinese stewards were employed on the China trade ships, on Atlantic coasters and Californian clippers the stewards were more likely to be African, having been recruited in the West Indies and the Cape Verde Islands, as well as in American ports. Often these men had "come down in the world," usually because of the demon drink. The steward of the *Wild Ranger* was a man with an impressive past, having been on an Arctic expedition, and the awed cook called him "Sir," with a great deal more respect than he ever accorded to Bethia Sears, or even her husband, the captain. "Our crew is so & so," wrote Isabel Duncan in February 1891; "the Steward is a complete failure in breadmaking, we have not had a decent bit of bread since leaving Grimsby." Apart from that, however, he could prove passable, she thought, for "he has not had another opportunity of getting tipsy."

Perhaps because of this predilection for drink, stewards were very apt to fall inconveniently ill. "Steward sick," wrote Mary Ellen Bartlett of the 275-ton brig *American Union* on August 23, 1860, the day after departure from New York. Her husband "James got dinner, I washed dishes, and we both worked all afternoon cleaning up Galley. I made bread for supper—set table—washed dishes. Beat down to Sandy Hook," she added as a kind of after-thought, as if to prove they were at sea. Then, the day after that, Mary Ellen was seasick herself, so the mate, Mr. Bryant, took the steward's place—though not with any great talent, it seems, for though Mary Ellen was too seasick to sample his cooking, her little boy Bertie chose to eat the forecastle food, "forward with the men." However, Mary Ellen rewarded his helpfulness by sewing him "a pair of shirts" when she felt better, and her little girl Nellie made him a "needlework," perhaps a bookmark or sampler.

On the *Oriental* in May 1854, the steward was off duty sick, and the captain's wife, Fidelia Heard, recorded that one of the passengers, named Henry, "officiated in his place, & he certainly did very well. He set the table for dinner & cleared it away, gave out stores for the men to the cook, & got supper for us, trimmed the lamps, & lighted them, filled all the pitchers, with the greatest ease. . . . He takes great pride in being Steward," she elaborated. "Wears the coarse apron & will not sit down to the table until after we have done, preferring to wait on us & eat at the second table."

There was many a steward who had to be clothed by the captain's wife, having arrived destitute on board. Emma Pray, in fact, being a seasoned seafarer, always carried old clothes for the purpose. On the *Governor Goodwin,* the steward was rather short in stature, appearing in his "new" outfit "at teatime, having reefed the trousers." Kate Mallett wrote amusingly about an old specimen "by the name of Brown," who was sent on shore at Newcastle, Australia, with five shillings to buy himself some undershirts. "He returned about six fighting drunk," and went into the forecastle, emerging after a ruckus with a bloodied and battered face. Captain Walter Mallett put him on watch as a punishment, but not long afterwards they were all startled by shrieks for help, "and found that old Brown had taken a clipping slice (a thing about 4 ft. long with a handle, like a big dull chisel) and gone into the fo'castle and told a young man that he was going to kill him." Instead, however, Brown merely managed to chop off his own little finger, by getting it in the way of the blade as he chopped threateningly at the bulkhead. "PS, I forgot," wrote Kate Mallett at the end of the letter. "Needless to say that old Brown drank up his undershirts. He returned empty handed but with a bee under his hat and skates on his heels."

However reprehensible the sartorial state, sobriety, or skill of the steward, his mere presence led to the common belief among sailors that the captain's wife fared much better than they did in the way of daily grub—and often they were right. "In the cabin the living is different from the forecastle," wrote seaman Mark Haskell on the *Castillian,* on March 12, 1853. "They [Captain Alexander Graves and wife] have pigs, hens, ducks, turkies, which are killed as wanted, besides a large quantity of choice provisions put up at home."

Usually, these "choice provisions" were extra snacks, and were supposed to supplement—not replace—the regular meals. When Georgia Blanchard embarked on the *Bangalore* in 1906, she found that her brother-in-law Albert, a major owner in the ship, had put aboard "some goodies for me like a barrel of apples, ten pounds of candy, a big basket of fruit and a large box of all kinds of nuts." Once the "goodies" had run out, the captain and his wife subsisted on much the same menu as the men. Less than three weeks after the bark *Henry Warren* had departed from Bath, Maine, in January 1851, Mary Rairden recorded that "our chickens are all gone. And now for bread & beef one day & beef & bread the next," she wrote, adding in robust tones, "Suppose as I am to be a Sailor 'tis proper I should begin betimes to grow fat on Salt beef, begin to feel a little salt already."

The wives who sailed on the big square-riggers often ate a lot better than that. The diary kept in 1891 on the clipper *J. F. Chapman* by Kate Morse Thomson, gourmand supreme and bride of the captain's son, who was serving in the capacity of first mate, is almost entirely made up of lists of the bountiful dishes that arrived on the cabin table. "I got up this morning at 6 o'clock, took bath, ate an apple, hard bread, made my bed, all before breakfast," begins a typical diary entry, dated February 2. Breakfast was at eight, and consisted of "Steak, baked potatoes, fried onions, hot biscuits and coffee, cakes & honey. I was hungry," she added—which was lucky, as another huge meal was served at one-thirty in the afternoon. "Baked lamb, boiled squash, sweet potatoes, Irish potatoes, Soup first, bread & butter, squash pie, claret wine. After dinner," she went on, "Mrs. T. and I made candy, had splendid luck with it, had three plates full." Then "we had a lovely supper" at six-thirty—"Kidney stew, baked potatoes sweet & Irish, with cherry wine, white grapes, rolls and cake."

"Mrs. T." was Kate's mother-in-law, and so the new Mrs. Thomson had a privileged position on board. She did no work apart from keeping her own room in order and flirting with Albert during his off-duty hours, and so it seems likely that she was carried as a passenger, for the menus are certainly reminiscent of the lavish repasts served to the passengers on the packets in Alice Howland Delano's time, before competition from steam forced the packetboat owners to cut both standards and fares, in a vain effort to keep dominance of the transatlantic routes. Because Kate Thomson never mentioned the crew of the clipper *J. F. Chapman,* it is impossible to tell whether they were feasting as lavishly as their skipper and his family, or subsisting on a diet of salt beef and hard bread, but the latter seems much more probable, for the ship could surely not have had sufficient cargo space to carry such goodies for the entire complement on board. Obviously, this would lead to some dissatisfaction in the forecastle.

By contrast, when Hattie Atwood first embarked on the *Charles Stewart* in 1883, she found that the men ate more or less the same food as was served in the cabin, though not in exactly the same style, there being no chairs or table in the forecastle. Each crew member had to supply his own mug, plate, spoon, and fork, all made of tin; the mug had a hook to hang over the lip of the bunk and was therefore called a "hook pot." The sheath knife they used for rope work served to cut their meat. Their meals came from the galley in a big tin pan or wooden kid, and included bread, salt pork, bean soup, tea, coffee, molasses, and brown sugar, with duff once a week and on special occasions. Elizabeth Young Linklater remarked that the sailors were issued a ration of flour on certain days, and voted among themselves whether it was to be cooked into bread or duff. Isabel Duncan of the *Scotia* of Banff, Scotland, wrote to her sister in November 1884, "We have chops or beefsteak & boiled potatoes for breakfast, the former is sometimes of mutton, veal or pork, & coffee, never tea—dinner, soup, roast meat, potatoes, vegetables," adding that the foremast men were not denied these luxuries, for they all had "beef three times a day, that is always the way on board ship, each man gets 1 ½ lbs [of meat] besides potatoes and vegetables."

When this abundance is contrasted with the shocking conditions on board the *T. F. Oakes*, it becomes obvious that the provender varied greatly, according to the ship, the owners, the circumstances, the trade, the time, and the master. The first-class passengers on a transatlantic packet were entitled to expect a menu to match the significant sum of money they had invested in a ticket, while those on longer voyages were forced to become accustomed to coarse, salt, or—in later years—canned food, as the months went by and the fresh rations ran out.

Naturally enough, then, seasoned wives tried to plan ahead for some variety in the menu over the long weeks of passage. With the prospect of a voyage to Puerto Rico and the West Indies ahead of her, Isabel Duncan bought a bulk lot of chicks in Dundee, hoping for a regular supply of eggs. Instead, they all turned out to be "cocks, I never was so deceived. I made sure of one, and now it crows lustily. I have to undergo a good deal of teasing about them but it is nothing compared to the disappointment," she wrote to a friend. Similarly, on the 1883 voyage of the *Charles Stewart* of New York, Captain Atwood bought fifty fowls in the Mediterranean, "and we had chicken (?) all the way home," recorded his irrepressible daughter Hattie. At other times, however, "we were glad to eat salt meat and bread and still be able to hold on to the seat while we were eating."

In the absence of refrigeration it was only sensible to keep livestock on board to eke out supplies, to the extent that the decks might resemble a farmyard when the ship left port. In the late 1870s, when Captain Young's ship *Norval* was chartered by Shaw, Savill & Company to take passengers to New Zealand, his daughter Elizabeth noted that one sheep, one pig, and a dozen ducks and hens were

Feeding time in the poultry run: little Max Lembke, son of Captain Otto Lembke of the schooner Helene, *feeds the chickens.*
Courtesy San Francisco Maritime National Historical Park.

provided by the company for each cabin passenger. As Captain Young had to pay his wife's passage, and there were eight passengers in the cabin, quarters had to be found for nine sheep, nine pigs, and nine dozen poultry. On some ships special pens were made for larger animals; on others the ship's longboat was put into requisition, the pigs and sheep living on the bottom, and the hens in coops placed across the gunwales, though it was often recorded, too, that cages for poultry were hung over the transom rail at the stern.

On other ships, the animals were simply allowed to run loose, Maria Murphy exclaiming in a letter home, "you would have laughed" to see the children "racing with the pigs, who seemed to enjoy the fun as well as they." Little wonder, then, that when they were eating pork chops, Maria confessed that though they tasted good, "we feel something like cannibals." Incidentally, if a storm followed the killing of a shipboard pig, the sailors (and captains' wives) called it "piggy's revenge."

Feeding fowls gave the captain's wife a chance to take the air and feel useful, as well as providing food for the table, though many wives complained that hens did not lay well at sea, and Mary Congdon recorded that the yolks were white. Maria Murphy did have a good "layer" once, but the ship's cat frightened her overboard. On a later voyage, the Murphys let the hens run about in the dining cabin when the weather got cold. "Now, all we need is a little pig pen under the table to make the picture complete," Maria mused.

"When we first started I noticed some chickens and turkeys and a goose, also two sheep, one black and the other a white one," wrote Lizzie Edwards, describing her passage on the bark *Funny Major* in 1857, when she sailed from San Francisco to Honolulu to meet her husband. "At first I thought perhaps they had been taken along as pets, [for] they seemed so gentle and had the privilege of traveling around at will, tho' I soon found my mistake—for every day the first week out we had some kind of poultry."

Eliza, to her chagrin, had missed out on the poultry, being seasick. She was up and about, however, when "the white sheep was missing and we began to have mutton. It was mutton for breakfast, mutton for dinner and mutton for supper," while all the time she eyed the black sheep, "and he certainly did not look very appetizing, really the word <u>dirty</u> doesn't begin to express it. But I began to have an inkling as to what would soon be his fate and <u>ours too</u>—and sure enough one morning he failed to appear as usual on the deck, but he did not fail to appear on the table in sections." Years later, she confessed that she could not eat mutton without remembering that sheep.

It was usual to carry cats and dogs to protect the ship's store of rations from rats. In fact, according to Mary Rowland, "It says in our Laws that we must carry cats." She thought it more natural than trapping rats and throwing them overboard, "for, poor things, they turn about instantly and follow the Vessel a long time and try to get up on board and look up at us so pleadingly with their little bright eyes." Jack Russell dogs were particularly popular, being such good ratters. "Because I had nothing else to disturb me," wrote Mary Dow in ironic tones on the bark *Clement* in June 1838, after a series of restless nights, "the rats thought they would have a set down in the pantry last night, but <u>Spot</u> soon found out their plans, and walked in for a share; he killed no less than seven, he is death on rats." According to legend, Jack Russells were deliberately bred with a patch over one eye, to impart an appropriately nautical look. However, they were very apt to throw fits. "Our dog Jim had his first fit," Maria Murphy remarked in 1899. He had been chasing Cape Horn pigeons, which probably triggered the episode. "There was quite an excitement for a while, thinking he had gone mad."

Some animals arrived on board of their own accord. On the *Shenandoah* in 1896, Maria Murphy was awakened by the sound of a wail, to find that the steward's cat "had presented me with four kittens." Sadly, the lives of pets on board were often short. When the kittens were about three weeks old "the mother cat got caught in the wheel ropes" and was killed. "We felt so sorry for the poor little kittens, they missed her so—two have since died."

"We have lost our cat!" wrote Bel Wood on the *Sagamore* in April 1874.

"And we did feel real sorry to lose her, do not know what became of her. She used to watch the birds as they flew about, and would get in all sorts of dangerous places, and Aaron thinks she must have gone overboard." On the *Arthur Sewall* on the 1899 passage to London, the Murphys had a kitten called "Scrappy," who came to a very sad end. He fell overboard off Cape Horn, and though "the poor little thing got onto the rudder," and the second mate went down on a rope in a rescue attempt, Scrappy "was swept away." The ship was brought aback and a boat lowered, but though "they rowed a long way astern," the kitten was never found. "One would not suppose we would miss a little kitten so much, but we do." The fact that Shotgun Murphy was racing his rivals to port at the time, and yet delayed for this fruitless rescue mission, is a testament to how fond the family was of little Scrappy.

It was probably inevitable that some animals carried for food became pets, particularly if there were children on board. On the *W. F. Babcock* in 1883, the Murphys carried a legendary goose. She was intended for Thanksgiving, but became "a regular pet," the whole deck her domain. Somehow, Thanksgiving went by without roast goose, the bird being given a stay of execution until Christmas ("the children don't want her killed at all"), but on Christmas Eve hearts were hardened, and goose got the chop—to the regret of all on board but most particularly the cook, for he forgot the roast and burned it.

+ + +

"I feel sick and cannot drive it off," wrote Mary Dow in June 1838. "I wish for a good drink of cold water, and the Lord only knows what I do wish for, to tell the sum and substance, I wish myself at home." Freshwater "worked" in the casks, changing its nature drastically and growing various organisms as the voyage progressed. "Fresh, if you can call it that," wrote Madam Follansbee, in a rare outburst of passion, "when oftentimes one has to hold onto their nose while drinking it, and sometimes ropy, at that." Jane Barber wrote, "We have an excellent steward and I have missed no home luxury but water," adding, "Oh, how it has haunted my dreams, that old well" of home.

Refreshing the supplies of freshwater in port might not prove all that much of a relief. At Buenos Aires in December 1855, Mary Rowland recorded that all the ships took on water directly from the River Plate, the "same great well" that all the inhabitants used, "probably because it is better than any other." Though the water obtained in this way was very muddy, Mary did not express any of the squeamishness that modern, disease-conscious mothers and wives might feel, merely observing that it was "very soft and good for use after it has set a while and become clear."

At sea, a good solid shower of rain was a much appreciated blessing, even on the big windjammers like the *Bangalore,* where the donkey engine could be fired up to condense freshwater from salt. As Georgia Blanchard ruefully recorded, her husband ordered the engine started up at the last possible moment, and no sooner had they filled their casks by this expensive means than they had two days of solid rain, and nothing in which to catch it.

The usual means of catching rainwater was to stop up the scuppers once enough rain had fallen to wash the salt off the decks. However, water caught this way was often not very pleasant to drink. In September 1855, Mary Stark wrote to her little girl at home that it had been raining solidly—"but such water, Lizzie, as you & your grandmother would be very unwilling to drink. . . . The water in the new casks we started with tastes very strong of pitch pine & bilge water—& the rain water is caught off the cabin deck, & is strong of tar & paint, so I dislike that more than the other, until it has stood for a month or so, & worked itself good."

Various means of making water more palatable were tried out, such as sweetening it with lemon syrup. This might have helped to get the drink down, but the aftereffects could be awful, Elizabeth Marble writing on the whaler *Kathleen* that the mixture "keeps me distressed all the time." Isabel Duncan made hers into tea, which she served to guests with her own cake and tinned Huntley & Palmer biscuits, but found that Americans were not "great tea-drinkers." All in all, it is no wonder that ales, porters, beers, and wine were drunk by captains' wives in the after cabins of merchant ships, and not just in the cuddies of packets.

On islands near the Antarctic, such as Ker-

Washing day. Mrs. Montgomery takes advantage of a fine day after a night of rain to get her laundry washed and hung out to dry.
Ruth Montgomery Collection,
Penobscot Marine Museum.

guelen, where sealers and whalers gathered, local herbs were harvested and boiled up to make a kind of tea, which might taste horrible but was effective in preventing scurvy. While at anchor in the Falklands in January 1851, the steerage boy of the New London whaler *Hannibal* recorded that "Mrs. Gray went a fishing & gathering a kind of tea that grows wild here in great abundance." Sarah Gray seems to have been particularly resourceful. Two days earlier, he had noted that Mrs. Gray had gone "a fishing" in the evening, catching a fresh mess that fed them all, which he thought quite noteworthy, especially as earlier that same day she had gone "a gunning," returning with a bag of sixteen rabbits.

Fishing was a popular means of augmenting supplies. Traditionally, any of the fish that the men caught were retained by themselves, the exception being flying fish that became stranded on the deck, which by long custom were given to the captain's wife. When a lot of fish, or very large fish, were caught, everyone on board enjoyed a fresh mess. On the *Clarissa B. Carver,* Annie Dow kept a line trailing over the stern the whole time, baited with a piece of pork rind cut in the shape of a fish. Jemima Horton did the same, borrowing "a hook of one of the men." She did get a bite, but "the fish ran off with it, so Will made me one of a hair pin."

When the ship was moving along, however, the chances of success were small, and even when a fish was caught, care was needed, as some species could prove poisonous. Dolphin fish was a popular catch, changing colors as it died, but in some waters it was not fit to eat. It was cooked with a silver coin to check for poison; if the coin went black, then the fish was thrown away. At Kobe, Emma Pray noted that fish caught in the harbor were poisonous because of the copper salts in the water, leached from the coppered hulls of the sailing ships in port.

Even canned food had its hazards, as Emma Cawse described in 1877. "One of the large meat tins exploded, causing a great commotion in the back of the ship," she wrote ten days after departing from Shanghai. "Quietness was restored in less than two hours after the disinfectant & perfume was profusely used. No lives lost," she added, with the dry humor that was characteristic of women of the time. Emma, like many of her sister sailors, was not generally so lighthearted about wasted food, however, for she was acutely aware that the ship was almost entirely dependent on what provisions had been taken on before sailing from port. Scurvy and starvation were thus real possibilities.

Hannah Reed was by no means the only captain's wife to ration out scarce food to a sick and starving crew, and Emma Cawse had good reason to conclude many of her journal entries on the *John R. Worcester* by writing "Thank

God we are all well, and have plenty to eat." On the brig *American Union* food was becoming so scarce on the homeward passage from Galveston, Texas, in January 1863, that Captain James Bartlett dropped anchor in Greenport, Long Island, and took a party of seamen ashore to dig clams. They got none, but managed to buy eggs and butter, and the lighthouse keeper's wife sent Mary Ellen some apples. "Tomorrow," Mary Ellen wrote, "they are going eeling." Then, in Holmes Hole, Martha's Vineyard, they got "clams and milk and apples" from shore, and thus the crew of the brig *American Union* survived to make port in Boston.

CHAPTER SEVEN

Occupational Therapy

*It is quite still now above and below, except when the great main-
sail gives itself a shake, as if impatient for a gentle breeze, now it is
held in confinement by a reef or two. But I say, keep quiet mainsail
a little while, have patience, these black clouds will disappear e'er
long,*

> *Then Jack and Bill with Tom and Harry,*
> *Will loose and hoist you with a song right merry,*
> *But you must wait, so pray be still,*
> *Let tired sailors sleep that will.*
> —*Mary Rowland, January 5, 1857*

"Day after day goes by, and nothing in sight. How must
poor shipwrecked sailors feel, watching in vain for a
ship?" sighed Maria Murphy in May 1883. It was a malaise that soon spread
to them all. "It has been perfectly calm during the last 24 hours—not even one
squall has visited us to break this dull monotonous life," wrote Bethia Sears.

"It seems to take all one's life, ambition and courage away." Bethia, like many wives, worried that the superstitious sailors—including the captain—would blame it on her being on board. "Elisha says we are having hard luck," she wrote earlier in the voyage; "hope it is not because I am here."

"This afternoon we have been fishing," wrote Mary Rowland in the midst of an Atlantic calm, in October 1856.

> *It being very still and quiet on board as usual in calm weather, and not a ripple disturbed the surface of the mighty Ocean, we were all tired of ourselves, hardly knowing what to do to pass away the time. I had taken my sewing and found a comfortable seat on deck in the shade of the sails and H. had seated himself nearby intent on reading . . . one watch was below and the other busy. As for the man at the wheel, he had nothing to do. Some one says, just look at the fish, and one hardly thinks of looking at every fish that comes along, but sure enough all around the vessel the water was alive with fish of several kinds, great baracotas and Dolphin and small black fish and other kinds. Now for a chance—It really appeared as if they were sent to us, [though] we were rather scant for fishing tackle, but soon all hands were out of cabin and forecastle, and fishing for dear life.*

Catching sharks was an even more exciting means of breaking the monotony, though rather barbaric. "It is almost a calm, and is exceeding warm," wrote Emma Cawse on June 17, 1877. She and their passenger, Mrs. Hewitt, had "sat out the most of the day, reading & talking." Then

> *two large sharks came around the ship, so the sailors got a hook with a large piece of pork on it & a rope and in a few minuits one large one was caught (with two very small ones on its back) and pulled up on deck, it jumped and lashed its tail around and appeared to be very powerful. It was soon killed & washed & ready to cook, it created quite a sensation among the sailors, and in fact we were just as excited as the men, that is Mrs. Hewitt & I were.*

The two women had put their "hats on, & rushed around & back & forth as well as anybody." Such excitement was very welcome as a means to break the monotony. Captain Jim Murphy once took "three sharks of good size, and the mate, one," Maria recorded, and when they cut open the stomach of one of them "out came six baby sharks about two feet long and as lively as possible, so we had ten sharks at one time. Everybody was so excited, for it is quite a haul to pull in a shark, they struggle so. It seems almost cruel to treat them so." All sailors, however, "despise the very name."

Likewise, it was common for seamen to "fish" for albatrosses with a hook and line. Once on deck, the poor birds provided much hilarity, for they promptly became seasick, and were unable to take flight again unless thrown in the air. Late in the century, when it was fashionable to have hats, coats, and muffs trimmed with feathers and down, the birds were killed with a sail needle thrust through their skulls, and then skinned, so that five-year-old Mary Jarvis of the Dundee ship *Duntrune* remembered the hatches being covered with skins pegged out to dry. Annie Dow noted that the feet were skinned, too, "to make tobacco pouches."

Another strange diversion was to set light to a tar barrel and throw it overboard in the evenings, to watch the flames spread over the waves—surely quite a hazard for other ships down-current. More conventionally, ship models were created in abundance, and often presented to the captain's children, along with toys—some of which were potentially dangerous, such as the bow-and-arrow set that the carpenter of the *W. F. Babcock* made for five-year-old Wilder Murphy. Fancy rope work and macramé were enduringly popular spare-time pursuits, along with more temporarily fashionable ones, such as shell collecting and making pictures out of pressed seaweed. This last happened often in the Gulf Stream. Mary Jarvis reminisced that she liked to fish for seaweed out of the bathroom porthole, "with a hook made from two pieces of thick wire," while fastened to the lavatory seat by a rope around her waist.

Occasionally something diverting was found within the ship itself. "We have discovered a poet in the crew!" exclaimed Maria Murphy in May 1883. The sailor was a German who had been suffering from delirium tremens when he had first arrived on board. "He has composed a piece about the ship, and it is really good." It was so generally assumed that seamen were shiftless, unschooled castoffs of society that any wife who reported a well-educated man in the forecastle did so in tones of wonder. "He must be a man of good education," Maria went on, "for he writes a very fine hand in English and spells well."

In view of this preconception, it is probably not surprising that the wives did not interact with the sailors more, even if they were hard up for companionship. Victorian reticence was very inhibiting, along with the social ranking peculiar to the sea. Often, too, the sheer size of the ship meant that the crew seemed to live a long, long way from the afterhouse, and only the man doing his trick at the helm could be observed closely. "Sailors appear to be enjoying themselves forward," Bethia Sears wrote during the second dog watch on a calm, fine evening; "someone is playing on a flute and I can hear the others dancing, and occasionally comes a roar of laughter." Her tone was wistful, almost as if it was like overhearing a jolly party to which she had not been invited.

On a more reticent note, Charlotte Babcock described spending moonlit evenings sitting on deck, "singing or talking, or listening to the sailors on the forecastle singing, some of whom had very good voices—distance, of course, lending enchantment to the ear." Maria Murphy did rather better, encouraging crews to come aft in the dog watches, to entertain the family with songs and dancing at closer quarters. "They sing more than any other crew we ever had," she wrote on the *Arthur Sewall* in 1899. One wonders whether the men enjoyed it as much as the family did, though Maria often recorded being given gifts of models and other handiwork, which tends to indicate a spirit of good fellowship.

There was more chanteying on some ships than there was on others. "It is amusing to hear the sailors sing," Captain Stoddard's daughter Carrie wrote on the *Kathay* in March 1856.

> [O]ne of them takes the lead and the others join in. Last night they sang "I wish I had a wife and she was a lady." It sounded real nice, almost as good as a concert. The best of their singing is they never stop, but keep right on till they get through their work. One or two of them have accordions and they make it quite merry in the evenings by dancing and singing.

When Captain Henry Stark of the clipper *B. F. Hoxie* took on a freight of whale oil at Honolulu in late 1855, whalebone was included in the manifest. His wife, Mary, whiled away the homeward passage by carving a piece of bone into a corset busk and then decorating it with scratched and inked pictures. This kind of art, called "scrimshaw," was more usually associated with whalemen, but it seems likely that the men on board the clipper worked on their own bits of whalebone.

The hobbies popular with sailing ship crews were often surprisingly feminine, seamen being strikingly unconcerned about jeopardizing their manly image—perhaps because a personal sense of virility was bolstered by the prevailing ethos. It was common, for instance, for captains to help their wives with the laundry. Kate Thomson noted when she had done her washing that "Capt.

and Albert put line out and Albert hung them out for me." Even crusty Shot-gun Murphy was recorded helping out at the tub. "J. does the greater part," Maria noted in April 1884, "else I should be all day." When Horatio Nelson Gray was first mate of the *Charlotte Reed* in 1850, he dropped a spyglass overboard. So chagrined was he (it was the only telescope in the ship) that he "had a good crying spell," as he freely recorded.

The spare-time activities of many captains reflected the same carefree lack of concern about appearances. According to the testimony of Fred Essex, who took passage on the *Emma T. Crowell* in the 1880s, Captain Andrew Pendleton was "a wonderful and enthu-siastic hand at knitting slip-pers." Another writer, Joanna Colcord, recorded that An-drew Pendleton was also a dab hand at net lace, finishing a bedspread every voyage. Emma Cawse described sit-ting companionably with her husband on deck, with a sail for an awning. James was embroidering a sofa cushion that he was making out of cross-stitched canvas, while she was busy with her tatting shuttle. Seamen were used to plying needle and thread, of course, sails needing making and mending so often, but it

Sabbath reading—one sample of the many books the Seamen's Mission sent aboard.

still presents an amusing and engaging picture. Emma, like Bethia Sears, ap-preciated having a husband to sit by her and keep her company as she sewed, but it was not a scene that would happen on board either the *John R. Worcester* or the *Wild Ranger* on a Sunday. On the Sabbath, the seventh day of the week, the day of preacher-ordained rest, respectable women were supposed to set "work" such as sewing aside in favor of religious observance.

As it happens, the well-traveled women (excepting Calista Stover and a few religiously obsessive Nantucket wives) do not seem to have been obses-sively pious. Eliza Edwards of Sag Harbor, New York, waxed extremely crit-ical in a letter home as she described trying to buy milk when the ship was in

Lahaina, Maui. She found that the missionaries "will not allow cows milked on the Sabbath, so we couldn't get a drop. Now, did you ever hear anything so perfectly absurd in your life?" She herself

> *just longed to go on shore & tell those missionaries that I thought they were getting beyond infinate wisdom, for if the Almighty had not de-signed that cows should be milked on Sunday, he would probably [have] caused them to give no milk on that day, just as he withheld the manna on Sunday & caused a double portion to descend on Saturday.*

However, even the most pragmatic wives did not like to break the Sabbath, perhaps because Sunday was such an enjoyable day at home—a time for dressing up, listening to rousing sermons, singing inspirational songs, gossiping in the churchyard, and relaxing from the endless grind of housework. At sea, however, none of these were easily available, with the result that Sundays were tediously long and unrelievedly boring. "Sundays are long days at sea," sighed Mary Dow, "or at least they seem so, to me. I often wish I was where I could spend them more profitably, but it is useless to wish."

If there was a piano, parlor organ, or harmonium on board, religious tunes were tinkled, and sometimes women sang hymns to themselves. On the Boston ship *George Washington,* for instance, Charlotte Page noted that "as it is Sunday, I have spent the day in reading and practicing sacred music." The other recommended occupation was reading improving books, such as Bunyan's *Pilgrim's Progress.* These had limited appeal, however. Emma Pray tried to compromise by setting Sundays aside for rereading letters from home and penning replies, as well as catching up with her journal.

Unsurprisingly, many wives went gamely on with their sewing, knitting, or cooking, despite pangs of conscience. "I suppose you will think I am very wicked indeed, if you knew what I have been doing today," wrote Kate Mallett uneasily on Sunday, January 26, 1908. "Well! I'll tell you, and perhaps your sense of economy will soften your judgment." A man in Newcastle, New South Wales, had presented her with "a peck of green tomatoes" a day or two before they had sailed, and "they ripened off so rapidly" that she was forced to turn them into pickles in a hurry, even if it did mean breaking the Sabbath. "They are real good too, if they were made on Sunday," she wrote, with a touch of defiance.

The Sabbath was a much happier day for the sailors—a day, in fact, to be jealously guarded as one of their few legal rights, for a fine Sunday was a holiday for all. Work about decks and in the rigging came to a halt (except in times of storms and other emergencies, of course), and nothing was done for the ship save what was necessary to keep her in trim and on course. The sailors had no scruples about sewing, washing, and such homely tasks, however, not regarding them as "work"—and, in fact, on many ships this was the only day they were allowed to attend to their personal chores. As first mate Horatio Gray described on board the *Charlotte Reed* on Sunday, August 11, 1850,

> *No duty carried on this day—any more than trimming yards & sails*
> *& other actually requisite Jobs—But this day is generally devoted, by*
> *those who can, to reading—by others, sewing—washing—&c, over-*
> *hauling their little fortunes in the shape of chests—but too frequently*
> *it is the case, that the Fortunes are small indeed.*

It must have been quite provoking to watch the sailors happily busy with their small domestic tasks, when a woman was forced by her conscience to give up the sewing and recreational reading that passed the lagging time away. On the coasting bark *J. J. Hathorn,* Susan Hathorn betrayed a definite hint of irritation when she noted that her husband, Jode, had been reading *Old Mortality*—"finished it Sabbath day." Being a sailor, Jode did not share her scruples about reading for entertainment on the Sabbath.

On the other hand, this day of rest was exasperating for husbands who were eager for a fast passage. "Everything is quiet on board today," wrote Elisha Sears in his wife's journal on Sunday, October 28, 1855, "and the sight of a sailor or sailors laying about the forward deck makes me long for Monday or a work day to come. It seems as if we had Sundays about half the time since we left." His complaint was understandable, for his ship, the clipper *Wild Ranger,* was making very slow progress. But this work free Sunday was a hidebound convention, and there was nothing he could do to change it.

Carrying passengers made Sundays more homelike, for Sabbath services could be held, often with a sermon being delivered by a lay preacher, or even a real parson. The latter happened on the *Logan* in May 1838, when a missionary, the Reverend Lockwood, took passage from Batavia (now Jakarta) for Macao. On other days of the week, passengers often helped to alleviate the tedium and loneliness, as well. Two men went to California on the clipper *B. F. Hoxie* in 1855, and Mary Stark wrote to her daughter Lizzie, "Our passengers are very agreeable, & are a great deal of company for us," adding, "Your father appears to enjoy their society, & I am glad they are on board."

Emma Pray gave a hearty welcome to their passenger, George Goodwin, when he arrived on board the *Governor Goodwin* in April 1888—he perhaps having chosen that vessel because it had the same name as his own. Mr. Goodwin was a Quaker, and therefore very staid and a little odd in speech: "once in a while slips in a thee and a thou to me, which is quite amusing." However, he had one great redeeming feature. "[A] confectioner by trade," he had brought along candy enough "to set up a small establishment," and Emma had a very sweet tooth.

As it happens, his candy was left alone at first, as the first mate's wedding cake was consumed. He had married during their four weeks in port, but "seems to keep in very good spirits, considering the circumstances." Then Emma, freely aided and abetted by her husband and the mates, started in on Mr. G.'s caramels—which needed eating up anyway, she declared, becoming sticky as the weather warmed. Two weeks later, all five pounds of these had been consumed, and the after gang was making a start on his store of "mixed candies." Another fortnight, and they were moving onto his butterscotch, and Mr. Goodwin was teaching the steward how to cook confectionery. Lessons in popping corn came first, followed by demonstrations of how to roast salted peanuts, all of which the after gang sampled freely, with the result that "all are ready to drink the Ocean dry."

Mr. Goodwin provided much amusement as well, for he was so amazingly credulous. When they crossed the line Captain Samuel Pray handed him a spyglass with an invitation to view the equator, having put a hair across the glass. "Upon looking through, he said, 'Why, it's there sure enough!' " It was an old trick, and the Prays had not expected it to work. "We were so dumbfounded to see his earnestness that we couldn't say a word, and I was glad to hear the breakfast bell ring," Emma confessed, for it gave her a chance to get away while her face was still straight. At the table the equator formed the topic of conversation, however, "and I had all I could do to keep my countenance, to hear the absurd things said."

Mr. Goodwin seemed to be able to keep himself busily occupied, much of the time writing a newsletter intended for his bicycle club. Unfortunately, he was also morbid by nature, and had an endless fund of shipwreck stories, "all of which have a tendency to cheer one up," said Emma wryly. Still worse, he did not appear to trust the captain and kept Samuel Pray company on deck during nighttime storms, asking constant questions that must have been more than slightly exasperating. As Alice Delano and Cornelia Peabody had already found out on the transatlantic packets, passengers could be a very mixed blessing.

When young Bethia Sears embarked on the clipper *Wild Ranger* in October 1855, there was one passenger on board, a youngish man named Cartwright. He seemed amiable enough, playing backgammon with her husband, Elisha, in the evenings. However, it was Bethia's honeymoon, and she would have much preferred it if they had had the sitting room to themselves, and so she claimed whichever was the leeward side as "our side of the house."

Apart from little altercations over territory everything went well, however, until they arrived in San Francisco, and Mr. C. betrayed his true colors. On February 26, on the eve of leaving for Calcutta, "Mr. Cartwright was ashore all night playing billiards," and when he did turn up on board, he was carrying a large and suspicious piece of baggage, which *clinked*. For two weeks he partied in his stateroom, every night and all night long, very noisily and yet quite alone. And after that he sat about and pined for more liquor. "I wish he was out of the way," wrote Bethia angrily in April. "He says if he could have what he wishes it would be a two-gallon jar full of sherry cobbler." And, what's more, "He is always in the cabin and as stationary as a piece of furniture."

Lady passengers were best, for at least it meant that there was someone to sit and sew with, as Cynthia Congdon described on the *Hannah Thornton* in 1852. The sewing was for the steward, who was rather "destitute for clothes," and the women "had quite a laugh about our benevolent society." Sometimes this company was more theoretical than real, however. As Kate Mallett complained in January 1905, when their passenger, "Mrs. Monteith, poor soul,"

Kate Mallett and a lady passenger on board the
Guy C. Goss, Captain Mallett on the poop.
Peabody Essex Museum.

was flat on her back in her bunk, "I wish I could once have someone for company at sea who is well. I have enjoyed all I've had, but everyone was a fit subject for a sanitarium while with me."

In December 1837, Alonzo Follansbee and his Madam tarried in London while the quarters of the *Logan* were altered to make room for two passengers. One was a young man, "about 17 years old," named Cryder, who was going out to China to work as a clerk. The other was a Miss Emslie, who took over the mate's stateroom, the mate being shifted forward, and thus lived in close proximity to Madam. Eliza Emslie was headed for Canton, to join three brothers who worked for Lord Napier. While the *Logan* was in Portsmouth readying for departure, two members of Parliament with impressive titles—Sir James Duke and Lord John Russell—paid calls on her, and so her credentials seemed impeccable.

All went well at first. Miss Emslie was fluent in French, having been educated in that country, and was happy to teach Mrs. Follansbee the language while the ship breasted the Atlantic and Indian Oceans. Then, in the port of Batavia (now Jakarta) in the Java Sea, she proved to be generous to a fault, shopping freely for gifts for dear Madam. In fact, Madam was beginning to feel very uneasy about accepting them, for she was hearing rumors about Miss Emslie's behavior with the local gentlemen that reflected the young woman's generosity, too, but were not at all to her credit.

The idyll was lurching to a halt. Back on board and on the way to Canton, Madam overheard Miss E. using "vulgar, profane, and threatening language" in conversation with the steward one night, and became so "frightened" that she put on a wrapper and fled up to deck to search out her husband. Alonzo listened to her flustered account, looked down the skylight, and exclaimed, "Why, she is as drunk as an owl!"—and so the scandalous truth was revealed.

When they finally dropped anchor in Canton, Miss E.'s three brothers strode on board. They were "fine-looking men," but greeted their sister with the words, "Well, Lize, what the d—l did you come out here for?" According-ing to gossip, they packed her back to London on the first ship available, to rejoin the two members of Parliament, one of whom—also according to ru-mor—was the father of her illegitimate child. All in all, it is little wonder that ultra-puritanical Alonzo Follansbee (who had personally destroyed all those gifts) decided not to bother with passengers on the homeward voyage.

Not surprisingly, considering the tedium of a fair-weather passage, the sight of another ship was a noteworthy event. Some captains even put up a bounty for the first sight of "someone in the world besides ourselves," as Mary Henry of the *Cato* once put it. "I had the pleasure of discovering two sail be-fore any of the ship's company," wrote Mary Dow on the bark *Clement* in July 1838, "and of course had the promise of a bottle of grog."

To raise a sail that was close enough to "speak" was better still. In May 1837, right near the beginning of her voyage, Madam Follansbee described the process.

> *"Sail ho! Brig in sight!"*
>
> *"Where away?" says the Capt.*
>
> *"On the starboard bow," cries the mate, and all hands rush to the side of the ship. The Capt. with his trumpet calls out, "Ship ahoy!"*
>
> *Answer, "Hulloa!"*
>
> *"What brig is that?"*

"The brig May, *21 days from Portland, bound to Puerto Rico, where are you from?"*

"New York, bound to Havana!"

Then, as the ships slowly passed each other, a seamanlike conversation would ensue, usually with a request that the ship and company should be reported when the other captain arrived in port. On the *Logan* the exchange became so animated that everyone got distracted, and the two vessels collided. They had to be fended away from each other with mats and cushions, but this kind of lubberliness did not happen very often.

It is little wonder, then, that Mary Henry, who was voyaging with her husband for the first time in five years of marriage (and was not enjoying it very much, either), wrote with perceptible animation on October 28, 1851, that they had spoken "the English Barque *Sidney* of London 123 days from Calcutta bound for London, it was quite exciting to me, it being the first Vessel I ever saw Spoken at Sea, and it being nearly 4 weeks since I had seen any new faces." And, what's more, "the Captain was a fat jolly looking fellow."

On March 2, 1896, Maria Murphy was gladdened by the sight of the English bark *Mona*, which "passed quite near, so that we saw the captain's wife and children. As we passed the crew of the M. gave three cheers for the *Shenandoah*, which our boys returned lustily—and it did seem good to see someone outside of our own little world." When Bel Wood was on the *Sovereign of the Seas* in September 1879, she related that a ship

> *came very near us with a <u>lady</u> on board, the first one I had seen for four months, and I was glad to see her.*
>
> *After looking at each other with the opera glasses, I waved my handkerchief to her, she returned the salute, Oscar took off his hat to them, and they swung theirs to him. Then we began a conversation with black boards & chalk. Aaron wrote where we were from, where bound, and how many days out. They could read it readily with the glass. Then they wrote that they were from Rio Janeiro, for Havre, 38 days out.*

Another means of communication while speaking another ship was "signalizing" with flags. As Sarah Everett of the *Kineo* described in January 1860, "This mode of conversation with flags is a great invention." When they had spoken the clipper *Spirit of the Times* a few days previously, "the sea was rough and we were some distance from the Ship, yet exchanged names, where from, where bound, how many days out, longitude, & finally he wished us to report him when we got into port, then Timothy wished him a good voyage, & he answered many thanks for the favor."

This exchange of signals or chalked messages was usually the extent of the speaking, although it might happen several times over several days, as the ships kept pace with each other. This gave competitive skippers the opportunity to note how well their ships were doing, a particularly thrilling exercise if the other vessel was a famous one. When Emma Cawse noted that they had spoken the crack clipper *Cutty Sark* on July 3, 1877, it was in highly understandable tones of excitement. "James expected that she would be away ahead of us by this time," for the two ships had left Shanghai about the same time. "Perhaps we will get to London first after all," she exulted. "Hurrah for the Jack R.W. and her Captain!"

Next day, the *Cutty Sark* was still in sight, and the boy who came into the cabin to fetch the flags was in such an excited rush that he picked up Emma's bag of soiled laundry by mistake. "Hurrah for the Jack R. again," Emma wrote on the eighth. "We have beaten the *Cutty Sark*—so far, anyway, for she is away astern of us now, can just see her in the distance." On the eleventh, she was closing the gap, for "she sails better than we do in calm weather," but all they needed was a strong breeze, Emma declared, and "the Jack R. will leave her away astern again, you bet."

A week later, they were still racing. "It is getting quite interesting to have her come up so near to us and then run away from her again, and she considered such a grand smart ship. The Captain must feel wild." Wild, indeed. Legend has it that the *Cutty Sark* once overtook the *Shenandoah* with the hoisted signal "Would you like a tow?"—which must have ruined Shotgun Murphy's day. The *Cutty Sark* finally overtook the *John R. Worcester* on the twenty-first, but Emma did not record what signals—if any—were flying. In the meantime, however, the impromptu contest had provided much interesting stuff for her journal.

On November 6, 1851, by contrast, it was dead calm when the *Cato* spoke a ship, "and we saw them lower a boat and make towards us." Mary Henry, to her surprise and pleasure, was about to receive a visit, for "the Captain came in the boat and introduced himself as Captain Cox of the Whale Ship *Magnolia* of New Bedford." Captain Cox "staid and took tea with us, and invited us to come on board of his Ship the next day if it held calm." And, lo and behold, the next day dawned pleasant and still, and he sent over a whaleboat for the promised return call.

"We passed a very pleasant day," Mary reported, "despite my being a little Sea Sick"—probably caused by the rancid smell of the ripe old whaleship—and they exchanged visits over the next five days. Provisions were exchanged

Ready for visitors at sea. Artist: Ron Druett.

as well, "John letting him have a Pig & some Onions and he gave us 5 barrels of Potatoes & 6 Pumpkins. . . . He also asked me if I saw anything on board of his Ship that I would like—if there was, I should have it. I told him there was not, although it was a wrong story, for he had a Goat that I should have liked very much but I knew he thought a good deal of the milk himself, for they had very bad water."

Mary's wistful expression must have belied her tactful silence, however, for when Captain Cox arrived on board next day, he "to my great joy and surprise, brought his Goat with him, and made me a present of it, and he could not have made me a greater present." The goat was promptly christened "Mag," short for "*Magnolia,*" and carried onward through the Indian Ocean. She was so frightened during heavy rain "that she run into the cabin and got into my room and stowed herself away under my bunk"—giving Mary quite a start, for she "could not imagine what it was when I first heard her horns scraping underneath."

Captain Cox's openhandedness, as well as the exchanged visits by whale-boat, was characteristic of a staunch whaleman custom called "gamming." Because the whaling voyages were so long, and the ships were going nowhere in particular once they had arrived on whaling ground, other vessels were hailed with great delight, and mass mid-sea visits among a whaling fleet were commonplace. Merchantmen, on the other hand, had a destination that they wished

to reach as quickly as they could, for they would not get their money until the cargo was delivered. The women were very aware of the difference. As Caroline Stoddard remarked in April 1856, "We have not met with a single whaleman yet. I was in hopes we should, so that I might see some new faces, and have a chance to send a letter to the loved ones at home."

If the winds had allowed it, Captain John Henry of the *Cato* would most certainly have kept on his way, in preference to gamming with the *Magnolia*—for, as his wife noted, "John thinks he is the most unlucky fellow that ever was to be mak-

Whaleships speaking: sketches from a whaleman's journal, kept on the Richmond *of Rhode Island, 1845.* New Bedford Free Public Library.

ing such a long passage"—and so Mary would have been deprived of her visits. And, incidentally, Captain Gersham Cox of the *Magnolia* would have missed out on a series of visits he himself must have thoroughly enjoyed, for on the next voyage of the *Magnolia* he carried his wife, making it conceivable that Mary Henry was the unwitting cause of another sister sailor's roving upon the restless seas.

Mary Henry was to gam again that voyage, once—unusually—with another merchantman, the British ship *Conqueror*. Again it was calm. Captain Rennie and his wife both came on board the *Cato*, "took dinner with us" and then "insisted upon our going on board the *Conqueror* to tea." As it turned out, it was a fortunate visit, for when Captain Henry compared his chronometer with

Captain Rennie's, he found it was "out of the way." And so he was able to correct his clock, which could have saved him some critical mistakes in navigation.

Six months later, the *Cato* encountered the *Conqueror* again, and "she came alongside so that we could speak to each other; we could see Capt. & Mrs. Rennie very plainly & it really seemed like meeting old friends," wrote Mary. There was much "waving of hats & Handkerchiefs," but the wind blew fair and so, as much as Mary and Mrs. Rennie would have liked it, no enjoyable gam came about. Instead, they were forced to watch each other's ship draw away. "The *Conqueror* is a fine ship to look at & a sight worth seeing at sea," concluded Mary.

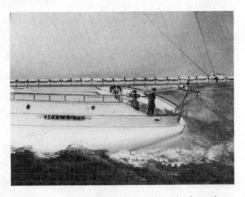

Martha, wife of Captain Herman Aldrich, on the poop deck of the brig Atalanta.
Artist: William York.

On Easter Sunday, 1885, in latitude 23"20', longitude 37"60', the ship *General Fairchild* was raised by the men on the *W. F. Babcock,* leading to a great deal of excitement, for the two ships had been in the port of Leith, Scotland, together. They were steering the same course at the same speed, and so "I invited them on board," wrote Maria Murphy. Captain Taylor and his wife accepted, coming on board and remaining "until six—it has been such an enjoyable day, such a treat to see new faces, particularly a lady!" Unsurprisingly, "our tongues flew fast all day"—and, best of all, thus passed a most unusually enlivening Easter Sabbath.

Christmas was a welcome break in the general tedium, along with New Year's Day and Thanksgiving. "We are trying to make this day seem something like a Holiday," wrote Maria Murphy on Christmas Day 1883, "although all hands are at work, there being painting necessary." In 1884 she made a Christmas tree and decorated it with tinsel, fringed tissue paper, and candles—and it promptly caught fire. On the *Shenandoah* in 1896, Maria recorded an extremely generous exchange of presents. Her husband, Jim, gave her an order for ten pounds to be cashed in Liverpool, and her son Wilder (now eighteen years old and serving as a seaman on board) gave her his earnings. "I gave Steward a pair of links, and Jane made him a linen picture frame. I made each officer and Carpenter a canvas cap—Jane made [up] a candy bag for everybody." Captain Murphy gave the men the day off, "and they fully appreciated it, by their actions. Jane and I went on deck to wish them a merry Christmas, and they gave three cheers for the 'Captain and ladies.'

"In the afternoon they had some very amusing races," Maria wrote, and went on to describe three-legged races, wheelbarrow races, obstacle races, and racing each other "with a potato in an iron spoon," all novelties she had never seen before. "They were so good-natured and happy—after the races I sent out some oranges—Jim ordered two turkeys killed, one for the cabin, the other for the men—and they had a fine dinner." Then, in the evening, they had a concert, finished off with another round of three cheers. All in all, that 1896 voyage of the *Shenandoah* seems to have been a happy one. "I nearly forgot to mention that Neptune came on board the night we crossed the line," wrote Maria.

The ceremony of crossing the equator was a particularly welcome interruption in the sameness of the routine, for it usually happened in the doldrums, a region of calms and adverse winds. It was a kind of initiation, in which a sailor who had been dressed up as King Neptune clambered over the bowsprit and came along the decks with a ragtag retinue, to interrogate new sailors—the "greenhands"—and then "lather" them with slush grease and tar, before "shaving" their faces with sheet-iron "razors" and dumping them overboard or into a tank. The process was a rough and rowdy one, sometimes with grog or bottles of wine handed out by the captain to the men.

When Captain Nathaniel Palmer's wife, Eliza, voyaged with her niece on the clipper *Houqua* in 1846, the ship's cannon were fired, there was "a first rate dinner & plenty to drink," and—in the words of the steerage boy—"the ladies in the cabin presented us with some fine Ginger cake." Eliza Palmer was a seasoned voyager, but her niece could well have been crossing the line for the first time, which would have meant that the ginger cake was a bribe to buy off King Neptune and his crew. On the *Kineo* in 1859, the cook played the part of the King of the Sea "in a Sheepskin suit, a mask on, the grains in his hand—and presented such a formidable appearance that I should have been frightened to meet him on a lonely road," confessed Sarah Everett. Her little boy Eddie had been looking forward to the event, but "the minute he heard him hail 'Ship Ahoy!' as he came over the bow, he run for the cabin, as pale as a Ghost." And so, taking pity on the boy, his father "bought him off with a bottle of wine."

A particularly lively visit from Neptune was celebrated on the four-masted "shipentine" *Arthur Sewall,* in June 1899. "Well," Maria Murphy wrote, "it was the funniest sight I ever witnessed on board ship." Neptune was wearing "a long beard of oakum, with a high hat of canvas," preceded by his "police—

with big badges," and joined by his "bride," who looked "too funny for anything—I laughed 'til I cried," wrote Maria.

Maria Murphy had provided the costume herself, for she had ripped the
tucks out of an old lavender wrapper and turned a piece of cheesecloth into a
veil, topped off with some old pink netting roses. "A short German boy was
the bride, and he had a wig of oakum that hung to his knees—it was so funny
the way he came dancing along, tossing up his ringlets." This comical pair set
off up the deck toward the ceremonial tank that had been made out of an old
sail, followed by "the barber with a razor about a yard long," and accompanied by music from a band comprising "a guitar, mandolin, banjo, concertina,
triangle, and harmonica."

Meanwhile the "seven victims" had been tied to the rail, ready for the initiation. "We stood on the top of the mid-ship house, to see the fun," Maria
went on. Then, when the last had been shaved and ducked, the crew handed
out programs to the captain and his family and proceeded to stage a concert.
"Some of them have fine voices, and the boys play well," Maria wrote,

> but the gem of the affair was a cake walk by our Steward and one of
> the men—they were blacked up, Steward had on a white suit with cane
> decked up with bright colors—the other had on the lavender dress, and
> as he was tall, it brought the dress halfway to the knees. I never saw a
> better cake-walk—Steward was a soldier and probably learned the
> walk down South—the men were so jolly it was a real pleasure to
> watch them.

And then, with a belated jolt of conscience, Maria added, "Some fun now
and then does one good, especially on board ship where life is so serious"—for
all this frivolous jollity had happened on the sacred Sabbath. "You must remember we are on the ocean, and things are different," Maria excused on behalf of them all. "Sometimes our crew sing 'Nearer My God To Thee,' and it
sounds beautifully."

CHAPTER EIGHT

Medical Matters

We heartily wish that H[enry] had some other business, this is so much care, and constant exposure to danger and sickness. [But] unless I can go sometimes, we must be separated most all the time, with the exception of one month or six weeks out of the year, and that is unhappiness to us both.

—Mary Rowland, January 1873

"Cook was taken sick last night," wrote Bethia Sears on the clipper ship *Wild Ranger* in December 1855. Her husband, Captain Elisha Sears, "who officiates as physician, attended him three times during the night. Said he had a bad pain in his heart. Several of the men are sick and E. is dosing medicine a great part of the time." This was not an unusual situation. Because on most ships no surgeon was carried, many a captain was forced to do his best with the medical chest that was legally required equipment on all American ships "of 150 tons and upwards, with ten or more people on board," and on British ships "in accordance to the Scale appropriate to the said ship," along with much reference to some terse guide such as William Hollis's *A Companion to the Medical Chest, with Plain Rules for the Taking of Medicines.* The cook recovered, but one suspects that he would have gotten better just as quickly without Captain Sears's well-intentioned but untutored treatment. It is probable, in fact, that more than a few captains killed their men while attempting to cure them, as William Cleveland did on the *Zephyr* in August 1829.

The *Zephyr* was a sandalwood trader, collecting cargo in the notoriously unhealthy Straits of Timor, when Captain Cleveland overheard a man named Cornelius Thomson complain that he had felt a little chilly in the night. On being cross-examined about it, Thomson protested that he felt perfectly well, and indeed was on the verge of going on shore with a sandalwood-cutting party. Cleveland, however, was determined "to be on the safe & cautious side"—as his wife, Lucy, put it—and commenced upon a ferocious course of treatment that started with "a powerful dose of Calomel of Julep," progressed through a "dose of castor oil" and several enema injections, to raising blisters "upon the calf of both legs after soaking them well in hot water," and culminated with "a blister on the breast, throat rubbed with linnament &c." Within hours the poor fellow was out of his head, and by morning he had breathed his last. It was the day after his twenty-first birthday.

Everyone on board was upset, for Thomson had been universally popular—"a correct, an amiable, respectful, very handsome young man, always ready at his duty, cheerful & obliging," wrote Lucy Cleveland; "he had gained upon our affections very strongly. On Wednesday evening he was dancing happily upon the forecastle, and Sunday at 8 in the morning he was carried on shore, [and] burried." Lucy certainly thought his rapid deterioration strange—"the shortest & most deceptive" sickness she had ever beheld—but it is doubtful that she realized that his death was almost certainly due to her husband's officious blundering.

Medicating the sick and mending the hurt constituted just another of the many challenges a sailing ship skipper had to meet when he was many miles away from home. However, the fact that he was in charge of the medical chest did not make him feel confident of his medical expertise—or reassure anyone else on board the ship, either. "Wish I was where I could have a doctor. Took some pills last night but they do not seem to be what I want," wrote Adelaide Hamilton in the middle of the Atlantic. Adelaide was constantly seasick, suffering also with the pounding headaches that often accompanied the complaint, but her husband could do little or nothing to help her—as usually was the case.

"I shall be thankful when we get in," wrote Maria Murphy when their first mate was very ill, "so that he can have medical attention." Likewise, other ships were hailed in the hope that there might be a physician on board, though the moral support of just another captain could be a distinct comfort, particularly if something tricky like an amputation was on the agenda. American craft under 150 tons might not even carry a medical chest unless the vessel was over seventy-five tons, had a crew of six, and was headed for the West Indies. When Charlotte Page was on the *George Washington* in June 1852, a schooner hailed them, for the captain was ill, "and not having any medicine on board they came here for some." What the captain of the schooner *really* wanted was a regular doctor, but even if the *George Washington* was one of the few to have a ship's surgeon on board, it was not likely that it would have made much difference to the patient's prognosis. Medical science was still in a primitive state, with no knowledge of antibiotics and little idea of antisepsis—or even basic hygiene—and many doctors blundered about as blindly as sailing ship captains.

Early in 1849, whaling wife Susan Veeder bore a little girl in the port of Talcahuano, Chile, a charming infant they named Mary Francis. At eleven months she had "7 teeth, Creeps all about the Ship, and is verry cunning. She is now on deck takeing a ride in her Waggon." Nine weeks later, the child was dead, killed by a bungling doctor. The ship had called at the island of Tahiti and Dr. Johnson sent for, as Mary Francis was a little feverish with teething. He prescribed two powders, and shortly after taking the second one, the little girl convulsed. A few hours afterward, she died. As her grief-stricken mother noted, there was no doubt that she had been poisoned.

Nineteenth-century doctors came in two types, based on the school of thought they favored. They either purged the patient violently, with castor oil, calomel, enemas, and bleeding, or else they believed in blisters. Blistering was achieved by burning the skin area closest to the pain—the back of the neck, for instance, if the patient had a headache—with raw mustard, burgundy pitch, or some other caustic substance. As we have seen, Captain Cleveland of the *Zephyr* "played safe" by employing both methods.

These strange measures must have seemed effective, for otherwise they would have not been standard practice. Perhaps after being purged the patient felt too weak to register pain, and maybe blistering was in itself so painful that the original soreness became insignificant by comparison. In Manila in November 1837, Captain Jos Winn suffered with a feverish cold, so "had fifteen leeches applied to his head," which from our modern point of view seems a thoroughly medieval practice. However, his wife, Hannah, saw no reason to object to the application of the disgusting, sluglike blood-sucking creatures—and was apparently proved right, for the patient got better.

And so the century drew on with very little improvement in medical method. For rich and poor alike, for both landlubbers and seafarers, good health was a rare and wonderful blessing, and life was definitely precarious. Ports—tropical ports in particular—could be very dangerous at some seasons of the year. When Captain Leroy Dow carried his wife, Ella Cora, on the *Clarissa B. Carver* in 1881, the ship sprang a leak a few days out of Hong Kong, so he put into Batavia for repairs, arriving August 18. Leroy left his wife in their hotel room on shore alive and well one morning, and got back in the afternoon to discover her dead.

It was a very unusual correspondent who did not finish off a letter with a prayerful hope that she and the reader would meet again. "If I meet you no more on earth," wrote Nancy Bolles to her family in New London, "I hope I shall meet you all in heaven, for we must all soon leave this world and try the unseen realities of eternity." Family medical guides were carried along in abundance, and journals and logbooks were used to jot down "receipts" for home remedies. Thus slotted into Cynthia Congdon's diary kept on the bark *Hannah Thornton* is a loose page bearing a "remedy" for cholera.

> *1 part laudanum*
> *1" camphorated spirits*
> *2" capsicum*
> *2" tinctur'd ginger*
> *Dose for an adult ½ teaspoonful in a wine glass of water. If the case is severe or obstinate repeat the dose in three or four hours.*

When Cynthia had a bad headache, her husband "bathed my head in vinnegar [and] I had mustard on my feet, and after a while the pain abated." On the clipper *B. F. Hoxie* in 1855, one of the seamen was dying of consumption (tuberculosis) and Mary Stark medicated him with a syrup of borage, catnip, and wormwood. "I don't know how good it might be," she worried, "but wish I had an armful of herbs, & knew the good of them, & other medicines."

Captains were also expected to cope with the many accidents that were almost inevitable on board a pitching ship at sea. On February 16, 1859, Captain Horatio Nelson Gray and his wife, Emma, were roused from sleep when

> *a great fat Norwegian managed to fall from the top-gallant forecastle to the main deck last night—just before midnight, and broke his col-*

larbone—Dr. Gray was called in and he immediately set about <u>*fixing*</u>
the man's arm or shoulder or collarbone—he hardly knows which—
however, the fellow says, "tish goot—verra goot, Coptin." Meaning I
suppose that the bone *is properly set, I have no doubt but what he is the*
best judge.

While this candid confession of anatomical ignorance is engaging and
amusing, it seems evident that Captain Gray would have greeted a "proper"
doctor with great relief at that moment—and very likely that the patient, despite his protestations, felt likewise. On the *Oriental,* in August 1853, a young
passenger named Henry who had gotten a fish hook embedded in his jaw
when his fishing line flew back did not feel at all confident in Captain John Jay
Heard's surgical skills. When the "Capt. took out his lancet & pliers to extract
it, Henry begged to be allowed to pull it out himself," Fidelia Heard recorded,
adding that the self-induced extraction, though painful, succeeded.

At times, seafaring wives and daughters were strong-stomached enough
to bear a hand and help. In April 1883 the *Charles Stewart* was swept by a gi-
gantic wave that broke the stateroom windows, poured into the cabins, and
carried away the wheel, breaking the helmsman's leg. It was a serious com-
pound fracture, with the bone sticking right through the skin, and it took Captain Atwood, his daughter Hattie, and the mate two hours to set it. It was a
grisly experience, and Hattie recorded that the mate "was nearly overcome."
It was the one and only time she saw his face—which was normally red to
match his hair—turn white.

If the ship was in port, the patients were often drunk, which did not help
the sorely taxed skipper. When the *Hannah Thornton* was in Valparaiso in February 1853, the second mate fell and cut his head, and Captain John Congdon stitched it up. "I do not believe I could have had so much patience with a
drunken man," wrote Cynthia with an audible sniff. Being towed by a steamboat in and out of port had its hazards, too, for it is surprising how many people got a cinder in an eye. Captain Thomson of the *J. F. Chapman* was one such
sufferer, and his daughter-in-law recorded getting it out "by putting in a hair,
and some Flaxseed."

Dentistry was yet another responsibility, and skippers became adept at ap-
plying oil of cloves and drawing teeth. Mary, the young daughter of
Bracewinch Jarvis, who sailed on the Dundee bark *Duntrune* in 1896, later
reminisced that she saw her father pull a tooth for one of the apprentices.
"There was a hatch in the after cabin," she wrote, and "the poor boy was on

his back on the hatch cover with my father's knee on his chest while Father struggled with the tooth. I hope it was the aching tooth that came out." She was understandably nervous when one of her own teeth gave trouble later in the voyage. Her father's "cure" for that was to bounce her on his knees and then suddenly part his legs so she thumped unexpectedly to the deck. Needless to say, it did not work.

Obviously, there was an even greater problem if it was the skipper himself with the toothache. "All this week J has suffered agonies with his teeth," wrote Maria Murphy in May 1884. "Neuralgia set in and for two days and nights the pain was terrible—he tried everything. The jumping pain is gone today, but the tooth is very sore and grumbles all the time—he has scarcely slept for a week. . . . Toothache and head winds are pretty hard to bear." Maria was unable to help much with either of these afflictions, though during the previous voyage on the same ship—*W. F. Babcock*—she was able to save her husband some distinct personal embarrassment when he was seized with a terrible pain in his bowels, for the only alternative would have been medication by the mate. "I was terribly alarmed, for I thought of stoppage," Maria wrote in a letter home. No "movement of the bowels" could be induced with pills, so finally she delivered an enema.

Shotgun Murphy was a man of no mean size, weighing 232 pounds, but Maria "made him stand on his head"—on a pitching ship—while she performed the operation. "His bowels were very sore for three days," unsurprisingly, but the procedure had the required effect. "I have never felt so relieved in all my life," Maria declared after the stubborn bowels finally moved, but did not bother to describe how Shotgun felt about it, probably not thinking it necessary.

Luckily, sailors were a generally rugged species, hardened by vigorous exercise in appalling conditions. A certain amount of hypochondria was inevitable, however. In January 1897 Maria Murphy noted that Shotgun was convinced he had diabetes. Then, a few days later, he informed her that he had leprosy, undoubtedly the result of overenthusiastic study of Dr. Thomas Ritter's *Medical Chest Companion for Popular Use on Ship-Board.* Sailors were equally prone to morbid imagining. In March 1856, Mary Rowland amused herself by recording that the whole crew of the brig *Thomas W. Rowland* had succumbed to hypochondria. "First one is ailing then another," she wrote, for it had become "fashionable" to be ill, and the whole complement was behaving as if "the Capt has nothing else to do but deal out medicine. I pity all that are really sick and am willing to assist all I can," she added, but at times it was hard not to laugh.

"Let me see," she wrote, "what have been the complaints generally and what they have originated from. First came Jack, wanted a dose of Salts, Blood out of Order. Second case Nick, with a sore leg, knocked off the skin on launching day and it never got well before he hurt it over. Thirdly Gardner. Taken cold and confined to the forecastle several days." Then came Lawrence, who had cut

Ship leaving port.
Courtesy Joseph D. Thomas.

his toe but fortunately not severely enough to cut it clear off. "Perhaps next time he will succeed better and not cut it at all," she commented dryly. Peter had "sprained" his ankle, but on investigation it "did not happen to be sprained after all and only needed to be bathed in Opodeldoc once, which proved an effectual cure, very favorable indeed."

So miraculous was this opodeldoc (a liniment composed of camphor and essential oils that was a Victorian standby) that a man named Frederick who was famous for fabricating illness immediately became "lame" himself, "but soon recovered from that, a powerful remedy that Opodeldoc. Thanks, Dr. Ritter." Offering opodeldoc did not please a man named Tom, for he preferred a ferocious, internally administered regimen of calomel julep, castor oil, and cream of tartar. "He actually requested a dose of each and took them in two days or less time. He did need some medicine, I suppose, for these cured Tom and I think might have killed me," Mary recorded with disbelief, and added a little ditty:

> *"Thus ends this day, so passed away—*
> *And may the patients soon get better*
> *Obtain relief from Dr. Ritter."*

Getting away safely from port with a healthy crew did not mean that no disease lurked on board, for a multitude of pests skulked in the holds and the bulkheads. Rats and fleas transmitted plague, while flies spread the germs of diarrhea and dysentery, and mosquitoes were the conduit for dengue fever, yellow fever, and malaria. "Rats are as thick as your fingers," wrote Bethia

173

Sears when she went back on board the *Wild Ranger* after a spell ashore in Calcutta in July 1856, and on the brig *Massachusetts* Katurah Pritchard found the fleas "so plenty, I sometimes fear for my life."

Hunting down rats, cockroaches, and other assorted vermin seemed to happen in sudden bursts of energy, Bracewinch Jarvis's daughter Mary remembering "a rat hunt" in the saloon organized by the apprentices and officers. They lifted her on top of the table before they began the attack so that she could watch the sport. These rats were no small foe. One night as Adelaide Hamilton was getting to sleep, "a rat got into the cabin through the bathroom window and got into my room under the bed." She grabbed her little boy and fled, and her husband Joe locked himself into the room with a cudgel. "[A]fter more than an hour's fighting Joe killed him, but not before the rat had left the mark of four of his teeth in Joe's arm." It had been quite a battle, and unsurprising that it was "such a looking room as it was afterwards."

More exotic pests could be nerve-rackingly likely to have a poisonous bite. Sarah Todd was once sitting on the cabin floor nursing her baby when she felt something crawling over her, and brushed it away. Then she looked to see what it was and discovered an enormous centipede. "It was four or five inches long, and such a frightful creature!" It got away despite her screams, and from then on she lived in a constant state of nerves, until they were south of Cape Horn and the cold-stiffened corpse was found by the men. "I have got him bottled up and shall take it home with me as a memento."

To her horror, however, it was not the only one of its species aboard. "Three nights since while sleeping in my bed with little Lelia [Ida Revely], I felt something crawling on my neck," she wrote on March 27, 1858. "I raised my hand to brush it away and O how frightened I was when I found it to be another of those awful centipedes. I screeched and caught up my babe who screamed to the top of her lungs." Sarah's husband Edward jumped up, "just in time to get a sight of the creature crawling over my pillow toward his berth. We could not find it that night, but next morning we found and put an end to it."

In Brisbane, Australia, a cockroach came on board that was so huge Hattie Atwood mistook it for a man's slipper. Oddly, many seamen believed that cockroaches ate bedbugs, and so while the bugs were hunted ruthlessly, the roaches were often left alone. Except, that is, when fishing, for a fat cockroach made capital bait. In October 1856, the brig *Thomas W. Rowland* was carrying a freight of fruit, which had commenced to hatch flies and mosquitoes the moment they left the port of Malaga. "And now besides these plagues we have still other ones on board," Mary Rowland wrote with very understandable squeamishness:

[W]hite crawling worms about an inch long come out of the cargo of figs and raisins, and large numbers make their appearance in the Cabin, and more particularly in my room. They keep hid during the day time and like the Cockroaches & musketoes make their Debut at night, they crawl up on the ceiling overhead and then fall down in a short time but Oh dear they like to hide in my mattress best of all places and although I watch for and destroy all that I can find before I retire, often I am awakened during the night by them as they drop down upon me and then commence to crawl over me occasionaly taking a nip as their appetites suits them.

It is disgusting to even think of these reptiles crawling over one's flesh while we are alive, but they are harmless and in a few days there will not be one to be seen—they soon die. They are always present when the Cargo consists of dried fruit. But enough of this, I'll write no more about it.

"All sail is set. All hands are well and can eat their allowance," she added—a blessing indeed, considering what a range of fevers this truly biblical plague could have been carrying.

In July 1858, the mate of the *Logan* terrified his grieving shipmates. They thought he was dead of Java fever and were preparing him for burial when he suddenly sat up, calling out hoarsely for "Black Betsy." This, it seems, was his nickname for his tea mug, and the event was considered a miracle. It was a very rare ocean-going voyage that did not record the death of at least one sea-man. Because of the small size and isolation of the ship community, the loss was felt deeply by all, and because of the hazardous conditions, it often came with shocking suddenness. Many a seaman fell to his death, sometimes right at the feet of the captain's wife or children. "A very startling and sad accident occurred at five minutes before 12 last night," wrote Fidelia Heard on September 25, 1853.

The boy Andrew Symonds fell from the mizzen top-mast crosstrees, onto the top of the house & from there to the deck. He was stunned by the fall, every effort was made to restore consciousness, and in fifteen mins. he ceased to breathe—if breathing it could be called, it was a choking sound in the throat, and when that ceased there was no other sign of life, his pulse gone, no breath visible on the mirror. . . .

His body was decently dressed, and wrapped up in a canvass with iron weights, and at nine o'clock A. M. the Capt. read the funeral ser-

*vice, & his body was committed to the great deep. . . . It was such a sad,
sad scene, all the men were assembled during the ceremony, standing
with uncovered heads—the flag at half mast, the ship hove to, all wearing a melancholy appearance.*

On April 10, 1878, Sarah Morgan of the *Bridgeport* reported in a letter
home that "the weather was frightful" the whole way across the Atlantic, "and
comfort was unknown to any of us." A sailor had fallen from the topsail yard
and "never breathed after he struck the deck, the whole back of his head was
crushed in." Not only was it "a sad sight to see his body launched into the
deep," but the storm was raging all the time. At any moment the whole complement on board might find themselves in the same watery grave, "for it
seemed almost impossible for any ship to stand such weather. I hope and pray
that we may be spared from ever haveing such a passage again."

At times no ceremony was possible, for the poor seaman had fallen from
aloft into the sea, and his body could not be retrieved. "This morning as I was
standing on the poop deck I heard the cry of, boy overboard!" wrote Carrie,
Captain Stoddard's daughter, on the *Kathay* in mid-Atlantic, in April 1856.
"Oh, no one who has never heard the sound can know how awful, how terrible it is at sea." The unfortunate fellow was the fifteen-year-old cabin boy,
George Washington Douglas, and though the ship was hauled aback and a
boat lowered immediately, it "all was to no purpose."

The wind was blowing a gale on the *Fanny Major* one day in November
1857 when "one of the men fell from aloft, struck his head against the rail of
the ship then into the water & was drowned," Eliza Edwards reported. They
were unable to lower a boat, but she doubted that it would have made any difference, for "I think likely the fall killed him, for we heard his head crack all
over the deck. It made us all feel very sad & whenever I think of the voyage
that scene comes right up before my mind."

Some journals report a series of deaths, where a mast had collapsed, a foot
rope had broken, scurvy had struck, or some exotic disease had been carried
on board. "Fuller & Pope very ill, Williams & others unwell," recorded Lucy
Cleveland on July 27, 1829, as the *Zephyr* left "Coopan" (Kupang, on the Island of Timor). "About seven o'clock in the evening poor Fuller breathed his
last death groans. Prayers were read over him & by the glimmering lamp light
on this gloomy & cloudy evening he was consigned to his watery grave." Pope
followed two days later, "relieved by death from his tedious suffering."

It was amazing how often nothing about the deceased was known. If he
had shipped under a pseudonym, which was common, it made it difficult to

Sarah Morgan.
Courtesy P. Bowen Briggs, Jr.

know how to word the usual notice to the newspapers when they got into port, or even how to report his death to the Seamen's Mission, which was the other way of letting his family know about their loss. Emma Pray, like many wives, recorded going through a deceased man's belongings in the hope of finding the names of family and friends, but without result, so that the only epitaph that could be given to the shrouded corpse that slid over the side was, "He was a thorough sailor, and a good man at his work."

Captain John Mathieson once described a farcical sea burial conducted by a Captain Butcher, who did not have a prayer book with him, or even a Bible. Butcher could not recollect the words of the Lord's Prayer, let alone the proper rites, though he tried hard for a little while. "Thy . . . thy will be done on earth . . . earth . . . as it is . . . is . . . ," he mumbled. "Oh, for God's sake," he finally exclaimed in disgust. "Let the bugger slide." Thankfully, this kind of fiasco was very much the exception. Most of the time the funeral was a decent one, with the flag at half-mast and the whole ship's company assembled to hear some kind of religious service—though one captain's wife is recorded as witnessing a similarly botched funeral.

Worse still, it was the burial of her own husband, Captain Jensen of the four-mast barkentine *James Johnson,* who died of heart failure while the ship was becalmed in mid-Pacific. Not only had he been the only person on board who could navigate the ship, but the instant he breathed his last, discipline collapsed, as the mates broke into the spirits room, and the crew shared out the liquor. A sea burial followed, but not one that offered much consolation to the grieving widow. The tipsy carpenter had forgotten to put weights in with the corpse, so that every time Mrs. Jensen came on deck she was confronted with the dismal sight of her husband's coffin bobbing pathetically along in the wake of the ship, while all the time the crew caroused and the mates wondered how to get to Honolulu.

It was a salutary lesson for Mrs. Jensen's sister sailors, not only to learn how to navigate but also to find some better means of disposing of the corpse. In Victorian times it was most emphatically not considered romantic to be buried at sea, though when the corpse was an ordinary seaman, there was very little choice. Captains' cadavers, however, were different, and many dutiful wives did their best to keep the body preserved for interment at home.

One such was Sarah Gray of Liberty Hill, Connecticut, whose seagoing career spanned twenty years, culminating in a voyage on the whaleship *James Maury*. It was a sad and eventful journey, for when they sailed from New Bedford on June 1, 1864, her husband, Captain Sluman Gray, had less than a year to live. The log for March 24, 1865, reads "Light winds and pleasant weather. At two PM our Captain expired after the illness of two days." Refusing to allow him to be slid into the sea like an ordinary man, Sarah insisted on pickling the corpse, and so the log for the following day reads, "Light winds from the Eastward and pleasant weather, made a cask and put the Capt. in with spirits."

This cask became quite famous. On June 28, the *James Maury* was captured by the Confederate raider *Shenandoah*, a warship that was commanded by a man who was just as flamboyant as Captain James "Shotgun" Murphy of the downeaster *Shenandoah* (a different vessel) a generation later. This was Captain James Waddell. The Civil War had been resolved in April, but Captain Waddell refused to believe it, seizing ships and burning them just as if battle was still raging. Accordingly, when first mate Lieutenant Chew of the Rebel ship arrived on board the *James Maury,* he found Sarah Gray in a state of some hysteria.

He was able to reassure her. Captain Waddell had heard about the cask and the corpse, and had decided to ransom the *James Maury* as a gentlemanly gesture. Accordingly, 222 prisoners were put on board the 395-ton ship, and the *James Maury* was sent off to Honolulu, the cask undisturbed. With such extreme overcrowding, it must have been a nightmare journey, but somehow Sarah got the cask home (the bill for cartage from New Bedford was $11) and buried her husband where he lies today, in the Liberty Hill graveyard. Local legend has it that he was buried cask and all, but it seems much more likely that the preserved corpse was taken out of the barrel and put into a regular casket.

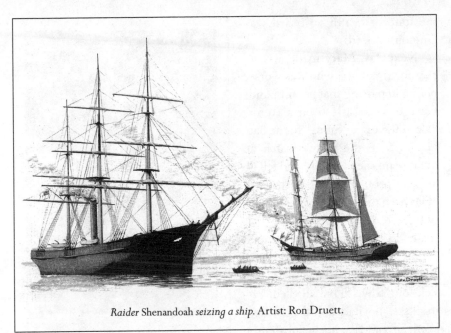

Raider Shenandoah *seizing a ship.* Artist: Ron Druett.

While the decease of anyone on board was tragic, the death or incapacitation of the captain was a crucial blow to the voyage. "Madam's duties are studying navigation, reading, keeping the ship's signals in repair, and walking decks with the Captain," wrote Madam Follansbee three months after departure from Boston. Some of this work could well have been performed under protest, for she disliked it so much. "Spent most of the day repairing signals and flags," she grumbled on June 30, 1837, "and no enviable job it was, for they were sure to get torn every time they were hoisted." However, Alonzo had informed her that knowledge of navigation and signal codes could make the difference between life and death. "All this, and ten times as much more, I have had to learn," she wrote, "in case it should fall to my lot to take charge of the ship!"

This tends to indicate that Captain Alonzo Follansbee enjoyed shocking his bride, but he did have justification, for there was a definite possibility that a captain's wife might be forced "to take charge." On the bark *Clement,* on passage to the Baltic in May 1838, Captain George Dow's wife, Mary, "threw up" her breakfast, but felt better after taking a nap, up to making "some plum-porridge" for the mate, who was also unwell, and feeding the chickens, that "have got the gapes and sore eyes; the sea does not agree with them, one or two have died already." She added on a domestic note, "Cut me out a night-cap," but the state of health on board was ominous indeed.

Next day, Mary made arrowroot for the mate, who was worse, noting in passing that her husband, George, was "asleep on a cotton bale in the upper cabin," for he had had to take the mate's watch at night. And then her husband fell ill as well, probably from overwork. "Has been in great pain most of the time," wrote Mary on a note of despair. "I do not know how he will get his strength again, for we have no dainties on board to nourish the sick, our fowls have all died. He thinks if he had a little chicken broth he could eat it," but obviously that was impossible.

Ship in a storm.
Artist: Ron Druett.

"It is a poor place to be sick, on board of a vessel at sea," she continued. "Any one suffers for proper medicine when sick, and proper nourishment when recovering. I have nursed him as well as I know how, with what I had to do with, and that is the most I have done, mended a few old duds, washed and ironed a few things, set up a cotton stocking, worked time twice a day." So Mary Dow was the only person on board fit and well enough to "work time" and find their position. Without her, the *Clement* would be drifting without guidance. "How glad I shall be to hear him giving orders again," she sighed, with good reason. Captain George Dow did recover and resume command, but in the meantime she had indeed been "in charge of the ship."

Mary Dow would have had a great deal in common with another captain's wife, Frau Meinders, who brought the Bremen barkentine *Johanna* into Fremantle, Australia, on July 9, 1890, with the aid of only one man, the mate. The vessel had sailed from Mauritius on April 1 with a cargo of sugar. She was well-crewed and well-provisioned, and the weather bid well for an excellent passage, but unfortunately one of the men they had shipped in that port was carrying "el vomito"—yellow fever. Within days Captain Meinders had buried seven men in the sea, one of them the second mate, and more were terminally ill.

Woman on deck during storm.
Artist: Ron Druett.

Because they had a very young baby with them, Meinders instructed his wife not to deal personally with the sick men, giving her other tasks instead. When they buried the cook she took over the galley, and then, as still more men died, her husband hurriedly taught her how to steer, so that he and the mate could work the sails while she took charge of the helm. Then, as the corpse of the last seaman slid over the side, Captain Meinders became so delirious that his wife was forced to lash him into his berth, and the baby became feverish, too. It is little wonder that the mate collapsed with exhaustion when they finally arrived in port, or that Frau Meinders wept with relief when the doctors at the hospital in Perth informed her that both her husband and her baby would probably recover.

It is pleasant to learn that Frau Meinders was hailed as a champion, but, as is so often the case with the seafaring sisters, what happened to her after that is unknown. The newspaper writers, in fact, neglected to note her Christian name. As we have seen with "Miss Arnold" of the *Rainbow,* it was common for the heroine of a sea drama to remain largely anonymous. Not being part of the crew list, the seafaring wives and daughters were unofficial participants in lives of isolation, routine monotony, sudden excitement, and fear, which rendered them strangely invisible. As Emily Wooldridge, captain's wife on the English merchant brig *Maid of Athens,* mused in November 1869, after describing the individual men of the crew in the pages of her diary, there was no point in describing herself, for she was "On board ship a Nobody." For this reason the female presence on board has gone almost completely unnoticed, unless the seafaring wife happened to star in some sensational tale of disaster or near-disaster at sea. Few people would be aware that Emily was on board, except for the fact that, when the *Maid of Athens* caught fire off Cape Horn,

Emily Wooldridge shared in the ordeal of the crew and played a part in their eventual rescue.

On January 10, 1863, during the height of the American Civil War, the brig *J. P. Ellicott* was captured by the Rebel raider *Retribution*. Both Captain Devereaux and his mate carried their wives, and the wife of the latter was left on board the brig to cook for the prize crew. In true theatrical style she got the Southern master and mate drunk, and persuaded the crew to take them prisoner, providing handcuffs for the job. Then she took command, navigating the brig to St. Thomas in the Virgin Islands, where she put her in the hands of John T. Edgar, Consul. No doubt he was amazed and the owners were very grateful, but the rest is lost to history, for the papers that printed this exciting yarn left the heroine completely anonymous.

Another who failed to get her name into the papers was Jennie Parker Morse, who voyaged on the ship *John W. Marr.* In 1881 her husband, Captain

Nancy Maria Babcock, of Greenport, New York, who sailed with her husband, Captain Hedges Babcock, on long whaling voyages in the 1850s, carrying a baby's trousseau with her in case she became pregnant. The only son she bore, however, died on the island of St. Helena, where they had called for the help of a doctor.

Captain Hedges Babcock.

Courtesy Society for Preservation of Long Island Antiquities.

George W. Morse of Bath, Maine, died of "bilious intermittent fever" off the coast of Madagascar. Being the only one on board who could navigate, Jennie took over command and steered for New York, delaying only to head up George's body in a cask of spirits and put down a mutiny. However, the papers merely noted the death of the captain, and the arrival of the ship, in late December 1881.

Bearing in mind the popular precept that men were strong and women were naturally frail, some kind of mutinous protest was probably inevitable when the captain's wife took charge of the quarterdeck. Lizzie Edwards and Mrs. Martin Palmer—both wives of whaling captains—were on board a schooner that plied among the Hawaiian Islands when the vessel was blown out to sea by a freak gale while both the captain and mate were on shore. Lizzie "went up on deck to make a few suggestions, and was told to <u>go downstairs and mind my business.</u>"

As it happened, the crew coped perfectly well, and having the captain on board the schooner made very little difference, for he was very green at the trade. When he arrived at his destination—Hilo, on the island of Hawaii—it was coming on dark, so instead of dropping anchor he tacked offshore, going out so far that by the time he made the port again it was growing dark the next night. And out to sea he tacked again, which indicates that he was either overcautious or else a very slow learner.

Naturally enough, Lizzie Edwards and Mrs. Palmer were growing thoroughly tired of this by the third night, so they "protested very strongly about going out to sea again all night, and gave a few very explicit directions." Lizzie concluded complacently, "The result was we got in about noon the next day." The captain, however, never forgave the insult to his masculinity, telling everyone in Honolulu that it was the last time he would go to sea with "She Captains."

Another woman to take command after the death of her husband was Mrs. Howe of the *Ellen Southard,* of Bath, Maine. "About the beginning of June last," a New Bedford shipping paper reported on July 30, 1867, "the *Ellen Southard* was seen by a schooner about 80 miles West of the Farallone Islands, flying a flag of distress.

> *The schooner at once went to her assistance, and found her in command of Mrs. Howe, her husband, the captain, having died when the ship was out a few days from Hong Kong. The ship was short of water, and the crew and Chinamen in a state of mutiny....*
>
> *The crew was picked up in a foreign port, and they, with the Chinamen, made threats against Mrs. Howe's life, if she did not get the*

ship into San Francisco by a certain time. Mrs. Howe was a good sailor, and she worked the vessel well. She stood her watch, and the Chinamen were so brutal that she was obliged to carry a revolver in her hand. . . .

The officer of the Wyanda says that he never listened to a more heartrending tale than that of Mrs. Howe, and he could not restrain his tears when she related her trials.

It was yet another story for the newspaper editors to relish—until another such yarn came along, as always happened. "HEROIC CONDUCT OF A WOMAN," headlines across the eastern seaboard of America announced in 1856, blazoning the story of Mary Ann Patten of the *Neptune's Car.* The clipper, a heavily masted vessel of 1,617 tons, had left New York in June, driven hard in a race to get to San Francisco first. Shortly after departure, however, Captain Joshua Patten found that his first officer slept through his night watch after ordering the sails shortened. This was no way to win the race, and so, after firing the lazy, chicken-hearted so-and-so, Captain Patten took over the first mate's duties himself.

Exhaustion caught up with him as they breasted Cape Horn, and Patten collapsed with a fever of the brain, probably meningitis. The second mate was no navigator, and neither was any other man on board, which should have spelled disaster for the ship. Fortunately, however, Mary Ann had been sailing since her marriage at the age of eighteen, and knew how to work up sights. In fact, Joshua Patten had once written in his log, "Mary Patten is uncommon handy about the ship, even in weather, and would doubtless be of service if a man."

At this time she was "but 25 years of age, small of stature, possessing much grace and delicacy of appearance"—according to the news reports. Mary was nursing her seriously ill husband, too, but nevertheless she took charge of the ship, not only bringing the *Neptune's Car* safely into San Francisco but doing it in the creditable time of 120 days, beating three of her husband's competitors.

It was a feat worthy of some quiet self-congratulation. Many a woman, having accomplished this, would have enjoyed her little spell in the public eye. Instead this "Florence Nightingale of the Ocean" felt embarrassed. She did not believe in women's rights, but nonetheless was hailed by the women's rightists as a shining example of women's ability to compete successfully in a field that traditionally belonged to men.

"Poor Mrs. Patten!" wrote Sarah Todd, after calling on Mary Ann in New

York. "Her husband is very near to death. How can she bear up under such affliction?" Captain Patten died in Boston on July 26, 1857, in his thirty-sixth year, so that Mary was not just a reluctant champion but a very young widow as well.

However, at least she has not been forgotten. The hospital at the U.S. Merchant Marine Academy, King's Point, New York, is named "Patten" in recognition of her truly remarkable feat.

CHAPTER NINE

Hazards of the Sea

The Sea is high and running in all directions as the wind has been blowing from all quarters of [the] Compass. The Vessel is both rolling and pitching. The lightning is flashing most of the time and an occasional clap of thunder rolls along the sky, and oh how we roll. H[enry] has just divested himself of oil Clothes and Jumped into bed. But alass there is no rest to be found in such weather as we are having.

—Mary Rowland, December 24, 1856

In 1820 a melodramatic account appeared on Boston bookstalls: *An Authentic Narrative of the Shipwreck and Sufferings of Mrs. ELIZA BRADLEY, the wife of Capt. James Bradley of Liverpool, Commander of the Ship* Sally, *which was wrecked on the coast of Barbary, in June 1818, WRITTEN BY HERSELF.* Mrs. Bradley's ordeal was lurid in the extreme, for when the ship was driven ashore on the north coast of Africa she "fell into the hands of the Arabs," and endured "incredible hardships during six months captivity (five of which she was separated from her husband)," until he managed to buy her back by paying a ransom to the Arab who had "enslaved" her.

In the meantime, Eliza had been stripped almost naked, had subsisted on a diet of insects, and—worst of all—had been the plaything of a tawny-colored "master" whose "red and fiery" eyes glared from above a black and curly foot-long beard. The most scandalous details were omitted. Suffice it to say that it was her Bible (which her "master," with most uncharacteristic generosity, had allowed her to retain) that sustained Eliza Bradley through this living hell.

Imaginative lady readers would have had no trouble filling in the gaps. And, while there is no evidence that Madam Follansbee had read this particular book, there were so many of its ilk that she must have seen others like it, prior to first boarding the *Logan* in May 1837. While Mrs. Bradley was English, the experiences of a fellow Bostonian, published in 1816 as *The Narrative of the Shipwreck and Unparrelled [sic] Sufferings of Mrs. Sarah Allen on her Passage in May last from New-York to New Orleans,* would certainly have been of interest. Accordingly, while Madam had been pleased enough at her first glimpse of the bedroom in which she was to spend so many seaborne hours— for it was "nicely fitted up" with "a large wide berth, with white drapery curtains, a bureau, washstand across one corner, chairs, and Brussels carpet"—she was somewhat disconcerted to find that one wall was "lined with muskets, pistols, cutlasses and boarding pikes!" Madam was puzzled at first, and then "horror-struck," for her husband lightly informed her that they were ultimately bound for the pirate-ridden shoals of the South China Sea.

Consequently, it must have been quite a moment when the man at the masthead of the *Logan* called out, "A pirate vessel in sight!" at dawn on April 22, 1838. Not only were they in the notorious shoals of the Straits of Sunda, but the ship was helplessly becalmed, while the pirate prahu had the distinct advantage of being propelled by a large number of oars. "Our cannon, swivel guns and pistols were soon got in readiness," Madam recounted. "Swords, cutlasses, boarding pikes and ammunition hustled on deck ready for them."

Nerve-rackingly, however, "there seemed little chance for us, as they were gaining on us every moment." By five in the afternoon they were less than a mile away, and Madam was bracing herself with the reminder that she "had practiced loading and firing guns and pistols at targets all the way out." Her tight-lipped husband informed her that her practice "would be of little use," however, and that when she fell into the pirates' hands, her fate "would be worse than death." By the grace of God, however, "a good breeze sprang up, and we were soon out of their reach."

Another wife to have a brush with Oriental pirates was Charlotte Babcock of the *Young America,* in the course of a comedy of errors that began in late 1854 when she was on shore in Shanghai. She had been set there by her husband to get on with bearing her third daugh-

Entering a bay on the China coast.
Artist: Ron Druett, after a sketch made
by Charlotte Babcock on the *Young America.*

ter. When the baby was about a month old, Charlotte received instructions from Captain David Babcock to charter a steam tug and travel with it to Ning-Po, some distance down the coast, where he was waiting with the ship.

This was quite an order, but Charlotte dutifully complied, discovering with pleasure that the captain of the steamboat, named Dearborn, carried his wife and small child. The quarters, however, were very cramped and hot, Mrs. Dearborn was promptly seasick, and it was not a pleasant trip at all. Then, when they arrived at Ning-Po, the *Young America* was nowhere to be seen. As Charlotte soon found out, "the wind coming out unexpectedly <u>fair and strong</u>," her husband had sailed north to Shanghai without the assistance of the tug. In fact, they must have passed the *Young America* in the night.

This cavalier attitude on the part of his fellow American must have annoyed Captain Dearborn greatly. Not only had he missed out on his towage fee, but he was stuck with Babcock's wife and screaming baby. Glumly, he turned back for Shanghai, but within a few miles was intercepted by a Chinese merchant vessel that was flying a flag of distress. The captain of the vessel spoke no English, and Dearborn did not speak or understand Chinese, but the river pilot he had just taken on acted as interpreter.

Thus Dearborn learned that the Chinese merchant had been robbed of a bag of gold by pirates, whose junk was still in sight. Next, he was offered a fat fee for retrieving the treasure, a bargain Dearborn agreed to very readily. Without any more ado—or even checking the facts—he chugged off in pursuit, meantime ordering his cannon run out, and ignoring the nervous protests of his passenger.

One shot across the bows was enough to bring about the "pirate" junk's surrender, which tends to make one feel suspicious about the story the Chinese merchant had spun. Mrs. Babcock, however, felt no doubts at all, saying that when the twenty-two men of the "pirate" crew had been handcuffed and paraded on deck, "a more villainous set of faces I never saw." And it was such a pleasure to see the Chinese merchant's delight: "he laughed and jabbered, rubbed his hands, and said, 'Hi yah!' and when they recovered his bag of gold seemed unable to contain his joy."

The rapture was short-lived. When the merchant called out that it was to be thrown to him from the deck of the junk, "by some stupidity it was thrown short, and fell into the water." His plunge into despair, it seems, was terrible to view, and meantime two of the "pirates" had jumped overboard and drowned, rather to Captain Dearborn's chagrin, as live pirates were worth a bounty. Twenty were left, though, so he steamed back to Ning-Po to hand them over—much to Charlotte's annoyance, for she was anxious to get back to Shanghai. However, within hours of arriving at Ning-Po the "pirates" had all been beheaded, and Dearborn was free to leave. There had been no kind of trial, but Charlotte saw no harm in that, merely observing, "Chinese justice is summary, but they well deserved their fate." After all, as she had remarked a few weeks before, after viewing three chopped heads on poles, "there are such multitudes of them, a few killed here and there are seldom missed."

Though this might seem callous, it was characteristic of Charlotte Babcock to do her best to look on the bright side of life, even when the shipboard existence was uncomfortable, frightening, or tragic. "In all my going to sea (seven years altogether)," she wrote another time, "we never had any signs of mutiny or insubordination"—something that a much later sister sailor, Mrs. "Sunrise" Clarke, would have greatly envied her.

Mrs. Clarke's adventure began just before Christmas in the year 1885, when the big 1,647-ton windjammer *Frank N. Thayer* set sail from Manila, bound for New York with a freight of hemp and tar. The shipmaster was Captain "Sunrise" Robert K. Clarke. Mrs. Clarke—a remarkable and yet semianonymous woman who had sailed on every voyage since marrying at the age of nineteen—was also on board, along with their five-year-old daughter, Carrie.

Cholera had broken out on board the ship, and Clarke had been forced to leave most of his crew in the Manila hospital. Their replacements were local Malays who became discontented soon after the New Year, when the captain handed out some rather summary medical care to one of their group who imagined himself mortally ill. Clarke had tried out all the contents of the medical chest on the patient, one vial after another, with varying results, some unpleasant, and had finished off the treatment with a kick. The Malay seaman recovered, but nevertheless he and his compatriots remained suspicious and moody. They seized the ship one night in January, in the course of a particularly bloody mutiny.

First the insurgents seized the quarterdeck, cutting the throat of the man at the helm with a handmade lance before tossing the body overboard. When Sunrise came rushing up to deck to find out why the ship had fallen off the wind, he was savagely slashed across the ribs. Mrs. Clarke, hearing the shrieks, dashed up the companionway just in time to grab the native's arm before he could thrust the lance again, and thus saved her husband's life.

"But by that time all hell was loose on the ship," reminisced one of the survivors, Andy Harris, to a reporter from the *Long Island Forum* fifty-six years after the event. Not only had the regular seamen retreated in disarray to the forecastle and the rigging, completely demoralized by the bloody slaughter of the first and second mates, but the cargo had been set on fire. Hemp and tar being so inflammable, matters looked exceedingly grim, so much so that Clarke handed two loaded revolvers to his wife, with the instructions to use them on herself and Carrie before falling into the hands of the pirates. Like Alonzo Follansbee earlier, he had "a fate worse than death" in mind. "By the grace of God I'll do it!" Mrs. Clarke reportedly vowed.

Instead, however, she held off the mutineers while the largest boat was hastily launched. At last they pulled away, with the captain, his family, and the original crewmen aboard, several of them injured. Sunrise himself was so severely wounded that his left lung protruded six inches through the hole the lance had cut in his chest. His wife pushed the slippery organ back inside and bound the gash with strips of cloth, which she then sewed tightly in place.

Clarke survived the ordeal, "but only because of his good wife's constant care," Harris claimed. And the little girl? Carrie had remained silent and still throughout the struggle on board the ship, and was equally quiet during the two-hundred-mile escape to the island of St. Helena. "Carrie was a well behaved child the whole time," the captain's wife was reported as remarking, in what must be a masterpiece of understatement.

And so it seems that Mrs. Clarke, like Charlotte Babcock, was a mistress of positive thinking—a distinct virtue, when the trials and tribulations of the seafaring existence are considered. "Though we sailed up and down the China Sea five different times in typhoon season," wrote Charlotte in her memoirs, "thanks to a kind providence we never experienced one, which was indeed wonderful, and something to be very thankful for, as they are terrible and many vessels have been wrecked by them."

She was right to count her blessings, for her luck was wonderful indeed.

When the *Governor Goodwin* was in Hong Kong during the typhoon season of 1888, Emma Pray watched as badly damaged shipping straggled into port. One in dire distress was the *Carrier Dove,* which had been swept and dismasted, and boats and cabins smashed by the tempest that had also broken the captain's leg in two places. For eleven days, Captain Forsythe had been carried up and down the deck in a litter, directing the struggle to get into port. The Forsythes were friends, so Samuel Pray went on board right away, finding Mrs. Forsythe in a dreadful state, "and sent her up here, while he sent ashore for a surgeon, and had the Capt. taken to a hospital."

Somewhat naturally, Mrs. Forsythe was "so nervous that I hardly knew what to do first for her." As it turned out, Mrs. Forsythe was mostly distracted about the state of her hair, which "had not been down for ten days, and was thoroughly matted & soaked with salt water." This, in an age when an abundance of long hair was a woman's crowning glory, presented quite a problem for Emma. However, "By perseverance I managed to straighten that for her, get her a cup of tea, and made her lie down."

Mrs. Trufant of the ship *Caspian* owed her life to a dog. She, her sister, and her two children were on board when the ship ran onto rocks near Bahia Honda, on passage from New Orleans to Boston, in January 1857. Captain Trufant was knocked overboard with the concussion as the ship struck. His body was found entangled in mangroves next day, but in the meantime there was no one to direct the evacuation of the ship, and the people watching from shore were unable to launch a boat. Mrs. Trufant, struck with inspiration born of desperation, tied the end of a ball of twine to her little dog's collar, and tossed him into the sea. He swam to the beach, and the twine was hauled in. On board, a thin line was attached to the string, and that in its turn hauled ashore. And so by degrees the rope was made

Ship in a storm.
Artist: Ron Druett.

thicker, until at last a cable stretched between the wreck and the beach, and the shocked women and children were rescued by means of a bosun's chair swung from the hawser.

On New Year's Eve, 1855, the tea clipper *Living Age* struck a reef in the South China Sea while under full sail. In a ghastly cacophony of tearing timbers she shuddered to a stop, pinned to the rocks and swept by a vicious surf that took the boats away. The men were yelling and running about in panic, convinced that they were about to be overrun by pirates, when the captain's wife, Mrs. Robert P. Holmes, hove into sight on deck.

Mrs. Holmes was wearing men's clothing and carrying a dirk, but her whole demeanor was so calm that the seamen were instantly ashamed, and made an effort to control themselves. As day dawned, the whole ship's company managed to make its way to the island, which turned out to be uninhabited by pirates—or anyone else. For more than a month, until February 25, 1856, when rescue finally arrived, Mrs. Holmes somehow survived on that island, a lone woman in a party of desperate men. Unsurprisingly, once they got back home, neither she nor her husband went on voyage again.

Being wrecked might be an efficient means of getting one's name into the papers, often with poignant details, such as the report of the discovery of the bodies of Captain Staples and his wife after the wreck of the *Golden Star* in February 1861, "found locked in each other's arms—and the capt. held in his hand a rope which he [had] tried to use for their safety." This was a mournful way of gaining the attention of the general public, though, and one to be actively dreaded. All the women feared shipwreck, and were reminded all the time that it was horridly possible, accounts of wrecks taking such prominence in the shipping papers.

When the 596-ton schooner *Nahum Chapin* was driven ashore on Long Island on January 21, 1897, watchers

Shipwreck.
Artist: Ron Druett.

on the storm-lashed beach could discern the figures of Captain Eugene Lavey, his wife, child, and the crew of eight men clinging to the foremast rigging, but nothing could be done to save them. Instead, as the papers reported, one by one the figures fell into the seething surf, to be washed up dead many hours later. Stories like these struck the seafaring communities hard, and so it was natural that any seafaring wife should suffer agonies of nerves in storms.

The English Channel was particularly notorious because it was so crowded with shipping. When she sailed on the *Clarissa B. Carver,* Annie Dow endured a terrifying storm in the company of fourteen other vessels in the Straits of Dover. She had already experienced one shipwreck, on her very first voyage, when her husband's brig, *Atlanta,* had run aground in the Tortugas in 1859. She and Sarah, aged one year at the time, had been housed by the lighthouse keeper while the cargo of coal was salvaged and so had survived quite comfortably, but it must have been a memory that sprang into vivid life every time the elements raged—and they were certainly raging, on this storm-racked November night in 1877.

The *Clarissa B. Carver* had three heavy anchors out, with plenty of chain, for the tempest was terrific. It was impossible to stand up against the wind, which came with pounding rain and towering waves. About midnight the ship directly ahead went down, and though the cries of the drowning could be clearly heard, nothing could be done to help them. Next morning, there was not a ship in sight. The *Clarissa* was the only vessel still at anchor. Of the fourteen other ships, seven had been blown onto the beach, one had gone down, and the rest had been scattered.

To Katurah Pritchard's horror, a sudden squall from the northwest tore through the fleet as her husband's brig *Massachusetts* was taking her departure from New York in January 1848, and two schooners capsized right before her very eyes—a most unlucky start to her first voyage, which meant that she was terribly scared whenever the wind blew hard. The brig was beset by a hurricane in September 1848, and she was so terrified that she sent repeatedly for her husband. It was impossible for him to leave the deck, so she "bore a torture for two hours indescribable." Taking on a pilot did not ease her suffering, for the one that came on board off the Hook of Holland was a nervous wreck. "It was first, luff luff and keep her away," and then loud cries of, "Mine God, we shall go ashore!—Mine God, we shall go ashore!" However, they "arrived safely at 2:00 p.m. at Helvoet."

Katurah Pritchard was a particularly sad case, though all the wives were anxious. On Tuesday, September 3, 1878, Isabel Duncan was scared by a sudden raging storm while the *Scotia* was lying in a bay at the island of St. Thomas. "Of course I was left alone and frightened enough," she wrote.

I held on to the bed until sickness made me get up and with great dif-ficulty I reached the basin. Oh, how sick I was, and such a noise, not only below but on deck, every moveable article was in motion, dishes crashing and tables dashing, the very drawers in the stateroom were slid-ing out and in as the vessel rolled; one time I was dead sick, next I tried to secure things and when all within my reach was fixed—jammed my-self into a place where I did not roll. I made several attempts to go on deck after some great crash above but was unable to crawl, leave alone walk.

In 1856 a lightning bolt flashed with a deafening report between two of the masts of the *Wild Ranger,* clearing Captain Sears's head by less than two feet. "What will happen next?" cried his terrified wife. "How shall we get through this night?" Off the Atlantic coast of South America, the strong, cold wind called the *pampero* was particularly feared. At two in the afternoon of No-vember 9, 1881, a *pampero* burst upon the *Eclipse,* the thunder continuous. "There was no lull, only that fearful boom—boom all the time, like thousands of cannons," wrote Adelaide Hamilton. Next morning, the ship was com-pletely encrusted with salt dried out from the storm's hurtling spray. The en-tire rigging glistened with white crystals: "When the sun shines it looks like frosting."

Oddly, many a wife found storms even more frightening when the ship was in port and she was on shore. When the *Governor Goodwin* was in Kobe in August 1888, a typhoon threatened, and Captain Pray made Emma, very much against her will, take up lodgings in the hotel on shore. Her only com-fort was that she had a room with a balcony, which overlooked the harbor and the shipping.

"About ten o'clock it began to blow very strong indeed," she wrote, "and by eleven it was a raging typhoon." Within three hours, it became obvious that she was in far more danger in the house than she would have been on the bat-tened-down ship. "The wind fairly screamed down my chimney, and the house and my bed rocked furiously." It was impossible to lie down, so Emma spent her time dashing in and out of the balcony, "but could not see anything on account of the pouring rain"—and all the time "I did not know but what the house would blow down." Eventually, however, the tempest abated,

Emma got to sleep after a session of killing fleas, and at dawn "jumped out to see if everything was all right in the harbor, and was glad to find the 'Gov' in her old place and everything apparently all right." And, indeed, no one on board was hurt, and the ship was unscathed.

Often the aftermath was even more taxing than the gale itself. In February 1874 Bel Wood had been around Cape Horn eight times, but she was still understandably nervous when her husband's ship *Sagamore* began to leak. Captain Aaron Wood, however, was a most resourceful mariner. "We have a windmill now to do the pumping," she wrote in May. "The tower is about twenty-five feet high. The arms extend eight feet above that. There are eight arms and it spreads over thirty yds. of canvas for sails. It is a big affair I assure you, and we think quite an invention." Not surprisingly, the windmill gained a lot of attention from other ships, and the ship's owners gave Captain Wood a purse of "fifty gold guineas in appreciation of his saving the ship."

Many cargoes were dangerous, not least the common cargo of coal. Lady Brassey, an Englishwoman who sailed about the world on her husband's luxury yacht in 1876, wrote after recording an encounter with a bark on fire that out of every three ships that carried coal or coke, one caught fire on the way round the Horn. One poor passenger, Mrs. Bates, set out from New York to San Francisco in 1849, and survived no less than three disastrous fires at sea before she finally arrived at her destination on the steamer *Republic* in 1850.

The drilling of the first commercial oil well in Titusville, Pennsylvania, in 1859 led to another popular freight—petroleum, or "case oil," called thus because it was packed in tins, which were packed in turn in wooden cases, that were sent to the Orient. There the oil found a good market as lamp fuel. On May 23, 1888, the ship *Governor Goodwin* was carrying a cargo of case oil, but, as Emma Pray documented, Captain Pray thought the ship had been overloaded. And so he ordered eight hundred cases thrown overboard. Each case held ten gallons, and so—as Emma quipped—"eight hundred of these ought to smooth the troubled waters for those who are coming behind us." He should have saved the oil. Within two days, "Oil bags were hung out," wrote Emma, "as the sea is getting pretty high. We brought oil for that purpose— fish oil—and it is put in two canvas bags and hung on each side of the bow of the ship." Then, on the thirtieth, "The oil bags were out, but the sea was terrific," she continued. "All hands were on deck all night, each one lashed with the exception of those who were below between decks, passing out oil cases, for we used it that night with good effect to smooth the water. Men stood on each side of the ship pouring out oil, while others handed up the cases, and burst open the tins."

In just one night, 150 cases—fifteen hundred gallons of oil—were used to save the ship. The *Governor Goodwin* took the remaining case oil to Kobe, Japan, took on a cargo of coal for Hong Kong, and exchanged it for a holdful of firecrackers for New York, along with eighteen hundred tons of matting. The prospect of a spark straying about any of this must have been ominous, but Captain Samuel Pray had a living to make, and a ship to pay her own way, and so such quibbles apparently never occurred to him. Mary Stark did express nervous doubts in April 1855, when she found that the cargo they had picked up in Philadelphia was gunpowder, "but they all say it is safe enough— as good as any other cargo." The *B. F. Hoxie* was by no means the only vessel to carry this unstable freight to California. Mary Congdon recorded her relief when the *Caroline Tucker* discharged her freight of gunpowder there in June 1861.

Collision was another hazard, as sailing ships were unpredictable when the breeze flirted about the compass. This often happened in harbors, especially those surrounded by hills. On October 16, 1856, the *Kathay* sailed from Shanghai for home, in a commotion of colliding spars that the port must have remembered for quite some time. "The first thing we did was to take the jibboom off of the *Spirit of the North,*" Carrie, the captain's daughter, recorded; "the next to run into the *Levant.*" Captain Thomas Stoddard was so embarrassed he decided to pay for towage after all, and "we had the small steamer *Antelope* to tow us down." The *Kathay* might have been a particularly unhandy vessel, for she had run into a junk in Hong Kong earlier, carrying away his mast, "but the pilot said he did not care if he carried away all the junk masts in the river," recorded Carrie, so the cluttered state of the harbor might have accounted for it, too.

Colliding with a steamboat was a nerve-racking possibility for the coasters, which often plied the same regular routes as the steamers. Among the coasters were the vessels that carried cotton from New Orleans to the textile mills of Massachusetts. Certain days of the week were worse, as Mary Rowland noted in July 1867, writing that on "Saturdays so many Steamers leave NY for all parts of the world there is great danger to be feared from them." Fog greatly increased the danger of running afoul of another vessel. Fifteen-year-old Nancy Latham described a collision with another sailing vessel in a heavy morning mist in 1900: she and her girlfriends "heard a great crash, men running, and lots of noise. Gert and I got out of bed and looked out and saw two masts sticking up by the bow." Then the wreck drifted away in the fog and they saw no more of her. Within moments she had become another statistic of the sea.

War was yet another threat, doubly ominous because communications were so bad that the details of the conflict were quite unknown. In August 1838 Madam Follansbee had to pick up her week-old baby and flee from Canton to Macao, as an opium war was threatening. In February 1862 the *Kineo,* on passage to London, passed a Dutch vessel that telegraphed, "Bad news, prospect of a war between England & North America." The Everetts were so alarmed that they asked the Dutch captain to come on board, "the two ships keeping along side by side, going about 1 knot an hour. The news was that an American man of war fired into an English mail steamer & caused considerable excitement." There was some compensation, however, in that "the Capt'n took dinner with us & it did seem a treat to have company at sea."

Nevertheless, it was a worry—though not as great a concern as the American Civil War, which was raging at the time. As Mary Rowland wrote, "Merchants dared not ship their property, fearing it might fall into the hands of the privateers that had begun their devastations on vessels bound into or owned in northern ports, and the southern ports were many of them under a blockade." The Southern ports had been so dependent on Northern-based shipping for importing and exporting goods that when hostilities broke out, the Northern states had many ships, while the Confederation owned very few. And so the Southerners tried to remedy the imbalance by sending out raiders—the *Shenandoah,* the *Alabama,* and the *Florida* being the most famous—to destroy as much north-based commercial shipping as possible.

As a program, it was spectacularly successful, for more than two hundred Northern vessels were seized. Naturally, insurance premiums became very high, and many owners were forced to sell their ships to other countries, primarily Britain. No vessel was immune, no matter how humble: the Confederate bark *Tacony* wreaked havoc among the fishing schooners of Gloucester. The whaling fleet of New Bedford was decimated as Captain James Waddell of the *Shenandoah* made a fiery business of chasing, ambushing, and setting alight the ships in the North Pacific. Merchant vessels were desirable prey because of their valuable cargoes.

In March 1862, Captain Cooper of the English bark *William Durnley* signalized the *Kineo* "that your civil war is ended," but he was wrong. Ironically, on his next voyage Timothy Everett was forced to surrender the bark *Greenland* to the Confederate raider *Alabama,* and watch as his ship was burned. It is not known if Sarah was on board the *Greenland,* but Mrs. William Nichols was certainly on board the bark *Delphine* of Maine when the Rebel cruiser *Shenandoah* fired a shot across the bows. According to the stories told, after directing the transfer of her six-year-old son, the steward's wife, their gear, and their canary to the Rebel ship, Mrs. Nichols turned to Lieutenant Charles Reed of the cruiser and gave him a piece of her mind. "Young man, you should be ashamed of yourself!" she exclaimed. "What would your mother say?"

Even stranger tales are told of the twenty-two-year-old wife of Captain Edward Robinson of Thomaston, Maine. While in Liverpool in 1860, Robinson's 1,193-ton ship *Frank Flint* was commandeered by the British government to carry cavalry and troops to China for the Opium Wars. When they arrived at Tientsin, the troops disembarked and marched off into the flat hinterland to meet the enemy, and the crew of the *Frank Flint* clambered into the rigging to watch the battle. Mrs. Robinson wished to see what was happening, too, so she was hoisted aloft in an armchair.

When the skirmish was won, the captains and wives from the fleet toured the battleground. Later, when Mrs. Robinson was asked by folks at home if there had not been a lot of dead people lying around, she reportedly replied, "Oh yes, but we just ignored them." In spite of this insouciance, Captain Robinson left her behind when he went along with the troops to Peking, mollifying her by carrying back a great deal of loot, which included an inlaid rosewood cabinet, four lacquer tea tables in a nest, a gold lacquer writing desk, embroidered robes, and bolts of silk, much of it now in the Knox Museum in Thomaston.

It does seem remarkable that shipmasters should expose themselves to exotic dangers so needlessly, for life in the decks and rigging was hazardous enough already. If they wanted conflict, there was often plenty of that on board, for sailors were naturally aggressive, especially when drunk. Brawls were common, and murder certainly not unknown. On New Year's Eve, 1859, the mate of the *Kineo* was slaughtered, as described by Sarah Everett.

The ship lay at the Chincha Islands, off the southern coast of Peru, fully loaded with guano fertilizer and ready to sail in the morning. "It has been a custom at the Chinchas the night a ship was loaded for the mates to go on board & spend the evening," wrote Sarah when she related the gruesome details in a letter to her sister. Mr. Bartlett, their mate, had asked permission to entertain other mates on board, and Timothy had readily consented, with the proviso that the seamen who rowed the officers' boats should be given no more than one glass of grog each.

The party went well, with much singing and playing of the accordion. However: "Just as they were nearly ready to leave, a sailor from the ship *Hippograffe* came aft & wanted some liquor, said it was a poor ship that could only give the sailors one glass of grog when loaded—with a great deal of abusive talk." His mate "drove him forward & our mate went forward with him to see about it—when he run his sheath knife, a very sharp pointed one, into his bowels & clean into his stomach."

Sarah herself had only just come on board, for she had been on board the *Moses Wheeler,* helping deliver Mrs. Whitman's baby. "I put away my things and had got undressed when I heard a strange sound on deck," she wrote.

> . . . the door was opened & they brought him with his wound bleeding & his entrails hanging out, oh dear, what a sight, I ran on deck bare-footed & screamed for the Capt'ns . . . & we got the Dr. there directly, he sewed up the wound & said he feared he could not live. . . . he was a great sufferer for 12 hours, when he got easier, & so patient a person I never saw. He told me about writing to his family, and talked very calmly about dying. . . . you may be sure it was a solemn scene, there was Mr. B. lying on his bed in the cabin, a mate on each side of him fanning him, Capt'n Phinney kneeling by him praying, & such a prayer I never heard.

The fact that captain, wife, and officers often hailed from the same community made such situations even more moving. "We did everything that could be done, for we were both very attached to him, I never saw T. feel so badly," she grieved.

Mary, daughter of Cynthia and John Remington Congdon, was on board the *Caroline Tucker* when the ship was dismasted by a storm in August 1862. It happened with terrifying suddenness. "By breakfast time all light sails were furled, by 9 we were a wreck," she wrote. Both fore and main topgallant masts had come crashing down, along with all their rigging, the sails were blown into threads, and the air was so full of vapor and rain that it was impossible to see twenty feet. Captain Congdon managed to get the ship into port under jury rig, but on April 16, 1863, Mary must have vividly recollected that storm, for she and her mother had just been informed that Captain John Remington Congdon had been washed overboard during a storm off Cape Horn, and drowned. "Such a death, such a grave," mourned Mary in her shore journal. "My dear father, I cannot realize it." There was "not a shadow of a hope that he might have been picked up, for in such a sea it would be impossible to lower a boat," she wrote later. "My poor mamma has been almost beside herself."

"The wind blowing furiously," wrote Mary Rowland in March 1856. "Nothing can be heard but the awful roaring of the wind, rain, and the sea, the latter appears ready to swallow down our vessel at once, which indeed seems like but a mere speck upon the mighty raging deep, pitching and rolling at the mercy of the waves. How grand, yet how terrific the scene." Thirteen years later, Mary still could "never get accustomed to [storms] enough to not suffer fear during these times when all the elements are at war . . .

> *The loud roaring of the great waves, the lightning's flash & thunder's roar are not pleasant company. The tempestuous sea seems trying to swallow us up or rather down, I should say. And then O don't the sharks have a glorious feast. Sometimes I wonder if they do not have an idea of what is going on above them, and so get the great whales and mermaids to assist them to set the waves in commotion. . . .*
>
> *At such times as these the sailors say, who would not sell a farm and go to sea? I say the person that wrote the lines "A life on the ocean wave" ought to spend a day with us here, then be sent to the state prison for life. Their experience in a sailor's life probably amounted to a row around in a bay some calm delightful evening, then went home and writ those lines with the assistance of books to get his sea phrases from, and then I suppose it was like the quack medicines, made to sell. For myself just now, I had much rather be in that old farm house in the Valley, and sitting around those morning glories.*

"The wind shifted round to the north east," recorded Mary Dow on the bark *Clement* in June 1838. Clouds gathered blackly, and "the cross sea made the Barque dance on tiptoe a short time, but she soon got tired of that and went to diving. A north-easter has a mournful sound on land, but here under these black skies and still blacker waters it sounds Dismal, Dismal."

After a particularly horrible passage around Cape Horn in 1883, Maria Murphy confided, "Some nights, I stowed away behind the bed in our room—there was just space to crowd in—and I stop up my ears so that I can not hear so plainly." Yet Maria had been nine years at sea, having first shipped as a bride, in 1874. "During this siege I have felt that I never could go another voyage," she confessed, "but as the weather brightens my courage gets stronger." And so her seafaring career eventually spanned thirty-five long and tempestuous years.

Similarly, Mary Rowland resolved, "I'll try and make the best of it, if it is my lot to go." It was easy enough in fine weather, but—like Maria Murphy—Mary Rowland often felt as if she did not have enough fortitude left "to ever cross the ocean again. I have not the nerve to listen to the roaring of the Tempest and the huge billows that seems ready to swallow us up at times, and the nights of care and fear during these awful thunder storms."

Mary's twenty-two-year seafaring career did not come to an end until June 7, 1876, however, when her beloved husband, Henry, died on voyage of an unnamed disease at the age of forty-nine. Sadly, her daughter Henrietta died just weeks afterward, on August 20, leaving an eight-month-old baby, also named Henrietta. "I took care of her till she was nearly 4 years old," wrote Mary later. "I think she was my solace in my great loss."

CHAPTER TEN

Dropping Anchor

*I manage to go around on shore more or less in every Port, and
learn the different manners and customs of different Nations and
the works of God & Man, both Nature and Art, and find much to
amuse, edify, and interest us, and see what so many Travelers pay
large sums for, while Henry makes us a living and the Brig is our
Hotell, and even what is much better, our Home.*

—Mary Rowland, January 1873

The *Kathay* dropped anchor in the green and "cheerful" port of Sydney, Australia, in June 1856, and "it seemed so good to see a horse
and cow again, and it was as good as any Opera Singing to hear a hen crow!"
wrote the captain's daughter in her diary. When the brig *Massachusetts* arrived
in Cuba in June 1848, "Oh, who can describe the joy one feels, on seeing land
after being toss'd about on the Occan," exulted Katurah Pritchard. It was a
moment that made the frights, the privations, the storms, and the monotony
of passage all at once worthwhile.

The first visitor to the ship (not counting the pilot who had guided them in) was usually the port doctor, who came to check on the state of health on board. If there were any sick men, or the vessel had come from a port where there was known to have been an outbreak of fever, he put the ship in quarantine, which meant that a guard was put on the vessel to make sure that no one left or came on board for a specified number of days. If everything looked good, he issued a clean bill of health. There was a fee for this, which varied from port to port. In New Orleans in 1873, Mary Rowland recorded that the fee for a brig was ten dollars—"easily made, I think"—while larger ships and barks cost up to fifteen or twenty, depending on tonnage.

At Cadiz, on April 28, 1881, Hannah Morgan remarked that when the doctor came on board, "Mama and I had to go up on deck and show ourselves. I never was up for a show but once before, and that was when we were in Genoa." When the Scottish ship *Scotia* arrived at St. Thomas island in August 1878, Isabel Duncan was amused and a little scandalized when the doctor immediately asked for a present of salt fish. They had none to give him, but "adjourned to the cabin and had some music, the Doctor and I being the performers." Then, when Captain William Duncan offered the physician a glass of wine, he immediately asked for the bottle. The wine was plentiful, so Willie Duncan did not begrudge the little bribe. Indeed, the episode became so convivial that it is not surprising that the rest of the ship's business had to be postponed to the morrow. "So much for my first day," Isabel summed up.

Similarly, when Dr. Lockhead came on board the *Governor Goodwin* in Hong Kong in 1888, Emma Pray decided that he "looked just the same as when I saw him six years ago." The good physician returned the compliment, saying, "Well, with the exception of a little more settled look, you haven't changed a particle." Emma took this with a grain of salt, for "everyone who comes here knows how fond Dr. Lockhead is of American ladies," but bridled happily nonetheless, for Dr. Lockhead turned to Captain Pray and informed him that he didn't feel like discussing such small matters as the state of health on board right now, having "so much to say to Mrs. Pray." And then the two of them settled down to a session of enjoyable gossip.

"As soon as the Dr. visits us, Andrew will go on shore to get our orders," wrote Helen York, on arrival in Buenos Aires on New Year's Day, 1886. While their husbands were on shore entering the ship's papers at the Custom House, seeing the ship's agent for orders, and collecting the ship's mail, the women were busy in a ship that was at long last lying still, in a happy frenzy of sprucing up the cabins to make them fit for visitors. The *Charles Stewart* arrived in Brisbane in 1883, and Hattie Atwood set to work at once, "put down the cabin carpet and polished up in fine style." An exception was Emma Pray, whose first job was to address the letters she had written on voyage, for she believed that if she got her letters ready to post before the ship dropped anchor, they were bound to get a head wind.

Letters were first and foremost in the minds of all the wives—letters that had been longed for all the months of voyage and yet, strangely, had been dreaded, too. In San Francisco in February 1882, Adelaide Hamilton was in a state of nervous tension as she busied herself "fixing our rolling home up in her best clothes," feeling "very blue and nervous, long for letters and yet dread to get them, afraid of bad news." Then, at last, her husband Joe came back on board, "and I am too full for utterance," for "Thank God, all are spared. I feel as if I could go up on the sky-sail yard this morning, I am so glad to have had news from home." In 1856 a stevedore came on board the *Wild Ranger* with a bundle of letters, and Bethia Sears wrote, "You can imagine how I seized them and ran below. I was so nervous I could scarcely open them. I ran through them hastily and found all well, which was a great relief."

Captain Aaron Wood "went on shore yesterday as soon as the anchor was down, and last night brought off about thirty friendly letters," wrote Bel. "I laughed and cried by turns, and was so excited that I could not sleep a wink until four o'clock, and was awake again before six." Letters arrived while Emma Pray was in Kobe, in September 1888. "I read & re-read them until I was fairly homesick," she wrote, "and had to pinch myself back to life in a heathen land."

In these days of instant communications, it is hard to realize how intensely the seafaring wives felt about receiving mail. Bad news might be dreaded, but it was far, far worse not to get any letters at all. In January 1870, aboard ship in Melbourne, Anne Augusta Fitch Brown was acutely disappointed when her husband, Jacob, came back "without one letter for any of us" after she had waited for him an entire day. "How sweet to be remembered," she bitterly penned.

This did not mean, necessarily, that no letters had been written and posted, for the way mail got around could be eccentric as well as slow. In the port of Anjer, Java, in July 1888, Emma Pray noted that the mail came overland by cart from Batavia—forty miles through jungle and mountain passes. In Hong Kong, in June 1838, Mrs. Follansbee was handed a bundle of letters she had written to Alonzo before they were married, and which he had never received. To her surprise, she found that they had all been opened and read, one captain assuring her that "they were the best love letters he ever read, not a word of nonsense in them." Somewhat chagrined, Madam observed with unusual tartness that she was "very thankful" she had not written nonsense, not knowing who might peruse them.

As soon as the captain was back on board—or, in some parts of the world, even before he managed to get on shore—he was besieged by all kinds of tradesmen. When Hannah Winn arrived in Manila in October 1837, a flock of natives raced the doctor to the ship, so that Hannah's first visitor was a market woman who "came off to the ship in her Banca (a Manila canoe). She was attired in a Purple and White plaided skirt, White grass cloth Short Gown, with small sleeves, White handkerchief in her neck, her hair combed back plain," recorded Hannah, who was always fascinated by dress and fashion. Then she turned her attention to the swarm of official boats that arrived in the market woman's wake. "The oarsmen in the health boat were all attired in Blue pantaloons, White Shirts, and no hats," she wrote. "Next came the Custom House boat with its officers who came on board and cleared the Ship *St. Paul.* The oarsmen of the Custom House boat were attired in various colours. Some wore Pink, some Blue, and others White Shirts, likewise the pantaloons differed in colour, according to the taste of the wearer."

On entering exotic ports, women often recorded amazing sights. Here, in the Indian Ocean, a local dhow is engaged in fishing for sharks.
Courtesy Joseph D. Thomas.

In Havre, France, in April 1848, Katurah Pritchard described a similar rush of entrepreneurs. No sooner had the custom house boat gone "than we were so swarmed with Boats, Brokers, Tailors, Carpenters, Sail Makers, Boardinghouse runners, that my husband had his hands full of cards in five minutes, and then I had an opportunity to learn how so many cards came home with my husband's things." When the *Kineo* dropped anchor off Mapoor Dock in Calcutta, "we were beset with Butchers, milkmen, taylors (all who sew are called so) &c., trying to cut down one another," Sarah Everett reported in August 1861, adding, "& I could hardly get rid of them."

Officialdom kept on arriving as well, often proving troublesome. In Buenos Aires in January 1886, Helen York "was quite disgusted with the officers that came on board. They called for Brandy. I thought they had more than was good for them already." When the *Logan* was in the port of Kronstadt, Russia, in August 1837, Madam Follansbee complained that she was the particular target of rudeness from the customs men, but then found out that an English captain's wife had been smuggling china plates into the country by baking them in pies.

Once the legalities had been satisfied, the next challenge was getting on shore to see the sights—or, alternatively, out to other ships, to call on friends. This often involved a ride in a boat, usually one propelled by oars, though if the ships were anchored well out and there was a fair wind, a sail could be set. Mary Rowland definitely preferred "to go with oars," but admitted after a visit under sail in Palermo that it had indeed been enjoyable, though when they arrived in the city square, it was to find a scaffold up and a man executed for murder.

Getting into the boat could prove a challenge. Madam Follansbee described the way it happened on the *Logan*—a complicated and cautious process that illustrates both Alonzo's pomposity and Madam's unassailable dignity. First, the captain's gig was lowered, "and brought around to the gangway" in readiness, and then "Madam's armchair was carried on deck, all covered with the Stars and Stripes." This was not a mere patriotic gesture, for once Madam had seated herself, the edges of the flag were brought up and tucked in all around her by the captain himself, as a precaution against any wind that might get under her flounces. Then, limbs thoroughly protected from the common gaze of sailors, Madam sat like an upright corpse as the chair was "secured to a windlass, and hoisted up over the ship's rail, and then lowered away down, down, down into the boat below," where the captain stood in readiness to receive this strange bundle.

"This is the way I was always taken on board the ship and taken off," Madam recorded complacently. "The boat was all cushioned, and carpeted expressly for Madam, and a nice awning over the whole." Madam sat in the bow, and Alonzo sat in the stern to steer, "while two sailors, all dressed in clean suits, sit in the middle of the boat, to row. And," she added, "this is the way my lady visitors were always taken on board the ship, and taken off."

She did not mention whether any of these callers expressed astonishment, but most of them were accustomed to a lot less formality. When Bethia Sears was "lowered down in a chair into the Dinghy," after the *Wild Ranger* arrived in Calcutta, she explained this unusual luxury by adding, "When I got ashore they carried me over the mud in the chair," which indicates that the tide was out. Mary Rowland certainly never enjoyed the privilege of a chair, for though she disliked "getting down the Side ladders into the boat," the only other choice was to "remain a prisoner" on the ship.

In the middle of the nineteenth century, when the ships collected at the off-shore islands of Peru to take on guano, ships' boats plied constantly back and forth about the fleet, and any woman who wanted a ride to another ship waited at the gangway until a boat came along, then braced herself and jumped. Hattie Atwood reminisced that it was as good as a circus to watch Mrs. Fulton (the same woman who pulled lines with the sailors and weighed three hundred pounds) poise herself for the drop. On one occasion the boat had to make the pass ten times before the lady finally made the leap, nearly swamping the boat in the process.

Victorian boating party, from a contemporary women's magazine.

Sometimes the boat was a hired one. In Hong Kong new arrivals were immediately surrounded by a host of sampans crying out for custom, "each one wishing the Capt. to hire his—his being 'No. 1,' and the rest no good," wrote Emma Pray. Captain Pray "chose a neat-looking one, No. 75, and the rest soon after dispersed." These sampans were quite large, having two masts and a whole family of three or four generations on board. "The mother of the family usually steers the boat," despite the host of children at her knee, Emma Pray marveled. "It is a mystery where they stow themselves," she went on—but room was always found for the hirers of the boat, who were seated under a bamboo awning amidships.

A similar custom prevailed in Genoa, Italy. In July 1856, Mary Rowland noted, "There are licenced watermen who keep a regular line of Boats, and generally all vessels employ one of these boats to attend to them while in Port," adding "There seems to be quite a strife among the boatmen" for custom. Understandably, a captain preferred to hire a man who could speak some English, because then he could be used as an informal interpreter while conducting the endless ship's business in port. Often he kept the boatman so busy running "to the market, the Consignees, brokers, ship Chandlers &c &c" that the boat might not be available when his wife wished to go ashore. That was the time for women to link forces and hire a boat of their own, as Mary did with Mrs. Montgomery of the brig *Torrent* during that spell in Genoa, their main object—like Emma Pray's in Hong Kong—being "to look for a good awning against the hot burning Sun."

At other places, there was a gangplank to the wharf to be negotiated—in full regalia of buttoned boots, corset stays, shawls, tippets, elaborate basques, four layers of petticoats, ten yards of skirts, a huge hat or bonnet, and often a parasol. Rebecca Stoddard objected strongly to the thirty-foot plank that had to be walked to get on shore in Sydney, but was forced to do it or else stop on board. "It did one good to see her coming up holding onto the skirts of Father's coat and looking as if she thought she should tumble over every step she took, although there was a rope on each side," commented her irreverent daughter, Carrie. Mary Rowland remarked that women who lived on shore were "often very timid when they come to call on me in my floating home," but with long practice she herself could "step on shore very easily."

The next priority was to remedy the damage that life at sea had wreaked. Making her first landfall was often the signal for a novice seafaring wife to get her hair professionally dressed for the first time in her life. Bethia Sears noted not just that her hair had gone dry, but her husband had told her "it grows red." Many women cut their hair short, because it was more comfortable in the tropics, which gave them another problem when getting gussied up for port visiting.

Once they had made themselves presentable, the wives called on one another just as they would in their houses at home. Many stag captains were highly delighted to entertain lady callers, too, which added to the social whirl. "Keeping a journal in port is very hard work," wrote Emma Pray in Kobe, Japan, after a hectic round of visits. "I have spent one day in making calls, and am thankful to say that they are now all returned. There are two or three of the ladies in the fleet who spend all their time in just going from one ship to another. How they keep it up in this hot sun is a mystery."

Sometimes the ships were moored so closely together that it was possible to jump from deck to deck. In San Francisco in April 1853, the *Hannah Thornton* was moored up against the clipper *Alcyone,* and Cynthia Congdon recorded, "We were so deep in the water, and they being light brought the top of our house about on the level with their decks." Captain Littlefield of the *Alcyone* "put a plank over and handed me on board," so that the two wives could get together. "They invited me in the Cabin," wrote Cynthia, "where they had supper waiting."

The women served up nice little repasts to one another, which included a surprising amount of alcoholic drink. When sixteen-year-old Charlotte Page entertained Liverpool friends and business associates of Captain Cummings on board the *George Washington,* she served "cake, wine and champagne." In Brisbane seventeen-year-old Hattie Atwood called on board an English vessel, and was served a "dainty lunch" of cold chicken, bread, and wine. Then she visited a Bremen ship, where the skipper served her schnapps, and after that she entertained them all on the *Charles Stewart,* where she served them "Yankee food." In Shanghai in 1856, Rebecca Stoddard also regaled her callers with the dishes of home, such as New England chowder, along with wine and brandy, her fifteen-year-old daughter Carrie "doing the honors" when her mother was too ill to preside in the cabin.

Sherry and gin were popular in the East because of the adventurers that had arrived there on East Indiamen from the Netherlands, Spain, and Portugal, bringing their national tipples. Because the British had taken part in the recent history of the region, beer, too, was a staple drink. A popular jaunt in London was to explore the remarkable, brick-vaulted wine cellars beneath London Docks, where all ships with cargoes of tobacco, rice, wine, and brandy had to unload. Part of the fun was the wine tasting, and in 1827 twenty-year-old Alice Delano was delighted when their guide "opened a cask of Sherry, the best I ever tasted." She had a cold, so had a good excuse, she thought, to drink as much as she was offered.

Hattie Atwood remarked on a strange custom she noticed while in Australia. At formal dinners, the men had a session to themselves in the host's study before the meal was served. When she asked her father what went on there, he told her they were given gin, salt fish, and crackers, which puzzled her greatly. She couldn't understand why the ladies were barred, as most would not say no to a little tipple, even if it might only be sherry with water and nutmeg. According to Carrie Stoddard, this last was a very popular female drink in the ports of Shanghai and Hong Kong, though Hattie Atwood noted that gin slings were all the rage with the people on the ships that were loading guano from the offshore islands of Peru. When Hattie was in Brisbane she went on a picnic, and apart from backing into a prickly cactus during a game of hide-and-seek, she had a first-rate time, for they took along "three kinds of meat, bread, cake, oranges, bananas, hard bread, pale ale, brandy, gin, wine," and "not a crumb or drop was brought back." And so it would not be surprising if some of the seasoned seafaring wives were also seasoned drinkers. "Very often take a glass of wine after dinner to cheer up my spirits," confessed Mary Snell of the ship *Victoria* in February 1839, "or perhaps something a little stronger." When young Benjamin Doane of Halifax, Nova Scotia, was on the eve of his first voyage in July 1845, he called on a relative, Olive Doane Kenney, who had sailed with her husband, Captain Simeon Kenney, on several voyages. "Handing me a glass of wine," he wrote, "she took up another and said: 'Cousin Ben, before we say goodbye, I am sailor enough to take a parting glass with you.' "

*Gathering of captains
and wives on the
Electric Spark.*
Peabody Essex Museum.

Local foods from shore were something to marvel at and write about. Hattie Atwood was intrigued with the roast of beef she sampled in Hobart, Tasmania, the first sirloin she had ever seen rolled up. In Macao, Mrs. Follansbee was given "great milkpans of brown sugar, with chopsticks to eat it with." The women were often squeamish about what they put in their mouths. When Carrie Stoddard was told that the Chinese ate insects, she exclaimed, "Oh gracious, I didn't believe they were so nasty." A great deal of ice cream was eaten, even in tropical places like Mauritius, where Mary Henry bought it at an "ice house." And most of the women loved tropical fruits, Mrs. Follansbee being particularly fond of mangosteens. Some of them ate unwisely of such treats as figs and melons, and had their portside round of activities interrupted by a bout of diarrhea—or, as Sarah Everett put it, "a visit from Mr. Dyer."

It was striking how often the women met up with old acquaintants during this ship-to-ship visiting in port. When the *Hannah Thornton* dropped anchor at the Chincha Islands off the southern coast of Peru in July 1853, Cynthia Congdon was delighted to find Mrs. Littlefield, for they had become very friendly just three months earlier, when the two ships were in San Francisco. Arriving in Anjer, Java, in June 1888, Emma Pray was pleased to see the *Eclipse* and the *Creedmore,* "both of which ships were with us in Calcutta last voyage," and so she was able to renew her friendship with Mrs. Shillabee of the *Eclipse.* Then, arriving in Kobe in August, she was very glad to find Mrs. Daly of the *W. H. Lincoln,* whom she had last seen in Calcutta five years before. In San Francisco in April 1859 Sarah Todd met a Mrs. Sherman whose company she had enjoyed in Sydney in October 1857.

Because intermarriage among seafaring families was so common, it was almost impossible to keep secrets, for there was so much gossip to be exchanged, and communicated in letters home. In October 1860 Sarah Everett wrote to her sister Hattie that she had met up with Captain Charles Patten and his wife—"you know who he is, the one who married the English girl." Earlier that year, in Melbourne, she had met up with "Mrs. Capt'n Kellum, who is very pleasant, she is Catherine Dodge's daughter of S. Boston." The fleet might even include neighbors from home. Helen York of Portland, Maine, met up with Mrs. Race and Mrs. Montgomery of that same town in the port of Buenos Aires, Argentina, in 1886. "Have had a real family gathering, a real Searsport crowd," wrote Annie Dow of Searsport, Maine, to her daughter Kate from Yokohama in August 1878; "all together with the children we number 13." There were occasional disappointments. In 1881, Laura Bagley met up with Captain Joseph Stover of the *Daniel Barnes* in Surabaya, but Calista was at home in Bucksport, Maine, awaiting the birth of her second baby.

Occasionally, though, a wife would have much preferred it if a certain other vessel had not been in port. Emma Pray found it very hard to like a certain Mrs. Colby, who came on board in Hong Kong and proved to be a garrulous gossip. She "informed me of everything that our neighbors have done, just how many calls I have had, and so forth, *ad infinitum,*" Emma wrote in exasperation. "Really, what that woman doesn't hear and see is hardly worth having anything to do with." Sarah Everett became very upset in Melbourne in April 1860, writing that she had been snubbed by Mrs. Hooper, who was "too busy (her husband said) to call on me." Mrs. Hooper had entertained other wives in port, so "I conclude I have got the cut direct," wrote Sarah angrily. "It is not the first time a Hooper's wife has done the same thing, but I guess it will be the last as far as I am concerned." It was a family feud that could well have had its roots in Honolulu, where an Everett had been a merchant, and a Hooper had been the U.S. commercial agent and acting consul.

Port of San Francisco in the 1850s.   Port of San Francisco in the 1850s.
Contemporary lithographs.

On the whole, though, relationships were amiable, for the wives were prepared to be tolerant, having so much in common with their "sister sailors." As Mary Rowland remarked in October 1856, "When we meet in foreign ports it is very natural and easy for us to become acquainted, after the first introduction and the usual compliments passed—which are generally, How do you like the sea? And is this your first voyage? Are you troubled with seasickness, &c &c."

Getting up groups of women made it easier on the husbands, too, for they were usually too busy in port to squire their wives around—and as for shopping, it was much more fun to cruise the shops and markets in the company of another female, for "most all men are apt to dislike the business," wrote Mary Rowland. "They willingly afford us any reasonable amount of pocket change to make our purchases with, but they can never have the patience to stand in a store and parley with the knights of the tape and scissors about the quality of such and such an article, as they think it is of no consequence at all." Mary Rowland and Mrs. Montgomery certainly took full advantage of their good fortune in being in the port at the same time, refreshing themselves between shopping sprees at the English Arms Hotel, "where the capts. usually go." This was yet another advantage of being in company with another woman, for it would not have been "proper" to go to a hotel on one's own.

Being together gave the women the confidence to deal with people who spoke an unintelligible foreign language; though several wives mentioned learning Spanish, most relied on friendly locals to translate. Going about in groups also made it possible to tackle local public transport without the supporting presence of a man—which could be quite a proposition, though in Melbourne in the 1860s the town authorities made it easy, by giving shipmasters' wives free tickets for the train that plied between the city and the port. In Sydney in June 1856, Caroline Stoddard and her mother found that the common means of transport was "an omnibus, the dirtiest things that ever was, and small, so they will only hold six inside, and crowded a little at that." A twelve-year-old boy stood on the step in the capacity of conductor, and when he had taken their fares they set off up George Street, "but only a little way," for then the horses balked. The conductor got off and whipped them savagely, so that they "kicked and cut up all sorts of capers," and then to the consternation of the passengers "set off full gallop"—in the opposite direction to the one they had been going, with the conductor sprinting behind. After two or three blocks they crashed to a halt, and Caroline and her mother made a judicious escape, even though the boy did not want them to go.

When Hattie Atwood arrived in Boston she remarked with some wonder that the horse cars had lots of yellow straw in the bottom to keep the passengers' feet warm, and in Valparaiso she observed that these "omnibuses" had a "top story" on them. Mrs. Follansbee rode a "droschy" in St. Petersburg, and in Java rode in a boat that was towed along the alligator-infested canals of Batavia by a horse.

Just like today, shopping for certain famous local products was a large part of the fun of being in port. Indeed, many women—such as Lucy Smith of the whaling bark *Nautilus*—bought large quantities of native handicrafts with the intention of selling them at a profit after getting back home. In 1855, according to Cornelia Peabody, Paris was the place to buy corsets. Cloisonné, embroidery, and porcelain were purchased in Japan and China, often via visits to workshops. "This morning we have been purchasing some crockeryware," wrote Carrie Stoddard in Shanghai, "such as Father brought home last year, and everybody admired." Buying animals was surprisingly common. When the *Levi C. Wade* was in Surabaya, the Bagleys' little girl, Hilda, was given two monkeys, "and the Steward has a large one." In Calcutta in 1877, the Dow family bought two monkeys, but one jumped overboard and swam for shore as they were taking their departure. Then the other one fought with the goose, until the goose flew overboard, so they sold it for ten dollars when they got to New York.

Caged birds were very popular, and it was fun to buy them in Canton, China, for the bird seller washed them before he handed them over by taking a big mouthful of water and then "spurt it out at them," as Carrie Stoddard described, adding, "I thought I should have died of glee, he looked so ridiculous, but the poor birds seemed to like it very much better than I should under the circumstances." In Palermo, the ships were constantly visited by sellers of birds in cages, who would leave them in the cabin on approval, hoping that the captain's wife would become so enchanted that she would persuade her husband to buy. In May 1867, Mary Rowland described a cabin that looked "quite ornamental," for six cages were hanging in the skylight. Altogether, there were "5 canaries and 3 goldfinches in them. This is the place to get good singers," she recommended. "They are brought onboard and left for trial."

In Palermo, as in the Orient, having portraits of ships and people painted was enduringly popular, too. In 1867 Captain Henry Rowland commissioned a painting of his brig, *Thomas W. Rowland,* which his wife, Mary, thought "quite ornamental." In China, captains who did not have their wives with them would hand the artist a daguerreotype, or even just a verbal description, and the painter would happily comply. As can be imagined, these were not very close to life, but having the subject sitting in front of the easel did not seem to make much difference, for Chinese artists labored under the fixed misconception that Europeans, no matter their sex and coloring, were all large-nosed, hirsute, and red-haired. Thus when Carrie Stoddard had her portrait painted in Shanghai, she was not at all "flattered" with the result. "It had bright red hair," she wrote, "black eyes, and something that looked like whiskers."

Markets were fun, as well as being exotic, and the wives usually got to know them well, helping to purchase supplies for the ship. In 1837, Hannah Winn found the Liverpool markets both colorful and scandalous, for "the porters were females, not so very agreeable to see our own sex carry burdens." Bricks were made by women, too, and Hannah saw "many females in Liverpool who gain all their livelihood from gathering manure from the streets, while others pass from street to street, crying, fish, apples, oranges

Women sifting brick dust.
From *Mayhew's London.*

&c &c to sell, which they carry on their heads." Similarly, when Mary Rowland was in Genoa in April 1867, she observed that all the sail making was done by women, "who only get 40 cents a day by working late and early," while the men "get better pay at something else."

In June the previous year, Mary Rowland watched some even more enterprising females at work, while her husband's brig *Thomas W. Rowland* was "lying out in the stream abreast of the City" of Antwerp. "The people here have a strange way of carrying on some of their farming," she wrote, "especially of carting their hay . . .

> *It is cut and at high water a galiot sails up into the field and is loaded and then at high water again off she goes and takes it over to the City. I have been watching them as the vessel lies near. The Galiots sail up and down and numbers are passing us continually, they look as if they would last for centuries before they would be wore out for they are so strong or appear so.*
>
> *The women manage these crafts as well as the Men and apparently as easily, on board of many are the whole family, and I see the frows make themselves very useful, help hoist the sails, steer the ship, do the cooking, and in port assist to take out Cargo &c., each dressed in their short pet-*

*ticoats—with wooden shoes and white night-caps. It is really amusing
for me to watch them as their Galiots glide swiftly past the vessel.*

"The people here seem to think nothing of murder or suicide," mused
Scotswoman Isabel Duncan when she visited New York for the first time, in
June 1886. On the same morbid note, the favorite sightseeing place in town
was Greenwood Cemetery, which Isabel visited twice, even enjoying a picnic
under the trees on the grounds. Interesting, too, was the chance to hear
William Talmadge preach to a congregation of five thousand, the hymn being
"Home, Sweet Home." The streetcars were a novelty, the fare a modest five
cents ("a cent is a half-penny"), and the Staten Island ferry (fare two cents) was
much appreciated, as the ship discharged her cargo there. "Driving is the only
cheap thing here except beef, which is 11 cents per lb & splendid quality." Then
the ship moved "over to the New York side to our loading berth," and the situation was splendid, too: "we have a fine view of the bridge & the large river-
boats besides vessels of all description passing up and down."

Visiting graveyards was a surprisingly popular pursuit, often being a pilgrimage to the graves of friends and relatives. Thus when Mary Henry of the
Cato arrived in Mauritius, one of her priorities was to see "Paul & Virginia's
grave." More sadly still, when Bel Wood arrived in Liverpool, in June 1874,
she "rode out to the cemetery where our dear little baby lies." In 1848 Katurah Pritchard had the odd experience of exploring the burial ground in Havre
in the company of a Captain Colby, who pointed out a gravestone "like unto
the one Capt. Colby erected to his wife." It seems that he and his wife had often walked there, and Mrs. Colby admired this stone so much that when she
expired it "was the occasion of his building one for her in that shape."

While the ship was anchored in the Thames at Gravesend, England, in
1900, the Murphy family rode out to the local burying ground to see the grave
of the Indian princess Pocahontas. In April 1837, Hannah Winn visited the St.
James Cemetery in Liverpool, and wrote a detailed description of everything
she saw. Particularly intriguing was a memorial to "Mr. Huchinson," who
"passed the first bill in Parliament for the railroad to Manchester" and was
killed when the first train ran over him. In Manila, Hannah boarded on shore
with an old Salem friend of her husband's, an entrepreneur by the name of
Peel. Then once she got settled she sallied out—to have a look at the graveyard. In Buenos Aires in 1886, Helen York found the way the Argentinians
buried their dead somewhat odd: "They put the coffins down under ground
& place a grating over them so you can see them quite plainly."

Batavia had a bad reputation for being "a hotbed of sickness and death," as Madam Follansbee phrased it. Built on low, marshy land, it was intersected with canals, which she described as being "inhabited by alligators and all kinds of venomous reptiles." This network of channels also served as the city sewer, "and it is no uncommon sight to see dead horses or even corpses floating down them." Perhaps it is not surprising, then, that the *Logan* left port with "Java fever" on board. Two men died, and the rest were so sick that Captain Follansbee had to call on the Chinese passengers to help work the ship to Hong Kong.

Hong Kong, however, was not much better. When Mrs. Follansbee arrived in July 1838, the rocky, sterile coast was inhabited only by fishermen and farmers, and all the business was done in the harbor, which was "crowded with ships of all nations." Even duck farming was conducted from a boat. The duck farmer "lets them out every morning, to swim about and get their own living," and then at night he let out a whistle and the ducks obediently came home.

Deals—many of them in opium—were transacted in so-called Receiving Ships, which were nothing more than floating offices. Hong Kong boasted "no commercial warehouses, schoolhouses, mosques or pagodas," so there was no other sightseeing to be done, and if Mrs. Follansbee went on shore she had to withstand mass curiosity from the locals, "who commenced to examine every part of my dress, from my head to my feet, and appeared very much surprised that my hair was short and curly and that I wore a cap, also that I wore no earrings."

And so the people on the ships had to create their own fun, Madam recording a dinner party on board the bark *Linton.* Even in the middle of the century, when Hong Kong became a major destination, the biggest and best parties were held on board the anchored vessels. In 1859, Captain Linnell of the *Flying Mist* gave a great ball. Invitations had been issued freely, to everyone of note from the governor of the colony downwards, and stag shipmasters turned up en masse. Unfortunately, according to Captain Joshua Sears of the *Wild Hunter,* there were "only about fifteen ladies" in the fleet, "and some of them have got such d——d jealous husbands that they cannot let them dance with anyone else," he griped. One "poor Devil of a captain" had a wife who was only eighteen, "and he can't bear for anyone else to look at her. Another poor fellow, six feet, four inches tall weighing two hundred and fifty pounds, has got a wife four feet, two inches tall, weighing eighty-three pounds. He, too, cannot let his wife out of his sight." So it seems that Captain Joshua Sears missed out on a dance—but not on the gossip, for how else could he have known the little woman's exact dimensions?

In ports where large numbers of ships assembled for a specific cargo—such

as tea in Canton or Yoko-
hama, coal in Newcastle,
New South Wales, or guano
in the Chincha and Lobos
Islands off Peru—corre-
spondingly large affairs
would be arranged, the
Fourth of July being a popular excuse for a party with
Americans. On June 30,
1878, the captains held a
meeting in the port of Yokohama, "to decide what ship
has the best accommoda-
tions for the Fourth of July
celebrations. They have
been on board our ship,"
wrote Annie Dow proudly,
"and say we have the best by
far." And so it was decided
to stage the big bust on the
Clarissa B. Carver, picnic
style, all contributing.

A social gathering of captains and families.
Courtesy San Francisco Maritime
National Historical Park.

The *Clarissa* was "gaily
decked with bunting," and all the ships were decorated. "I never saw so many
flags flying in one day before. We had but 25, some had 50." Great platters of
roast pork and roast turkey were carried on board, and several stewards from
the other ships came to help. Dinner was served to a great host between decks,
and music was furnished by the bands from the various men-of-war in port,
"that came on board at different times of the day."

Another anchorage where the fleet had to make their own fun was at the
Chincha Islands, off the southern coast of Peru—or, alternatively, the Lobos
Islands to the north—where the piled excrement of many generations of sea
birds was dug by teams of coolies in appalling conditions. These guano islands
were not pleasant places, for the air was full of fine yellow dust, and the sky
teemed with screaming birds. "Such a lonesome looking place, bunches of
rocks," wrote Hattie Atwood at Lobos de Afuera. "The sea lions vie with the
waves, seeing which can make the most noise." As Sarah Everett of the *Kineo* attested, everything stank highly of ammonia, too. "If you should hold a

Sunday in Yokohama. Artist: Sadahide.

bottle of hartshorn to your nose you can judge how our cabin smells," she wrote to her sister Hattie in January 1860. "I can hardly get my breath, sometimes."

Nonetheless, during the middle of the century the ships gathered at the Chincha and Lobos Islands in great numbers. When the bark *Hannah Thornton* arrived in September 1853, Cynthia Congdon wrote to her mother that there were "more than a hundred vessels" there, and "quite a number of ladies, too." Loading guano was slow, taking up to eighty days to fill a ship, and so there was a lot of time to pass. Mass picnics on the mainland were organized, though the terrain was barren and formidable, including a

Ships collecting guano at the Chincha Islands. Currier & Ives lithograph, 1860.

field "of human bones and skulls" that had been a battleground in Pizarro's time. Cynthia Congdon's party stayed overnight at a village, though the locals were so startled and fascinated by these unexpected visitors that "we found we could not sleep at all."

The land might be barren, but the sea teemed with life. Shooting parties were forbidden by the Peruvian authorities because the birds were the source of the valuable dung, so the captains went fishing and boating, sometimes staging regattas. Hattie Atwood saw a fight between two whales, "and they made the water fairly foam with their great tails." When Mary Congdon was at the Chincha Islands in 1861, two whalers came in "after recruits," and while they were there a whale was raised and chased, which made for great excitement. Then two British men-of-war steamed in, followed by a naval vessel from Bristol, Rhode Island, which proved even more enlivening, especially when a "secessionist" arrived, and threatened to fire on the fleet.

The women of the guano fleets often met up again in the port of Callao, Peru, where the payment and negotiations for the guano were made. Here were more of the macabre sights that the Victorians seemed to find so fascinating. Many of the ruined churches were buried so deep that only their crosses showed above the ground, and there were drifts of human bones in the gullies, all apparently the result of a great tidal wave that had devastated the coast 120 years earlier. On September 30, 1860, Sarah Everett recorded that

Mrs. Crabtree and Mrs. Whitman—the latter of the *Moses Wheeler*—were there for company. They paid visits on one another's ships, or else gathered in the ship chandler's store. The chandler, Mr. Crosby, who was also the U.S. consul, kept "beautiful apartments above the store where we are always welcome to stop, his wife has gone home to Nantucket." The women sewed and gossiped, though "part of our amusement consists of flea-catching," wrote Sarah.

In Callao in January 1862, Mary Congdon went to a bullfight. The arena, she thought, looked rather like a theater, and the men were dressed like circus actors. "They had a band, and ever so many soldiers." Then the bull was let in, and the soldiers dispersed in a hurry, leaving the bull to stick his horns into one or another of the horses, of which there were four. However, "it was not half as cruel or dangerous as I thought," so the horses must have been padded in some way.

A couple of months earlier, Mary Congdon had received a letter from some of her school friends, in which "they write they want me home. How strange," she commented, "when I am traveling to finish my education." Her tone might have been ironic, but it is little wonder that the women all thought at one time or another, "I surely have been well repaid for my determination to go to sea"—as Hattie Atwood put it, after riding on a jackass on the island of Gibraltar. Not only was it educational, but often a lot of fun, too.

CHAPTER ELEVEN

On Shore in a Foreign Land

This afternoon we took a Carriage which soon brought H. and myself and Children to the Hotel St. Antoine, where most of the Capts come, and here is a number staying at present who have their Wives with them, thus I shall find it very pleasant to have company from home, and some females that I can speak to.
—*Mary Rowland, in Antwerp, May 15, 1856*

*I*t was cheaper to live on the ship in port, but oftentimes it was not very pleasant, and at other times it was not possible. Often, the cargo was dusty and dirty, or it was very noisy to unload, or the ship was berthed a long way out of town—or else, as in Antwerp, staying on board was forbidden by the port authorities, because of the risk of fire. And so, for some reason or another, the captain would have to find someplace for his wife and family to stay. Occasionally, he could arrange board with a local resident, often an expatriate national. In St. Petersburg, Russia, Madam Follansbee boarded at a house kept by an American woman, Mrs. Wilson, who kept "slaves" (serfs) for servants, and in Macao, China, she stayed with Mrs. Pierce from Salem, a "lovely lady," who was "delighted to see a lady from Massachusetts."

There were favorite hotels in every port, including the Hotel Fonde in Manila. In New York, the Pearl Street House was recommended because it was close to both Broadway and Wall Street, where most of the ship business was transacted. When Laura Bagley arrived in Liverpool to join her husband on the *Levi C. Wade,* she stayed at De Silva's Hotel. In Havana, the Washington Hotel was patronized, being in walking distance of the square, where the bands played in the evenings.

The place to stay in Hilo, Hawaii, was the boardinghouse owned by a Bostonian named Pitman, who had married a mission-educated Hawaiian

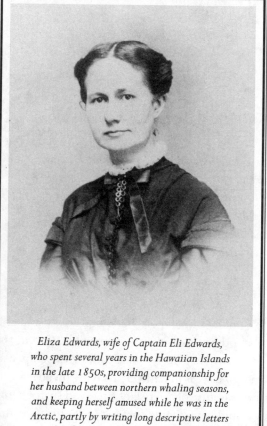

Eliza Edwards, wife of Captain Eli Edwards, who spent several years in the Hawaiian Islands in the late 1850s, providing companionship for her husband between northern whaling seasons, and keeping herself amused while he was in the Arctic, partly by writing long descriptive letters to her family in Sag Harbor, Long Island.
Courtesy Audrey Hauck.

woman and was doing well out of the lodging trade. Many wives rhapsodized about his beautiful gardens, while others liked his backyard, which had washtubs, bleaching tubs, laundry lines, "& an abundance of soft water," as Lizzie Edwards noted. The facility that Lizzie found most wonderful, however, was his bathing house. "'Tis quite a large room where we undress & dress, then we go down a flight of stairs into the water, which comes pouring in equal to Niagara Falls. The water gets about 4 feet deep, then there is an opening to let it off, so that it cannot get any deeper," she described in a letter home, in January 1859. At first Lizzie was too scared to go in, but "as it didn't drown" the three other seafaring wives who were lodging there, she thought she would give it a try. All four women went in together, holding hands, "& such a nice time as we had. The way we danced around in the water & enjoyed it is better realized than described."

Because trading with the captains was so lucrative, many chandlers, port physicians, and shipping agents took lodgers on the side. In Anjer, Java, the Dutch pilot kept the one good hotel, which must have been beautiful, for Laura Bagley of the *Levi C. Wade* described a front yard that was "heavy with the fragrance from the roses and other flowers, and was shaded by coconut, banana, tamarind, banyan." All the captains and families gathered there, though the provender was "purely Eastern in its style," which few of them appreciated.

Consuls often took in boarders, too, as happened in Cork, Ireland, in September 1848, when Katurah Pritchard took lodgings with the American consul there, mostly because a fleet of men-of-war was in port, with attendant flocks of beggars and prostitutes. The girls first arrived while Captain Pritchard was on shore entering the ship, so that Katurah was alone when "we were completely swarm'd with boats from the shore, chiefly females— and they were the worst creatures in female attire I ever saw. Two of them were down in the forecastle when my husband and the Mate return'd, and then such language as they used, is dreadful to think of." Worse still, they

Honolulu, 1847.

Boardinghouse in the Hawaiian Islands.

had brought rum on board with them to sell to the men, one of whom got "crazy drunk."

For much the same reason, Katurah stopped in a hotel in The Hague while the brig was being recoppered in Rotterdam, but "what is worse than all, my husband went over again to stay on board the Brig overnight." Perhaps because of this, or perhaps because of something she ate, Katurah woke up in the middle of the night in violent pain, with the conviction she was dying, "and to die alone, was dreadful." Servants were summoned, but could not speak English, and when a doctor arrived he dosed her with brandy, when what she wanted was hot gin. In the morning her husband arrived in a hurry, having received her message, and promised "he would not leave me again in a foreign Hotel, if they stole the Brig and Cargo."

In 1838 Madam Follansbee stayed with the American consul in Manila, Mr. Sturgis, who had a large, echoing mansion with bedsteads that had their legs standing in china bowls of water. The American consul in St. Helena, an island the American wives loved to visit because of its associations with Napoleon Bonaparte, was a famous fellow named Carroll, with sixteen children. The Follansbees were delighted to stop with this character when homeward-bound in February 1839, finding him eager to please. Their enjoyment, however, was abruptly dashed when Carroll handed them a hefty bill as they were taking their leave; one of the smallest charges was twenty-five dollars for a ride in a carriage.

In October 1837, Madam stayed in London at "the American Captains' boarding house at No. 8 Circus Minories, kept by Mrs. Stephenson," a Scotchwoman who weighed 402 pounds. These were very popular lodgings, with the result that the latest news of Mrs. Stephenson and her avoirdupois was always of interest to the American fleet. In April 1848 the Pritchards stayed there, too. Mrs. Stephenson was sitting on the sofa when Katurah entered the parlor, "so that she did not appear to me so large as I expected she would, her weight being 437 lbs, but when she arose from her seat, I could see her full size, and she was truly a sight to behold."

The Minories was within walking distance of the ship brokers, insurance houses, banking houses, and chartering agents of Leadenhall, Cornhill, and Threadneedle Street, which would account for Mrs. Stephenson's place being so popular with the American captains. Certainly, it was vastly preferable to finding lodgings within the appalling slums that surrounded Shadwell Basin, where the *Logan* was docked in 1837. Ten years before, the packet ship *Columbia* was moored in the Upper Pool of the Thames, abreast of the Tower of London, and Alice Delano took a boat from the ship to the Tower stairs, walking from there "with my basket on one arm and my dressing box in my other hand," to a lodging house at 16 Cannon Street, within sight of St. Paul's. The proprietress of this establishment, a Madam Bowles, was not very clean, however, so when Captain Delano joined his wife, he promptly moved their lodgings to Finsbury Circus, which was "a fine airy & delightful situation," and still within walking distance of the ship.

In 1855, while the Black Ball packet *Neptune* was lying at Liverpool, Captain Enoch Peabody took his bride Cornelia on a jaunt to London, where they stayed at the London Coffee House on Ludgate Hill, just a step from St. Paul's.

Grandly advertised as "the most elegant and extensive" coffee house in "the three kingdoms" of the world, the London Coffee House was very popular with Americans, too. It had a long history and a distinguished guest list. Benjamin Franklin, a frequent customer in the eighteenth century, had belonged to a club that met there to discuss social and philosophical issues. In 1851 George Peabody, the U.S. philanthropist, gave a banquet there for Americans who exhibited in the Crystal Palace at that smash hit of the century, the Great Exhibition.

Nineteenth-century sightseers to the Tower of London were apparently more credulous as well as more ghoulish than tourists today. In October 1837 Madam Follansbee described "the block on which the beautiful Ann Boleyn was beheaded in 1536, also the identical axe, with the hair and dried blood sticking to it, which is sickening to behold." Back in 1827 Alice Delano saw that "identical" axe "that Ann Boleyn was beheaded with," and in 1848 it was still there for Katurah Pritchard to view, along with "the Block on which Mary, Queen of Scots, was beheaded."

In Bombay, Charlotte Babcock visited the "Tower of Silence," where bodies were left for vultures to clean, and found it just as predictably nasty. Even more exotically, she was disgusted by the sight of a hermit who had been standing still with his right arm held out horizontally for an unknown number of years, so that the "flesh had all dropped off" the bones. In Calcutta, on the same macabre note, the captains and their wives got up parties from among the number that were staying at the same hotel to go and see the cremation grounds. "Took a ride to the Burning Gout," Bethia Sears recorded in June 1856. She went in company with Mrs. Patten and Mrs. French, with Captain Dow as escort. "Saw three bodies burning, it was horrible, horrible."

A more genteel pleasure was to visit an art gallery, though in Copenhagen, in September 1837, Madam Follansbee found that the pictures were so densely surrounded by "copyists perched on step-ladders" that they could not be seen. In London in 1827, Alice Delano went to the Covent Garden Theatre, which was modeled after the Temple of Minerva in Athens—"splendidly fitted up," she thought, even better than the Park Theater in New York. The play was *School for Scandal,* which she enjoyed very much. She also attended the opera, where she saw Rossini's *Thieving Magpie,* with Miss Fanny Ayton in the soprano role.

Westminster Abbey and St. Paul's (admission twopence) were popular sights in London. Alice Delano enjoyed the "fast stairs" in the cathedral, "where four persons may take hold of hands and come down full speed without danger." Most wives liked to tour cathedrals, and, surprisingly, many were as happy to attend a Roman Catholic service as they were a Protestant one. Charlotte Page went to a Catholic mass in Mobile, Alabama, in the morning, and a Presbyterian meeting in the evening. "This was the first time I ever was inside a Catholic church," wrote Carrie Stoddard of an experience in Hong Kong; "of course everything was Greek to me, but I found it very amusing, almost as good as a play."

Palaces were equally interesting, particularly for the democratic Americans, many of whom had parents and grandparents who had fought in the American Revolution. When Annie Dow toured one of the six palaces of Naples in February 1867, she described "the walls all inlaid with china and gold and beautiful mirrors," but also took note that she "saw not less than 15 beggars" outside. Mrs. Follansbee was impressed and yet somewhat scandalized by the grandeur of the Hermitage, writing with some bemusement that "everything seemed to be made of gold and precious stones."

Native chandlers and shipping agents would occasionally entertain the captains and wives, which could prove a most interesting experience. In Bombay, Charlotte Babcock was treated to cake, wine, and fruit in a Parsee house, where the parlor was "a square room with a very high ceiling." They all sat on a wooden platform that was suspended from the ceiling beams by a silk rope at each corner "and gently swayed" to create a refreshing current of air. The beds were hard, having only a thin silk mattress over an openwork bottom, but were perfectly suited to the hot climate, Charlotte decided.

"I waked this morning & found myself on Shore for the first time for 6 Months lacking 3 days," wrote Mary Henry in February 1852, the day after taking lodgings with "Mrs. Porter, No 7 Sooterkins Lane" in Calcutta. She had slept very badly, being "a little excited after liveing on board Ship so long"— and she must have been confused as well, for she dated the entry the thirty-first. As she became accustomed to stopping on shore, Mary Henry found she liked Calcutta "much," though there were two plagues to contend with, one being mosquitoes and the other servants, "for you cannot move without one at your heels."

Like all the other wives, she went riding on the Strand in the cool of dusk or dawn. Riding out was popular while on shore in Manila as well, where the wives took the air in a vehicle called a "Barouche," which—as described by Hannah Winn in 1837—was "drawn by two horses. The coachman rode on the left horse. He was habited in a Black Straw hat, Blue jacket edged with Buff, with Red collar & cuffs, White pantaloons, with Boots that come up to the knee, buttoned on the outside, and spurs." The riding ground was called the Calsada, set on the beach outside of the city wall. The view must have been spectacular, for the beach, edged with thatched houses where the local fishermen lived, faced the bay where the fleet lay at anchor.

While in Liverpool, Hannah Winn was much amused to see men and women "leading species of the Jack Ass, which they call Donkas, ready saddled. They accost every one they meet, 'Won't you have a ride?' " So Hannah paid over a coin, gamely picked up her skirts to jump on board of one of these animals, and found "they are so small my feet almost touch'd the ground." In London in 1827, Alice Delano was amazed by the coachmen who thronged the streets outside the theaters at the end of the performance, crying out, "Want a coach, a coach, gentlemen, a coach!" Once she hired one, and it got stuck in the mud, "the driver as insolent a dog as ever lived."

In October 1837, Madam Follansbee disliked London greatly. The streets were so muddy and slippery the local women wore the wooden-soled pattens that Madam used on shipboard, so that they clattered along like horses, and the herds of cows that were driven from door to door to be milked according to the needs of the customer added still more to the farmyard air. "Of all the dark, dismal places I have seen, London bears the palm," she wrote—but wooden footwear was common in other places, too. "I am sure—let me go where I may," wrote Mary Rowland in July 1856, "I shall never see a more odd dress than is worn by the old Country frows at Antwerp, when they come into the City mornings to sell their Marketing, some of them riding about in small carts drawn by dogs. . . . And then the wooden shoes and enormous white lace caps with such long broad ears to them, hanging down over their bosoms. . . . the wooden shoes have to be very large in order not to pinch the foot, thus they slip on the heel at every step with a continual click clack from morning til Night. I should think it would be intolerable to wear them and have such a noise at their heels."

"The Japanese, who wear high wooden clogs which they leave outside when they enter a house, unwittingly left them on the platform when stepping onto the carriages," wrote Maria Stover (Calista's daughter) in January 1890, after seeing her first Japanese train. "And great was their dismay when the train moved off and carried them away without those necessary appendages for the muddy streets!"

A ride in a rickshaw was de rigueur for the seafaring women in Japan, but the rickshaw men set such a rattling pace along the cobbled streets that the vibration "shook my hat off and my hair down," related Emma Pray in Kobe, "doing the same with the other ladies." Unsurprisingly, "all along the route the men, women & children would rush from their houses to look at us, the children shrieking and clapping their hands, while the older people just stood still with their mouths wide open and the greatest look of astonishment on their faces."

The popular conveyance in China was the sedan chair, which was normally carried by two men, though Charlotte Babcock had the disconcerting experience in Shanghai of being dropped by her two bearers, who ran off without explanation. She sat there in the middle of the street for some time, not knowing what to do. A couple of English sailors came by, lifted the curtains for a peep, but went off without offering assistance, and then a coolie did the same thing, except for uttering a startled "Hi yah!" Eventually the sedan bearers came back, bringing two of their fellows to help carry the load, explaining in gestures that Mrs. Babcock (who was in the eighth month of her pregnancy) had been too heavy for just two men to lug.

Being keen observers of other womenkind, the wives were very interested in dress and fashion. Alice Delano, "scudding about the streets" of London in February 1827, thought the females she saw had wonderful complexions, considering the soot in the air, but "they do not mind showing their legs, hold their dresses up in a most awkward manner. For my part, I almost blushed for them." It seems, however, that the women of London found Alice equally odd, for she noted, "The most impudent starers I ever met with are here. I have half a mind to ask if we owe them anything."

Also in London, in October 1837, Madam Follansbee managed to see the young Princess Regent, Victoria.

She wore an elegant white satin dress, and a robe of rich crimson velvet trimmed with gold lace, and a large crimson cape. She had a diamond tiara on her head, diamond earrings and diamond finger rings. She looked very fine, of course, as almost any young girl would, in such fine feathers, but she is very short and plain-looking. Victoria was born May 24th, 1819, and succeeded her uncle William IV, June 20, 1837, but only as Princess Regent till next year, when she will be crowned queen of Great Britain.

In Liverpool that same year, Hannah Winn saw "many ladies, some very richly dressed. Children dressed in mourning. Welsh women with men's hats on, rich fur capes, shawls of every variety, cloth boots of every discription, every kind of cloak, collars, ruffs, handkerchiefs, work bags, vails &c. &c. &c."

In New York, in June 1886, Isabel Duncan was rather chagrined to find that "Black silk seems to be the favourite here, or silk of some kind," for she had only one silk dress to her name, which "looks all right, only I am tired of it." All of them were astonished to see women use tobacco—an amazement that was mutual, for Hattie Atwood observed in Valparaiso that when she was offered cigarettes but declined, everyone was "surprised to find I did not smoke, as they thought all American ladies smoked." While the *Caroline Tucker* was in Callao, Peru, in August 1861, Mary Congdon announced in her diary that they were going to go sightseeing in Lima next day, "though they are expecting a revolution every moment. . . . I would not like to live in such a country, though our own is not much better at present." The jaunt did have its hazards, for "they would not let us enter the Church with our bonnets on. None of the ladies wear bonnets, some a little bit of a hat, but most all a shawl." Similarly, in Havana, Katurah Pritchard noted that "the Ladies were all dressed in white and wore no bonnets."

Naturally enough, some ports were liked better than others. San Francisco was visited so frequently in the latter half of the century that the city was regarded by many as a second home, often with relatives in residence. During the mad gold rush years of 1848 and 1849, however, it was inevitable that some of the captains' wives were stranded, just like their husbands, when the crews of all incoming vessels deserted ship and headed off for the mines. The Australian bark *Eleanor Lancaster* dropped anchor at Benecia at the mouth of the Sacramento River on April 2, 1849, and Captain F. W. Lodge instantly lost all his men. Undeterred, he set up business as a water man, securing enough crew to man the oars of one of the ship's boats by dint of offering exorbitant wages, and then ferrying miners up and down the river, while his wife turned the abandoned ship into a grog shop, also offering nursing facilities. Her only complaint, apparently, was that she did not have her piano—perhaps because it would have been so good for business.

On May 30, 1838, Mary Dow "bid good bye to the city of New Orleans" without any tears of regret, dubbing it "a den for the reffuse of every nation; it is a place where religion and law are forgotten, or laid aside, and where he that can swear the most, drink the most mint-juleps, or in short, he that can sin with the highest hand is the best man." By contrast, Mary Snell (who had a very individual sense of humor) declared after being "gallanted on shore by My Husband" on February 12, 1839, that she was "much disappointed in this place, it is not so bad as represented." Back on board, she regaled her visitors in the true spirit of the city—not with mint juleps, though, but with wine, cake, and cheese.

Another popular activity was visiting zoological gardens, such as Regent's Park in London, where Madam Follansbee saw "the largest elephant in the world," and "the largest hippopotamus in the world." In Calcutta in early 1852 Mary Henry saw an elephant that smoked a hookah and drank a bottle of brandy. In 1837 Hannah Winn was "much delighted" with the Liverpool zoo, which Charlotte Page described in 1852 as being "a beautiful place, where there are all kinds of animals and birds; also a great variety of amusements," which included a replica of Shakespeare's house. In 1857 Mary Rowland was extremely diverted by the zoological gardens at Antwerp.

"This garden is well worth the franc it costs for admission," she decided. Not only was there a wonderful "collection of parrots, parrotquets and cockatoos, of beautiful plumage," but there were cages of

> *ferocious wild beasts and huge Serpents, some of which were devouring beautiful rabbits, swallowing them down alive for one mouthful but with apparently great exertion. These were put in their cages while visitors were present but it seemed to be cruel amusement. The snakes after finishing their meal rolled themselves up in one huge Coil resembling a Ship's great hawser, only they were much larger in diameter.*

There were two lakes, where one could see "different species of Ducks, Swans, pelicans, an Egiptian Goose &c and the Banks served as a promenade for some wild turkeys and water hens and some small fowls, and amongst the rest a famous large Crockodile, sometimes seen floating upon the top of the water as if to obtain the rays of the Sun upon him, but when one approaches he dives into the water." There were Mandarin ducks as well, which were said to have cost "two hundred dollars, which I think is a good price for one pair, especially if one wants them for dinner."

In Kobe, in September 1888, Emma Pray visited a tea house. "The walls of the room were <u>sliding</u> panels of paper, there was straw matting upon the floor, and with the exception of one table, the room was empty," she recounted. Mats were brought for the wives to sit

Missionary house in Yokohama where Mary Swift Jones boarded while her husband carried freights between China and Japan. From Missionary World.

on, but "I felt it very back-breaking," she confessed, adding, "I never found my feet so much in the way before." Temples featured largely in the agenda. Emma Pray saw one in Kyoto with "33333 wooden joshes" and "a long line of Satans." In Bangkok, Laura Bagley saw an enormous reclining Buddha, "165 feet long, and well proportioned. The toes are three feet long & the width of one foot the height of a native man."

In Naples, in May 1867, Annie Dow woke up with "Vesuvius on the brain," and she and her husband, Jonathan, set off to climb the mountain, taking along

Buddhist statue in China.
Photograph by Ron Druett.

some roast chicken and doughnuts for provisions. As expected, the way was rugged, but a stop at the Hermitage for wine refreshed them. Near the top, they "were almost besieged with guides—men with chairs to carry us up; others with straps around them to drag us up, but we refused all help, although we found it very hard indeed climbing over the rocks and lava which was very sharp, would often slip back several steps." But it turned out to be as marvelously smoky, steaming, hot, and sulfurous as hoped, and the view was magnificent, too.

Jaunts like these might be dangerous, but they could certainly be counted— and recounted—as adventures, for all the women were very aware of owning a certain aura of romance, of being widely traveled and worldly wise, something in which they took perceptible pride. "I should like so much to visit Edin[burgh] during the Exhibition, I enjoyed it so much in Melbourne," wrote Isabel Duncan in sophisticated tones to her sister Nellie in 1886. Coasting past Brazil on an earlier voyage, in 1880, she wrote, "When the wind came partly

Kilauea volcano in Hawaii.
From a contemporary lithograph.

off the land the perfume was delightful," likening the scent to "the spicy breezes of Ceylon." When Emma Pray trekked the mountains of Japan in 1888, she reflected that they reminded her "very much of my trip in the Himalayas."

"Had I wit enough I might write quite a book during my travels by sea and in Port," mused Mary Rowland, "for I have had some opportunity of seeing the different manners and customs of foreign Nations." All in all, one can readily imagine the wide-eyed audiences that the women enjoyed when they got home, and how they must have enraptured children later with stories of these fabled anchorages. Strange indeed some of these stories must have been.

While staying on shore at Hilo, Hawaii, Lizzie Edwards and Mrs. Palmer decided to go out in a torrential downpour to see the Wailuku Falls, which were always spectacular but at that time in great flood. Donning their "Bloomer dresses" and rubber boots, and both carrying umbrellas, they waded along the overflowing tracks, until they hesitated at the brink of the river, not being able to discern the plank bridge beneath the torrent. Providentially, "a very tall native man came along—dressed in a long coat and a high silk hat," and absolutely nothing else. Undeterred by this odd outfit, Lizzie hopped on his back. "I carried the umbrella and we reached there in safety. And," she decided when they had arrived at the desired view, "we were well repaid." The river was twenty or thirty feet higher than usual, and Mrs. Palmer informed her it looked just like the rapids of Niagara.

In October 1855, the clipper *B. F. Hoxie* was more than a month in San Francisco looking for a cargo. Finally, Captain Stark decided to sail to Honolulu, looking for a freight of oil, and so his wife, Mary, was yet another seafarer to visit the exotic shores of the Hawaiian Islands. After a passage of only ten days they arrived, and found Honolulu instantly interesting. The harbor was fringed by a reef, along which oxen were driven, "& take a line from the ship which they make fast to wheels & draw the ships through the passage."

Better still, they had arrived at a most propitious hour, when the whaling fleet was coming in with oil from the Arctic season. All the whalers were looking for a captain willing to freight the valuable contents of their casks to New London or New York. "There are about 40 whaleships in here now, & more

*Whaleships gathering
at the Hawaiian Islands.*
Artist: Ron Druett.

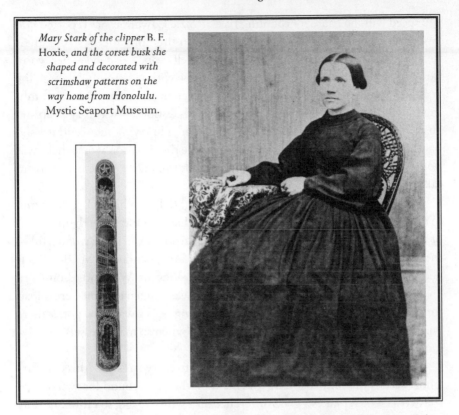

Mary Stark of the clipper B. F. Hoxie, *and the corset busk she shaped and decorated with scrimshaw patterns on the way home from Honolulu.* Mystic Seaport Museum.

are expected," Mary Stark communicated in a letter written on November 2, "& there is no other vessel here to load, so we shall not be detained here."

It took a month to fill the holds, however, which gave her plenty of opportunity to socialize with the wives who stayed on shore in the Islands while their husbands whaled in the Arctic. Mary Stark noted that the rich and the fortunate had a carriage. Captain William Clark of New Haven, Connecticut, had a house and five horses, "& has had a carriage sent out from home" for his wife to use, but Mary was happy to contemplate the other alternative. The other wives "ride horseback a good deal," she wrote, "& I think I shall try it while I am here."

This would involve riding sidesaddle, of course, though the Hawaiian women "ride horseback just like men, with a long loose strip of calico put around them on the saddle" for decency, "& look odd enough. They have a great fancy for yellow wreaths, which they wear on their heads, without bonnets, & large red & yellow beads around their necks." This must have presented a lively and exotic scene when combined with the Hawaiian love of riding at full speed with no pause for counting risks. Lizzie Edwards once reported that two riders who were galloping head-down in the rain "met & struck their heads together with such force that they both fell dead." As good as her word, however, Mary Stark was on the back of a horse within a month, "though the road was rough indeed," and by the second week in December she was climbing Punchbowl Hill, which—as Eliza Edwards testified—was very steep and rugged, "as I found to my sorrow one day, when in trying to ascend it I slid back 2 steps where I went up one, and to make the situation worse there was not a shrub or even a bit of grass long enough to grasp to save myself from falling."

Meantime, Captain Henry Stark was delighted with his luck, calculating in a letter to his father in Mystic, Connecticut, that it would show them a profit of $30,000, if "things go in the regular course." And—even more wonderful— the freight of oil was a home cargo. This was luxury indeed. "My dear Nellie," wrote Scotswoman Isabel Duncan from St. Vincent, West Indies, on April 30, 1886. "We could not get a freight for U.K., was obliged to come here & load for New York—a very poor freight, but nothing better was to be got, & there was no use hanging in hopes of freights rising when so many vessels were lying idle."

Captain William Duncan had contracted to carry sugar at "three dollars a hogshead," and only that day "a vessel took the same round for two dollars sixty cents which makes a good difference on a whole cargo, so I think he only fixed in time." New York was not home, but hopefully they would find a cargo for Britain there—"if not homewards we must just go away south again, there is no help for it."

This was the common situation. Alongside the excitements and pleasures of being at anchor, there was always the vexing problem of finding a freight to make the return voyage profitable. These freights were often so elusive, and competed for so vigorously, that individual ships might be away for several years, traipsing from port to port in search of business. In 1880, Laura Bagley took passage on the Cunard liner *Hecla* to Liverpool to meet her husband, Henry, for he had not been able to find a home cargo. Instead, the *Levi C. Wade* had been commissioned to carry a full load of coal from Cardiff, Wales, to Surabaya in the South China Sea, and if Laura had not consented to make the journey, it would have been at least a year before they were together again.

She was hopeful that he would find a cargo for New York in the South China Sea. Instead, the ship was then chartered to pick up a full cargo of rice in Bangkok. This set Captain Bagley an interesting test in navigation, for the river was only "thirteen feet five inches at the shoalest part," as well as being very narrow and winding. He went up in ballast, and then found he had to discharge most of it in the river before proceeding to the loading wharf, which cannot have helped to improve the depth of the anchorage.

The Thais were very expeditious, though, and lighters arrived alongside before Captain Bagley had returned from entering the ship at the Custom House. The working day was so long, in fact, that it was thought best for Laura and Hilda to take lodgings ashore, which she did with the Baptist missionary, a yellowed and elderly fellow by the name of Dr. Dean. Once the ballast was discharged, the ship was warped to Samson's Wharf where the rice was loaded, and despite the heavy rains—"excellent weather for frog concerts"—the whole process took less than three weeks. Meanwhile, Laura played croquet, shopped at the floating market, and attended many, many prayer meetings. Then, when they sailed for Europe, the ship sailed "dull"— which apparently was always the case when the cargo was rice—so that they took only just a few days under five months to arrive at Falmouth, England.

Arriving there in March 1881, Henry Bagley still could not find a homebound cargo, and so Laura left the ship, taking another liner to New York to visit her family for a spell, before rejoining her husband for yet another Oriental voyage. She should have stopped at home. On passage from Manila in 1884, Laura, her husband, and their small daughter Hilda drowned when the ship *Levi C. Wade* was lost with all hands.

"We have obtained a charter at last," wrote Sarah Everett of the *Kineo* to her sister Hattie (who was looking after Sarah's daughters) from Callao, in October 1860. "But it is for Mauritius, which will probably keep us a little longer from home." However, they were getting three pounds sterling freight, while the other ships were getting only two pounds ten shillings. Timothy Everett owed his luck to another skipper's misfortune. Three mutinous sailors had burned a bark that lay in the harbor, and her cargo had been offered to the *Kineo*.

"It makes us feel homesick to think of going farther off," Sarah sighed. "Timothy says he has been trying now for the last three years to get homeward bound, but don't see as there is much prospect of it yet." Prospects did not improve. "Homesick enough," Sarah wrote in August 1861. "Who would have thought when I left home it would be over two years?" It was longer than that. In February 1862 they were on the way to England, having picked up a cargo of teak in Bombay. They were steering for London, but had to detour to Cork because of headwinds and Timothy Everett's bad health, and were redirected to Liverpool for an unstated cargo. Unsurprisingly, Sarah wrote, "He is in hopes to sell the ship," for it seemed the only way of getting home.

For most, however—though perhaps not for several years—that longed-for home-port cargo was chartered and loaded, and the wives could actively anticipate stepping onto native soil, and seeing the old folks at home. When the *Logan* finally arrived back in Boston, on April 13, 1839, it was in the middle of a blizzard, "with our sails frozen stiff, the ropes, rigging, and decks covered with ice and snow." The pens of livestock had all broken away, and pigs and fowls were slithering and flapping all over the decks, but it was a sublime moment, an apt time for the captain's wife to pause for reflection. "I left Boston the first week in April 1837," Madam meditated on the last page of her journal, "and had been absent a little more than two years, during which time I had crossed the Equator 5 times."

Eighteen months earlier, at a dinner party in London, Mrs. Follansbee had made a prediction. Captains sitting about the table were discussing the relative merits of sail and steam, for the *Great Western* was a-building nearby. Forgetful for once of propriety and her audience, Madam had ventured a prophesy. Within a few years, she assured all those weightily opinionated sailing ship masters, more steamships than sailing ships would be crossing the Atlantic.

Not unexpectedly, the captains were highly derisive, and Alonzo Follansbee was doubtless embarrassed by his wife's temerity. Yet within one hundred years the sight of a cloud of canvas became very rare indeed. Madam had been right, though the changeover had taken longer than she had predicted. The transatlantic packet ships began going by the board as early as the 1850s—for when Cornelia Marshall Peabody sailed on the Black Ball Line ship *Neptune* in 1855, the steamships were already taking over the routes, not only leaving port on schedule, but arriving at the destination according to a timetable, too. For a while the captains of the huge square-riggers could freight cargoes of grain and fertilizer from Australia and Chile more cheaply than steamers, but only at the cost of mercilessly driving their crews. Understandably, good seamen became harder to find, and so the overall quality of the crews deteriorated, along with the substance of the ship's provisions.

And with the end of the story of the sailing ships that carried freight from port to port came the end of the story of the seafaring wives as well. For, unlike the owners of the clippers, coasters, downeasters, and windjammers, the men who held shares in the fuel-driven steamers did not allow their captains to take their wives and families on voyage. They said that living with his wife and children would distract a working captain from carrying out his duties. Which seems more than a little odd—for no one has ever said that about a man who lives at home and works on shore.

APPENDIX

Journals, Diaries, Letters, and Reminiscences Written by the Seafaring Wives and Daughters of Sailing Ship Captains

This list is intended as an aid for future researchers. It is therefore not confined to the seventy-five different sets of documents written by girls and women that were used as source material for this book, but encompasses all such manuscripts known to the author.

ALLEN, Harriet (Mrs. David). Travel journal kept on whaling bark *Merlin* of New Bedford, June 23, 1868, to April 12, 1872. Log 398–402B, The Kendall Whaling Museum, Sharon, Massachusetts.

ALLEN, Helen ("Nellie," later Mrs. Bradford). Child's partial diary, January 1, 1871, to April 12, 1872, kept on whaling bark *Merlin* of New Bedford, together with a retrospective essay called "When I was Seven, or, Sea Memories." Log 402, The Kendall Whaling Museum, Sharon, Massachusetts.

ALLEN, Sarah. Letter to her sister detailing voyage and shipwreck. Published as *Narrative of the Shipwreck and Unparrelled* [sic] *Sufferings* . . . Boston: N. Coverly, Jr., 1816.

ALMY, Almira (Mrs. William). Journal on whaling bark *Cape Horn Pigeon,* 1854–55. Nicholson Whaling Collection, Providence Public Library, Rhode Island. Also logbook kept on whaling bark *Roscoe,* 1859. Old Dartmouth Historical Society–New Bedford Whaling Museum, New Bedford, Massachusetts.

ASHLEY, Adra (Mrs. Edward). Partial journal on whaleship *Reindeer,* 1856–59. Baker Library, School of Business Administration, Harvard University, Boston, Massachusetts.

ATKINS, Mary. Private journal kept on brig *Advance,* sailing November 10, 1863, arriving off Woosung March 4, 1864. Published as *The Diary of Mary Atkins, A Sabbatical in the Eighteen Sixties.* Introduction by Aurelia Henry Reinhardt. Oakland, California: Eucalyptus Press, Mills College, 1937.

ATWOOD, Hattie (later Mrs. Freeman). Reminiscent account of a voyage with her father, Captain Horace Atwood, on the bark *Charles Stewart* of New York, voyage commencing January 30, 1883. Privately published in Bangor, Maine, by On Furbrush in 1907 as *A Trip Around the World on Board the Merchantman Bark "Charles Stewart."*

BABCOCK, Charlotte A. Noyes (Mrs. David). Memoir, headed "Life on the Ocean Wave: Reminiscences of my Voyages Around the World, 1851–8." Typescript transcription by Elizabeth W. Fuller, dated "Xmas 1908," held at The Huntington Library, San Marino, California.

BAGLEY, Laura M. (Mrs. W. Henry). Travel journal kept on ship *Levi C. Wade,* 1880–81. G69.3279, Maine Maritime Museum, Bath, Maine.

BAKER, Eleanor (Mrs. Michael III). Journal on whaling bark *Gazelle,* 1857–61. Owned by Dietrich American Foundation. Held at Old Dartmouth Historical Society–New Bedford Whaling Museum, New Bedford, Massachusetts.

BALANO, Dorothea Moulton (Mrs. Fred). Intermittent diary, June 21, 1910, to January 6, 1913, partly on shore and partly on her husband's coasting schooner *R. W. Hopkins.* Original held by Elsie Balano. Published as *The Log of the Skipper's Wife.* Edited by James W. Balano. Camden, Maine: Down East Books, 1979.

BARBER, Jane (Mrs. William). Two letters written to parents while on board her husband's coaster *Ocean Eagle,* the first written from Galveston, and dated October 18, 1852, the other written from St. Mark's, dated March

30, year not given but probably 1853. 6 pp. Manuscripts Collection, VFM 1100, G. W. Blunt White Library, Mystic Seaport Museum, Mystic, Connecticut.

BARTLETT, Mary C. (Mrs. Samuel B.). Discontinuous records of several Bath, Maine, vessels, 1849–71. MS95.16, Maine Maritime Museum, Bath, Maine.

BARTLETT, Mary Ellen (Mrs. James Brooks). Diaries kept on board brig *American Union,* 1860–62. Courtesy Everett White. Typescript copy in Maine Maritime Museum, Bath, Maine.

BECKERMAN, Rachel (Mrs. John). Journal on whaler *Live Oak,* 1869–72. The Kendall Whaling Museum, Sharon, Massachusetts.

BEEBE, Lydia (Mrs. John). Diaries written on the whaling bark *Brewster,* 1863–65, and on the whaler *Xantho,* 1867–69. Nantucket Historical Association, Nantucket, Massachusetts.

BLANCHARD, Georgia Maria Gilkey (Mrs. Phineas Banning). Typed memoir headed "Our Wedding Trip Around Cape Horn." 12 pp. Stephen Phillips Memorial Library, Penobscot Marine Museum, Searsport, Maine.

BLIVEN, Harriet (Mrs. George). Journal kept on the whaling bark *Nautilus,* 1865–66. Peabody Essex Museum, Salem, Massachusetts.

BOLLES, Nancy (Mrs. John). Letter to "Dear Sisters," written from "Mowee" (Maui, Hawaiian Islands), and dated March 25, 1851, describing her voyage on the whaleship *Alert* of New London. 4 pp. Manuscripts Collection, VFM 1655, G. W. Blunt White Library, Mystic Seaport Museum, Mystic, Connecticut.

BRADLEY, Eliza (Mrs. James). Memoir of voyage and shipwreck, 1818. Published as *An Authentic Narrative of the Shipwreck and Sufferings of Mrs. Eliza Bradley . . .* Boston: James Walden, 1820.

BRASSEY, Lady Annie (wife of Sir Thomas Brassey, M.P.). Discursive memoir, published as *Around the World in the Yacht "Sunbeam," Our Home on the Ocean for Eleven Months.* New York: Henry Holt & Co., 1878.

BRAY, Elizabeth. Diaries 1854–55 and 1860–62. Custom House Maritime Museum, Newburyport, Massachusetts.

BREWSTER, Mary (Mrs. William). Journals kept on the whaling ship *Tiger,* 1845–48 and 1848–49 (voyage ended 1851). G. W. Blunt White Library, Mystic Seaport Museum, Mystic, Connecticut. Published by the museum in 1992 as *"She Was a Sister Sailor": The Whaling Journals of Mary Brewster, 1845–1851.* Edited by Joan Druett.

BROCK, Eliza (Mrs. Peter). Journal kept on the whaling ship *Lexington,* 1853–56. Nantucket Historical Association, Nantucket, Massachusetts.

BROCK, Susan E. Memoir of a voyage on the merchant ship *Midnight.* Privately published in Nantucket in 1926 as *Doubling Cape Horn.*

BROWN, Anne Augusta Fitch (Mrs. Jacob). Travel diary kept on the *Agate,* 1870. Privately published in a limited edition as *Diary of 1870.* Edited by Agate Brown Collord.

BROWN, Martha Smith Brewer (Mrs. Edwin). Journal kept on the whaleship *Lucy Ann* of Greenport, October 18, 1847, to February 8, 1849. Oysterponds Historical Society, Orient, Long Island, New York. Published by the society in 1993 as *She Went A-Whaling: The Journal of Martha Smith Brewer Brown from Orient, Long Island, New York, Around the World on the Whaling Ship "Lucy Ann," 1847–1849.* Edited by Anne MacKay. Foreword by Joan Druett. Introduction by Donald H. Boerum.

CASH, Azubah (Mrs. William). Diary kept on whaleship *Columbia,* 1852–53. Nantucket Historical Association, Nantucket, Massachusetts. Comprehensive extracts published in *Women of the Sea,* by Edward R. Snow. Boston: Dodd, Mead, 1962.

CAWSE, Emma (Mrs. James). Two journals kept on ship *John R. Worcester,* 1876–77. Courtesy of James N. Cawse.

CHURCH, Charlotte (Mrs. Charles). Diaries and logs kept on the whaling bark *Andrew Hicks,* 1907, 1908. Also on the whaling bark *Charles W. Morgan,* 1909. G. W. Blunt White Library, Mystic Seaport Museum, Mystic, Connecticut. Also on the whaling schooner *A. M. Nicholson,* 1914–15. International Marine Archives. Old Dartmouth Historical Society–New Bedford Whaling Museum, New Bedford, Massachusetts.

CLARK, Maria (Mrs. James). Logbooks kept on the whaling bark *Nimrod,* 1863–65, and on the whaling bark *Orlando,* 1867–70. G. W. Blunt White Library, Mystic Seaport Museum, Mystic, Connecticut.

CLEVELAND, Lucy Heller (Mrs. William). Discontinuous travel diary kept on the sandalwood trader *Zephyr,* 1829–30. 11 pp. Log 656 1829Z, Peabody Essex Museum, Salem, Massachusetts.

COLCORD, Mrs. Andrew. Journal kept on the missionary brig *Morning Star,* 1875. Log 656 1875M, Phillips Library, Peabody Essex Museum, Salem, Massachusetts.

COLE, Sarah (Mrs. Frederick). Journal kept on whaling bark *Vigilant,* 1860–62. Phillips Library, Peabody Essex Museum, Salem, Massachusetts.

COLSON, Mary (Mrs. Herbert). Journal on whaling bark *George & Susan,* 1877–81. The Huntington Library, San Marino, California.

CONGDON, Cynthia Sprague (Mrs. John Remington). Private journal kept on shore, beginning January 8, 1841, ending 1844. Also travel journal kept on the bark *Hannah Thornton,* October 6, 1852, to January 11, 1854; also letters written to her mother on voyage, dated March 4, 1853, and September 9, 1853. Rhode Island Historical Society, Providence, Rhode Island.

CONGDON, Mary Remington. Child's diary kept on the bark *Hannah Thornton,* November to December, 1854; private journal kept on the clipper *Caroline Tucker,* March 29 to September 5, 1860; private journal kept on the clipper *Caroline Tucker,* December 21, 1860, to July 5, 1861; private journal kept on the clipper *Caroline Tucker,* August 9, 1861, to September 4, 1862. The collection also includes shore diaries kept by Mary over the next fifty years. Rhode Island Historical Society, Providence, Rhode Island.

CRAPO, Lucy Ann Hix (Mrs. Reuben Williams). Private journal, kept on the whaling bark *Louisa* of New Bedford, January 1, 1866, to August 16, 1867. Log 944, Old Dartmouth Historical Society–New Bedford Whaling Museum, New Bedford, Massachusetts. Also letters written on the whaling bark *Linda Stewart* to "Dear Sister Ellen," dated January 15, May 24, and September 27 ("at Tumbez"), 1878; April 17 (at Talcahuano, Chile), April 22, July 13, October 10, 1879; April 8, May 22, May 24, June 18, June 20, October 11, 1880. Mosher Family Papers, 1865–88, MSS 56, Sr. M, S-s 32, Old Dartmouth Historical Society–New Bedford Whaling Museum, New Bedford, Massachusetts.

DAVIS, Carrie Hubbard (Mrs. Charles). Diaries, January 1, 1870, to November 1881. Much correspondence is included in the collection. William Steeple Davis Trust, Orient, Long Island, New York. Carrie's story published as *Captain's Daughter, Coasterman's Wife: Carrie Hubbard Davis of Orient.* Written and designed by Joan Druett. Maps, illustrations. Orient, Long Island, New York: Oysterponds Historical Society.

DEBLOIS, Henrietta (Mrs. John). Journal kept on whaling bark *Merlin,* 1856–59. Newport Historical Society, Newport, Rhode Island.

DE FREYCINET, Rose (Mme. Louis). Journal kept on the French exploratory ship *Uranie,* 1817–20. Published in 1927 by Charles Duplomb as *Journal de Madame Rose de Soulces de Freycinet, d'après le manuscrit original accompagné de notes.* An edited translation by Marc Serge Riviere was published in 1996 by the National Library of Australia, Canberra.

DEHART, Charlotte (Mrs. Abram). Journal kept on whaling ship *Roman,* 1857–61. Privately held. On loan to Old Dartmouth Historical Society–New Bedford Whaling Museum, New Bedford, Massachusetts.

DELANO, Alice R. Howland (Mrs. Joseph). Private journal kept on honeymoon voyage on the *Columbia* to London from New York and back, beginning January 1827. Courtesy Mrs. Dorothy Weeks Buck. Typescript copy in the collection of the Oyster Bay Historical Society, Oyster Bay, Long Island, New York.

DICKERSON, Lulu. Letters to "Dear Ones at Home," June 6, 1878. Nickels Papers, Penobscot Marine Museum, Searsport, Maine.

DOW, Annie Black (Mrs. Jonathan). Diaries and letters written on various voyages from 1858 until 1879, when her husband died in San Francisco, comprehensively quoted in a retrospective account written by her son Scott Dow, headed "Captain Jonathan Dow—the Seafaring Days of Our New England Family," dated May 1948. Held at the Penobscot Marine Museum, Searsport, Maine.

DOW, Mary (Mrs. George). Informal journal on bark *Clement,* 1838, from New Orleans to the Baltic. Log 656 1838C, Phillips Library, Peabody Essex Museum, Salem, Massachusetts.

DRINKWATER, Alice Gray (Mrs. Sumner). Journal kept on the *Grace Deering,* January 26, 1898, to March 5, 1899, on a voyage to New Zealand and around the world; two sea letters, the first addressed "Dear Hattie" and started at sea, August 20, 1900; the second addressed "My Dear Sister," and begun August 26, 1900, also at sea. Published as *A Seafaring Legacy. The Photographs, Diaries, Letters and Memorabilia of a Maine Sea Captain and His Wife 1859–1908.* Interpreted for a general audience by the author, Julianna FreeHand. Illustrations, ship plans. New York: Random House, 1981.

DRINKWATER, Lydia E. Diary 1880, logbook of the ship *San Joaquin,* book 3. Maine Historical Society, Portland, Maine.

DUDLEY, Hattie. Diary 1884, Dudley letters, collection 50, Box 4, Brick Store Museum, Kennebunk, Maine.

DUNCAN, Isabel (Mrs. William). Three diaries, 1878–82, and eighty-one letters written from 1880 to 1886, and from 1888 to 1893. Aberdeen University Library, Scotland, MSS 2526/1–6. Photocopies of six letters and two diary fragments, January 1880 to February 1891, Manuscripts Collection, VFM 1011, G. W. Blunt White Library, Mystic Seaport Museum, Mystic, Connecticut.

EDWARDS, Eliza Wheeler (Mrs. Eli). Letters written on passage from New

York to Honolulu, Hawaiian Islands, via the Isthmus of Panama and San Francisco, to join her husband, Eli, master of the whaling bark *Black Eagle,* and while in residence in the Hawaiian Islands: dated San Francisco, September 17, 1857; Honolulu, November 9, 1857, November 25, 1857, November 26, 1857, November 27, 1857, April 2, 1858, April 30, 1858, August 1, 1858, September 14, 1858, October 3, 1858, October 24, 1858, November 30, 1858, December 19, 1858; Towahia, January 23, 1859; Hilo, January 31, 1859, February 28, 1859, July 15, 1859; Honolulu, October 23, 1859, December 8, 1859; Tahiti, January 7, 1860. Also undated typescript headed "A few Reminiscences of a Trip to the Sandwich Islands." Courtesy Audrey Hauck. G. W. Blunt White Library, Mystic Seaport Museum, Mystic, Connecticut.

ELLIS, Cynthia (Mrs. William). Journal kept on bark *Kate Williams* and whaling bark *Ohio,* 1877–78. The Kendall Whaling Museum, Sharon, Massachusetts.

EVERETT, Sarah L. Hudson (Mrs. Timothy). Letters written to "My dear Sister" aboard clipper *Kineo,* at sea in "long 28 West Lat 4 South," January 1, 1860; Callao, January 8, 1860; at sea "Lat 32 50 S Lon 16 11 West," January 22, 1860; at sea "Latt 45 16 South Long 47 50 East," February 12, 1860; Melbourne, March 15 and April 17, 1860; Callao, September 30, October 27, and November 20, 1860; sea letter started at sea "Latt 2 00 North Long 75 53 E," July 28, 1861, with entries for August 4 and 11; together with a letter to her daughter, "My dear Ella," included with the April 17, 1860, epistle; and a sea letter addressed to "My dear Family," initially dated February 16, 1862, in "Latt 23 32 N Long 39 51 W." Maine Maritime Museum, Bath, Maine.

FISH, Frances Eveline (Mrs. Asa). Letters written at sea and from Honolulu, 1855–58. Privately owned. Photocopies at the G. W. Blunt White Library, Mystic Seaport Museum, Mystic, Connecticut.

FISHER, Susan (Mrs. Nehemiah). Letters written on whaling bark *Cowper,* 1854. Published in the New Bedford *Whalemen's Shipping List and Merchants' Transcript,* March 27, 1855.

FOLLANSBEE, Mrs. Alonzo. Typed transcript of journal kept on the ship *Logan,* 1837–39, two volumes, edited sometime after 1883. The whereabouts of the original is unknown. Log 656 1837–9L, Phillips Library, Peabody Essex Museum, Salem, Massachusetts.

FRASER, Margaret Youle (Mrs. George). Journal kept on the ship *Sea Witch,* 1852–53. Log 656 1852–3S, Phillips Library, Peabody Essex Museum, Salem, Massachusetts.

GELETT, Jane (Mrs. Charles). Diary kept on whaling ship *Uncas,* 1846. Extensive extracts published in her husband's book *A Life on the Ocean.* Honolulu: Hawaiian Gazette Company, 1917.

GIBBS, Almira (Mrs. Richard). Journal kept on whaling ship *Nantucket,* 1855–59. Whereabouts of original unknown. Microfilm copy in the Pacific Manuscripts Bureau collection (PMB 227), Australian National University, Canberra, Australia.

GRANT, Helen (Mrs. William). Collection of diaries and letters penned on bark *George* and schooner *Thomas E. Kenney,* both of Nova Scotia, 1873–86. City of Victoria Archives, Victoria, British Columbia.

GRAY, Emma (Mrs. Horatio). Travel diaries, 1868 and 1869. Manuscripts Collection, coll. 89, Volumes 11 and 12, G. W. Blunt White Library, Mystic Seaport Museum, Mystic, Connecticut.

HAMBLIN, Bertha. Reminiscences of a childhood on the whaling and trading bark *Islander,* 1871. Privately published in Falmouth, Massachusetts, in 1963 by Bertha H. Boyce as *Bertha Goes Whaling: Personal Memoirs of a Voyage Aboard the Whaling Bark "Islander."*

HAMILTON, Adelaide (Mrs. Joseph). Sea letter kept on unnamed vessel (probably the *Eclipse*), beginning Sunday, September 11, 1881, and ending on arrival in San Francisco, February 9, 1882. Addressed to "My own Darling Mother." Estate of Mrs. Hamilton Haskell. Typed transcript, 20 pp., South Street Seaport Museum, New York City.

HATHORN, Susan Lennan (Mrs. Joseph S.). Honeymoon diary kept on *J. J. Hathorn,* January 1 to September 8, 1855. Diary held at the Library Collection of Duke University, Durham, North Carolina. A discussion of the diary by Catherine Petroski was published in 1997 by Northeastern University Press as *A Bride's Passage: Susan Hathorn's Year Under Sail.*

HAWES, Jerusha (Mrs. Jonathan). Journal kept on whaling ship *Emma C. Jones,* 1858–59. Melville Whaling Room, New Bedford Free Public Library, New Bedford, Massachusetts.

HEARD, Fidelia (Mrs. John Jay). Journal of voyage on bark *Oriental* of Boston, to Australia, 1853. Courtesy Mrs. Elizabeth Heard.

HENRY, Mary Elizabeth Rugg (Mrs. John). Journal kept on ship *Cato,* October 2, 1851, to September 3, 1852, and a second journal kept from October 23, 1852, to January 12, 1854. Log 1851C, Phillips Library, Peabody Essex Museum, Salem, Massachusetts.

HEPPINGSTONE, Adaline (later Mrs. Matthews). Diary of the captain's daughter on whaling bark *Fleetwing,* 1882. Old Dartmouth Historical Society–New Bedford Whaling Museum, New Bedford, Massachusetts.

HORTON, Jemima Secord Wicks "Dime" (Mrs. William H.). Sea letter penned on passage to Rio, addressed "Dear friends," and initially dated July 26, 1876. Three Village Historical Society, East Setauket, Long Island, New York.

HOTCHKISS, Emma (later Mrs. Gray). Journal, February 6 to August 16, 1856, on ship *Harvard* of Boston, Captain Levi Hotchkiss (Emma's father). Manuscripts Collection, coll. 89, vol. 6, G. W. Blunt White Library, Mystic Seaport Museum, Mystic, Connecticut.

HOUDLETTE, Harriet. Diary on unknown ship, 1839–44. Phillips Library, Peabody Essex Museum, Salem, Massachusetts.

JARVIS, Mary (later Mrs. Frederick Robinson). Reminiscences of a voyage around the Horn in the sailing ship *Duntrune* in 1896 at the age of five. Courtesy Wilfred Robinson.

JERNEGAN, Helen (Mrs. Jared). Reminiscences of a voyage on the whaling bark *Oriole*. Dukes County Historical Society, Edgartown, Martha's Vineyard, Massachusetts.

JERNEGAN, Laura. Child's diary kept on the whaling bark *Roman,* 1868–71. Published as "A Child's Diary on a Whaling Voyage," M. W. Jernegan, editor. *New England Quarterly* 11:1 (1929).

JONES, Ellen Evans (Mrs. Benjamin). Travel diary kept on brig *Tri-Mountain* on a Cape Horn voyage, January 1 to September 12, 1875. Three Village Historical Society, East Setauket, Long Island, New York.

JONES, Hannah. Log of the brig *James Caskie,* 1849–50. Custom House Maritime Museum, Newburyport, Massachusetts.

JONES, Mary Swift (Mrs. Benjamin). Captain Benjamin Jones's first wife. Letters written on a voyage to the Orient from New York, including some penned in Japan, where the writer was living with the first missionary party at Kanagawa (Yokohama), dated November 4, 1859 (to "Mrs. Tyler"), October 1860 (to "Sister Ellen"), October 26, 1860 (to "Sister Eliza"), and December 28, 1860 (to "Sister Eliza"). Mary died shortly after arriving back in New York. Three Village Historical Society, East Setauket, Long Island, New York.

LATHAM, Nancy (later Mrs. Griffin). "My Trip on the Water." Typescript reminiscence of a seven-week coasting voyage with Captain William Potter's family, in 1900, when Nancy was fifteen. Oysterponds Historical Society, Orient, Long Island, New York.

LAVENDER, Sally Mayo. "Journey of a Voyage in the brig *Panama* from Boston to Marseilles 1854." Typescript. Penobscot Marine Museum, Searsport, Maine.

LAWRENCE, Mary Chipman (Mrs. Samuel). Travel journal kept on whaleship *Addison* of New Bedford, November 25, 1856, to June 13, 1860. Nicholson Whaling Collection, Providence Public Library, Rhode Island. Published as *The Captain's Best Mate: The Journal of Mary Chipman Lawrence on the Whaler "Addison," 1856–1860.* Stanton Garner, editor. Maps, illustrations, introduction, epilogue, appendices, index. Providence, Rhode Island: Brown University Press, 1966.

MALLETT, Kate C. (Mrs. Walter). Extract from sea letter written to brother, on passage from Newcastle, Australia, to San Francisco, dated January 26, 1908. Original held by Mrs. W. Percy Marks. Typed copy, SM 8/29, at Maine Maritime Museum, Bath, Maine. Also a paper called "Sea Reminiscences." Typescript. Pejepscot Historical Society, Brunswick, Maine.

MARBLE, Elizabeth (Mrs. John). Journal kept on whaling bark *Kathleen* of New Bedford, August 25, 1857, to January 2, 1860. Also journal on bark *Awashonks,* September 6, 1860, to April 8, 1862. The Kendall Whaling Museum, Sharon, Massachusetts.

MARSHALL, Malvina (Mrs. Joseph). Letters written on the whaling brig *Sea Queen,* 1851 and 1852. International Marine Archives. Old Dartmouth Historical Society–New Bedford Whaling Museum, New Bedford, Massachusetts.

McINNES, Emma (Mrs. John). Diary kept on whaling bark *Josephine,* 1891–92. The Kendall Whaling Museum, Sharon, Massachusetts.

McKENZIE, Susan (Mrs. James). Diaries kept in Honolulu and on the whaling bark *Hercules,* 1869–70, on the whaling ship *Europa,* 1872, and on passage on the *Comet* to San Francisco. Old Dartmouth Historical Society–New Bedford Whaling Museum, New Bedford, Massachusetts.

MOREY, Betsy (Mrs. Israel). Journal kept on the whaleship *Phoenix,* 1853–55. Nantucket Historical Association, Nantucket, Massachusetts.

MORGAN, Mary Hannah "Mamie." Diary from March 14 to August 1, 1881. Courtesy Rosenberg Library, Galveston, Texas. Photocopy in Manuscripts Collection, coll. 181, G. W. Blunt White Library, Mystic Seaport Museum, Mystic, Connecticut.

MORGAN, Sarah (Mrs. William). Letters written on bark *Bridgeport,* September 1870 to December 1880. Courtesy P. Bowen Briggs. Photocopy held in Manuscripts Collection, VFM 1602, G. W. Blunt White Library, Mystic Seaport Museum, Mystic, Connecticut.

MORRELL, Abby Jane (Mrs. Benjamin). Memoir based on her journal, published as *Narrative of a Voyage to the Ethiopic and South Atlantic Ocean, Indian Ocean, Chinese Sea, North and South Pacific Ocean, in the years 1829, 1830, 1831.* New York: J. & J. Harper, 1833.

MURPHY, Maria Sarah Higgins (Mrs. James). Collection of sea letters written on board the downeasters *W. F. Babcock, Shenandoah,* and *Arthur Sewall.* G91.111, Maine Maritime Museum, Bath, Maine.

NYE, Eliza (later Mrs. Dana). Journal kept on passage on whaleship *Sylph,* 1847. Old Dartmouth Historical Society–New Bedford Whaling Museum, New Bedford, Massachusetts.

OWENS, Ellen. Diary in Welsh kept on board the *Cambrian Monarch,* 1881. Gwynedd Archives. Published as *Gwraig y Capten* ("The Captain's Wife"). Aled Eames, editor. Archives Service, 1984.

PAGE, Charlotte A. (later Mrs. Franklin Johnson). Journal kept on the ship *George Washington* in 1852. Published by the Peabody Museum, Salem, Massachusetts, in 1950 as *Under Sail and In Port in the Glorious 1850's, Being the Journal from 1 May to 3 October 1852 kept by Charlotte A. Page.* Alvin Page Johnson, editor. Introduction and notes.

PEABODY, Cornelia Marshall (Mrs. Enoch). Journal April 26 to August 9, 1855, on board packet ship *Neptune.* Original held by Charles Runyon. Typed transcript in Manuscripts Collection, RF 521, G. W. Blunt White Library, Mystic Seaport Museum, Mystic, Connecticut.

PEIRCE, Harriet. Child's diary kept on whaling bark *Emerald,* 1857. The Kendall Whaling Museum, Sharon, Massachusetts.

PENDLETON, Marietta. Reminiscent account of her early life on the *Emma T. Crowell.* Oral history. Typescript headed "The Early Life of Miss Marietta Pendleton." Stephen Phillips Memorial Library, Penobscot Marine Museum, Searsport, Maine.

PENNIMAN, Augusta (Mrs. Edward). Diary kept on whaling bark *Minerva,* 1864–68. Cape Cod National Seashore, Eastham, Massachusetts. Published as *Augusta Penniman: Journal of a Whaling Voyage 1864–1868,* with a foreword by Dorinda Partsch. Eastham, Massachusetts: Eastern National Park and Monument Association, 1988.

PORTER, Sophie (Mrs. William). Journal kept on whaling bark *Jesse H. Freeman,* 1894–96. Old Dartmouth Historical Society–New Bedford Whaling Museum, New Bedford, Massachusetts.

POTTER, Addie (Mrs. Sylvanus). Fragment written in the logbook of the whaleship *Emma C. Jones,* June 1879. Old Dartmouth Historical Society–New Bedford Whaling Museum, New Bedford, Massachusetts.

PRAY, Emma S. (Mrs. Samuel). Journal kept on *Governor Goodwin,* 1888–89.

Log 1888G, Phillips Library, Peabody Essex Museum, Salem, Massachusetts.

PRITCHARD, Emily. Diary, 1865. Photocopied excerpts at Custom House Maritime Museum, Newburyport, Massachusetts.

PRITCHARD, Katurah (Mrs. Thomas). Journal kept on brig *Massachusetts,* 1848–49. Log 656 1847–49M, Peabody Essex Museum, Salem, Massachusetts.

RAIRDEN, Mary Tarbox (Mrs. Bradstreet). Travel diaries kept on board bark *Henry Warren* of Bath, Maine. The first begins January 21 and ends on September 26, 1851. A second diary was kept on the same vessel on a voyage to Havana, Cuba, beginning November 27, 1851, and ending April 5, 1852. G94.81, Maine Maritime Museum, Bath, Maine.

RAYNOR, Ettabel. Journal on board *Ruth B. Cobb,* Captain Eugene Raynor, 1915. Three Village Historical Society, East Setauket, Long Island, New York.

RICKETSON, Annie (Mrs. Daniel). Journal kept on the whaling bark *A. R. Tucker,* 1871–74. The Kendall Whaling Museum, Sharon, Massachusetts. Published in 1958 by the Old Dartmouth Historical Society as *Mrs. Ricketson's Whaling Journal.* Philip Purrington, editor. Also journals kept on the whaling schooner *Pedro Varela,* 1881–83 and 1885. The Kendall Whaling Museum, Sharon, Massachusetts.

ROWLAND, Mary Satterly (Mrs. Henry). Collection, including two journals, written on brig *Thomas W. Rowland,* October 1855 to July 1857, and brig *Mary E. Rowland,* January 17 to May 20, 1867, and May 25 to July 10, 1867. Also, a sea letter to Hannah Smith, February 10 to April 12, 1870, along with another initially dated January 1, 1873, and shorter letters home, several overlapping the *Thomas W. Rowland* voyage, June 1866 to March 9, 1871. Courtesy Rowland Randall family. Three Village Historical Society, East Setauket, Long Island, New York.

RUSSELL, Mary (Mrs. Laban). Sea letter written on the London whaleship *Emily,* 1823–24. Nantucket Historical Association, Nantucket, Massachusetts. Lengthy extracts published in Edouard Stackpole's book *Whales and Destiny: The Rivalry Between America, France, and Britain for Control of the Southern Whale Fishery, 1785–1825.* Amherst: University of Massachusetts Press, 1972.

SEARS, Bethia K. (Mrs. Elisha). Sea letter addressed to "My Dear Sisters," kept on clipper *Wild Ranger,* 1855–56. Log 656 1855–56W, Phillips Library, Peabody Essex Museum, Salem, Massachusetts.

SHERMAN, Marianna (Mrs. Wanton). Diary kept on whaleship *Nimrod,*

1848. Nicholson Whaling Collection, Providence Public Library, Rhode Island.

SLOCUM, Sarah Jane (Mrs. George). Logbook kept on whaleship *Mary & Martha,* 1851–52. G. W. Blunt White Library, Mystic Seaport Museum, Mystic, Connecticut.

SMITH, Lucy (Mrs. George). Journal kept on whaling bark *Nautilus,* 1869–74. Nicholson Whaling Collection, Providence Public Library, Rhode Island.

SMITH, Marian (Mrs. Horace). Letter dated May 16, 1895, in the Bering Sea on board the steam whaler *Norwhal,* quoted by Elizabeth H. Kugler in "Chasing the Bowhead: Letters from a New Bedford Whaling Captain's Wife," *Cape Cod Life,* vol. 13, no. 3 (July 1991): 41–47. Also logbook kept on whaling bark *California,* 1898–99. Old Dartmouth Historical Society–New Bedford Whaling Museum, New Bedford, Massachusetts.

SMITH, Sallie (Mrs. Frederick). Diary kept on whaling bark *Ohio,* 1875–78, and also on the whaling bark *John P. West,* 1882–84. G. W. Blunt White Library, Mystic Seaport Museum, Mystic, Connecticut.

SNELL, Mary H. (Mrs. Nicholas). Journal kept on the ship *Victoria,* 1839, from Boston to New Orleans. Log 1845A3, Phillips Library, Peabody Essex Museum, Salem, Massachusetts.

SORENSEN, Burgess (later Mrs. Coghill). Reminiscent account of a childhood aboard the *Snow & Burgess.* Published as *When God Was an Atheist Sailor.* New York: W. W. Norton, 1990.

STARK, Mary (Mrs. Henry). Letters April 5, 1855, to January 27, 1856, all written on clipper *B. F. Hoxie.* Manuscripts Collection, VFM 196, G. W. Blunt White Library, Mystic Seaport Museum, Mystic, Connecticut.

STARRETT, Ellen Cutler. Diaries, 1863–65. Privately owned. Refer to Penobscot Marine Museum, Searsport, Maine.

STETSON, Elizabeth (Mrs. Charles). Journal kept on the whaling bark *Elizabeth Corning,* 1860–65. The Kendall Whaling Museum, Sharon, Massachusetts.

STICKNEY, Mary (Mrs. Almon). Diary kept on whaling bark *Cicero,* 1880–81. Nicholson Whaling Collection, Providence Public Library, Rhode Island.

STODDARD, Carolyn A. Journal kept on ship *Kathay,* 1856. Begins March 23, ends November 2, homeward bound. Log 1856K, Phillips Library, Peabody Essex Museum, Salem, Massachusetts.

STOTT, Anna (later Mrs. King). Reminiscences of a childhood on the whaling ship *Northern Light,* 1851. Published in *Old-Time New England* 48:2 (1957).

STOVER, Calista (Mrs. Joseph). Various letters 1866–91, diaries 1876–82, June–July 1882, 1888–89, along with memoranda and various ephemera; also an essay written in 1888 by her daughter Maria, all on ship *Daniel Barnes.* Manuscripts Collection, coll. 105, G. W. Blunt White Library, Mystic Seaport Museum, Mystic, Connecticut.

SWAIN, Harriet (Mrs. Obed II). Journal kept on the whaleship *Catawba,* 1852–55. Nantucket Historical Association, Nantucket, Massachusetts.

TABER, Asenath (later Mrs. McFarlin). Child's diary on the whaling bark *Alice Frazier,* 1854–55. Mariners' Museum, Newport News, Virginia.

TABER, Sarah (Mrs. Daniel). Journals kept on the whaleship *Copia* and in Honolulu, 1848–50, on passage on the *Julian,* 1851, and on the whaleship *Alice Frazier,* 1851–55. Mariners' Museum, Newport News, Virginia.

THOMAS, Emma (Mrs. Albert). Letters written on the whaling bark *Merlin,* 1872. Old Dartmouth Historical Society–New Bedford Whaling Museum, New Bedford, Massachusetts. Quoted extensively in *Saga of a Yankee Whaleman,* written by Sylvia Thomas and published in 1981 by the Old Dartmouth Historical Society.

THOMSON, Kate Morse (Mrs. Albert). Partial journal on the *J. T. Chapman,* 1891. Courtesy Mrs. Edward Sewall, Jr. A photocopy is on file as SM 8/23, Maine Maritime Museum, Bath, Maine.

TODD, Sarah Hix (Mrs. Edward). Journal kept on *Revely,* April 17, 1857, to April 17, 1858; shore journal April 22, 1858, to December 15, 1858, then incomplete journal kept on clipper *Comet.* Collection includes a fifteen-page narrative based on the journal and family history, composed about 1923 by a descendant, Leanna Almy Hicks Hanson. Manuscripts Collection, Log 900, G. W. Blunt White Library, Mystic Seaport Museum, Mystic, Connecticut.

TOWER, Betsy (Mrs. William). Diary kept on whaleship *Moctezuma,* 1847–49. Old Dartmouth Historical Society–New Bedford Whaling Museum, New Bedford, Massachusetts.

TURNER, Carrie (Mrs. Charles). Journals kept on the whaling bark *Napoleon,* 1878–82 and 1885. International Marine Archives. Old Dartmouth Historical Society–New Bedford Whaling Museum, New Bedford, Massachusetts.

UNDERWOOD, Eliza (Mrs. Michael). Partial journal kept on London whaleship *Kingsdown,* 1830. Dixson Library, State Library of New South Wales, Australia.

VEEDER, Susan (Mrs. Charles). Journal kept on whaleship *Nauticon,* 1848–53. International Marine Archives. Old Dartmouth Historical Society–New Bedford Whaling Museum, New Bedford, Massachusetts.

WALDRON, Elizabeth (Mrs. Nelson). Diary kept on whaleship *Bowditch,* 1853. Privately owned in Chester, Vermont. Microfilm at New Bedford Free Public Library, New Bedford, Massachusetts.

WALLIS, Mary Davis Cook (Mrs. Benjamin). Detailed journals kept on trading bark *Zotoff,* the first beginning July 22, 1844, and ending June 23, 1848, the second beginning October 12, 1848, and ending July 18, 1850. These two journals were published in 1851 as *Life in Feejee, or, Five Years Among the Cannibals,* by William Heath of Boston. Her third journal, kept on the *Maid of Orleans* from May 20, 1851, to June 1, 1853, was published jointly by the Institute of Pacific Studies, Suva, Fiji, and the Peabody Essex Museum, Salem, Massachusetts, in 1994. Edited by David Routledge. Original held at the Peabody Essex Museum, micro. 144.

WEST, Gertrude (Mrs. Ellsworth). Diary kept on whaling bark *Horatio,* 1898. The Kendall Whaling Museum, Sharon, Massachusetts.

WHELDON, Clara (Mrs. Alexander). Sea letters written on the whaling bark *John Howland,* 1864. Location of originals unknown. Typescript copies at the Old Dartmouth Historical Society–New Bedford Whaling Museum, New Bedford, Massachusetts.

WICKS, Adelaide (Mrs. Rodolphus). Diary kept on whaling bark *Coral,* 1888–89. Published in 1980 by the Descendants of Whaling Masters in New Bedford as *My Dear Husband.* Edited by Genevieve M. Darden.

WILLIAMS, Eliza (Mrs. Thomas). Journal kept on whaleship *Florida,* 1858–61. Published as *One Whaling Family.* Harold Williams, editor. Boston: Houghton Mifflin, 1964.

WINN, Hannah C. Stimpson (Mrs. Joseph Jr.). Journal kept on ship *St. Paul,* 1837–38. Log 1837S4, Phillips Library, Peabody Essex Museum, Salem, Massachusetts.

WOOD, Isabel "Bel" (Mrs. Aaron). Letters 1873 to 1895 on ships *Sagamore* and *Sovereign of the Seas.* Manuscripts Collection, VFM 1496, G. W. Blunt White Library, Mystic Seaport Museum, Mystic, Connecticut.

WOOLDRIDGE, Emily (Mrs. Richard). Reminiscent account of voyage and shipwreck on the *Maid of Athens,* voyage beginning November 1869, on the way to Callao, Peru. Published as *The Wreck of the "Maid of Athens," Being the Journal of Emily Wooldridge, 1869–1870.* Edited and illustrated by Laurence Irving. New York: Macmillan, 1953.

WYER, Charlotte (Mrs. Samuel). Journal kept on passage on the *Harriet Irving,* 1853, and on the whaleship *Young Hero,* 1853–54. Nantucket Historical Association, Nantucket, Massachusetts.

YORK, Helen C. (Mrs. Andrew). Diaries kept on board coasting (tern) schooner *Benjamin C. Cromwell,* November 10, 1885, to May 19, 1886, and December 25, 1889, to January 11, 1890. Maine Maritime Museum, Bath, Maine.

YOUNG, Elizabeth (later Mrs. Linklater). Memoir of a childhood at sea on the ships commanded by her father. Published as *Child Under Sail.* London: Jonathan Cape, 1938.

Logs, Journals, and Letters Written by Seamen

BAGLEY, Captain William Henry. Log of the ship *Levi C. Wade,* 1880. MS–1–F17 G67.2234, Maine Maritime Museum, Bath, Maine.

BENEDICT, Thomas III. Journal on *Houqua,* April 4 to December 5, 1846, Captain Nathaniel B. Palmer. Manuscripts Collection, Log 951, G. W. Blunt White Library, Mystic Seaport Museum, Mystic, Connecticut.

BROWN, Captain Edwin Peter. Letter to his wife, Martha, written at San Francisco, June 2, 1853. Oysterponds Historical Society, Orient, Long Island, New York.

COFFIN, Captain James D. Journal on Canadian whaleship *Athol,* 1845–49, quoted at length by Rodrigue Levesque in "Canadian Whalers in Micronesia (1840–1850)," *Journal of Pacific History* 14 (October 2, 1989): 225–37. It begins July 22, 1845: "Well, I have commenced another long voyage, one that I hope may prove at least as satisfactory as my former ones. This is my 5th voyage. I began in 1834, when I was about 20 years of age. I was then fired with love and ambition. A good reputation was my aim. To make my fair one happy and to know that she thought much of me was my delight. It is now '45. Eleven years, eventful years have flown. I can not say but I have attained and enjoyed as much as I could reasonably expect, and I have now embarked on another voyage which has, for its only novelty, my having my wife and child with me. . . ."

CONGDON, John Remington, undated heading to logbook kept on brig *Sacramento,* 1850; letter to daughter Mary, dated September 5, 1862. Rhode Island Historical Society, Providence, Rhode Island.

ESSEX, Fred. Reminiscences of a voyage as passenger on the *Emma T. Crowell* from Shanghai to New York about 1886. Captain Andrew Pendleton had his wife, son, and daughter on board. A very amusing and quotable account, called "A Pilgrimage Across the Pacific." Stephen Phillips Library, Penobscot Marine Museum, Searsport, Maine.

GRAY, Horatio Nelson. Journal on ship *Charlotte Reed,* 1850. Journal on bark *Cossack,* 1859–60. Manuscripts Collection, coll. 89, vols. 7 and 8, G. W. Blunt White Library, Mystic Seaport Museum, Mystic, Connecticut.

HASKELL, Mark W. Journal on *Castillian,* 1853–54. Manuscripts Collection, Log 741, G. W. Blunt White Library, Mystic Seaport Museum, Mystic, Connecticut.

JONES, Captain Benjamin. Letters to "sister" and "Brother Scud," June 3, 1868. Three Village Historical Society, East Setauket, Long Island, New York.

JONES, Walter. Local diary, kept in Setauket, 1855–90. Notes of local inhabitants, mentions of Rowland and Jones families. Property of Steve Poulos. Typescript copy at Three Village Historical Society, East Setauket, Long Island, New York.

MORGAN, Nathaniel S. Journal kept on whaleship *Hannibal* of New London, Captain Sluman L. Gray, 1849–51. Manuscripts Collection, Log 862, G. W. Blunt White Library, Mystic Seaport Museum, Mystic, Connecticut.

MORTIMER, Edmund. Journal on *St. James,* 1893, Captain Fred Clifford. A greenhand's account. Manuscripts Collection, Log 775, G. W. Blunt White Library, Mystic Seaport Museum, Mystic, Connecticut.

MURPHY, James Wilder. Letter to "My dear mother," dated August 1, 1898. Hennessey papers, MS-53, Box 14, Maine Maritime Museum, Bath, Maine.

PULSIFER, Freeman. Travel diary, 1859–60. Peabody Essex Museum, Salem, Massachusetts. Pulsifer was a passenger on the *Mary & Louisa,* which had Mrs. Benjamin Jones on board.

SEARS, Captain Elisha. Undated letter detailing his wife's illness and death. With Log 1855–6W, Phillips Library, Peabody Essex Museum, Salem, Massachusetts.

Published Books and Articles

Albion, Robert G. *Square-Riggers on Schedule: The New York Sailing Packets to England, France, and the Cotton Ports.* Princeton, N.J.: Princeton University Press, 1938.

————, William A. Baker, and Benjamin W. Labaree. *New England and the Sea.* Mystic, Ct.: Mystic Seaport Museum, 1972.

Arro, Hans. "A Survivor's Account." In P. John R. Mathieson, *Master of the Moving Sea.* Gladys M. O. Gowland, editor. Flagstaff, Ariz.: J. F. Colton & Co., 1959. Pp. 65–77.

Ashworth, Diana. "Woman's Journal Tells of Hardship on a Whaling Journey of the 1800s." *Rutland* (Vermont) *Daily Herald,* August 22, 1994. Account of descendant's research on Elizabeth Waldron.

Atkins, Mary. *The Diary of Mary Atkins, A Sabbatical in the Eighteen Sixties.* Introduction by Aurelia Henry Reinhardt. Oakland, Calif.: The Eucalyptus Press, Mills College, 1937. Illustrations, map on endpapers.

Bailey, Paul. *Long Island: A History of Two Great Counties, Nassau & Suffolk.* New York: Lewis Historical Publishing, 1949.

Balano, James W., ed. *The Log of the Skipper's Wife.* Camden, Maine: Down East Books, 1979.

Barker, Howard C. "John Conway Took Wife on Voyage." *Inquirer and Mirror* (Nantucket, Mass.), December 14, 1952.

Bates, D. B. (Mrs.). *Incidents on Land and Water, or Four Years on the Pacific Coast. Being a Narrative of the Burning of the Ships Nonantum, Humayoon and Fanchon, Together with Many Startling Adventures on Sea and Land.* Boston: J. French, 1857.

Bateson, Charles. *Gold Fleet for California: Forty-niners from Australia and New Zealand.* Auckland: Minerva, 1963.

Battick, John. "The Searsport Thirty-Six: Seafaring Wives of a Maine Community in 1880." *American Neptune* 37 (1977): 203–18.

Bird, Isabella L. *Six Months in the Sandwich Islands.* 1875. Honolulu: University of Hawaii Press, 1966.

Bolster, W. Jeffrey. "Every Inch a Man: Gender in the Lives of African-American Seamen, 1800–1860." In Margaret S. Creighton and Lisa Norling, editors, *Iron Men, Wooden Women: Gender and Seafaring in the Atlantic World, 1700–1920.* Baltimore: Johns Hopkins University Press, 1996. Pp. 138–68.

Bone, Alexander H. *Bowsprit Ashore.* London: Jonathan Cape, 1932.

Bonham, Julia. "Feminist and Victorian: The Paradox of the American Seafaring Woman of the Nineteenth Century." *American Neptune* 37 (1977): 203–208.

Bordages, Asa. "Women Against the Sea." Series in the *New York World-Telegram,* May 1934.

Brassey, Lady Annie. *Around the World in the Yacht "Sunbeam," Our Home on the Ocean for Eleven Months.* New York: Henry Holt & Co., 1878.

Brewington, Dorothy E. R. *Marine Paintings and Drawings in Mystic Seaport Museum.* Mystic, Ct.: Mystic Seaport Museum, 1982.

Brewster, Mary Louisa Burtch. *"She Was a Sister Sailor": The Whaling Journals of Mary Brewster, 1845–1851*. Joan Druett, editor. Foreword by Honore Forster. Introduction by Benjamin W. Labaree. Mystic, Ct.: Maritime History Association, 1992.

Brock, Susan E. *Doubling Cape Horn*. Privately published. Nantucket, 1926.

Brown, Anne Augusta Fitch. *Diary of 1870*, Agate Brown Collord, editor. Privately published in a limited edition.

Brown, Martha Smith Brewer. *She Went A-Whaling: The Journal of Martha Smith Brewer Brown from Orient, Long Island, New York, Around the World on the Whaling Ship "Lucy Ann," 1847–1849*. Anne MacKay, editor. Foreword by Joan Druett. Introduction by Donald H. Boerum. Orient, N.Y.: Oysterponds Historical Society, 1993. Includes biography, genealogical charts, letters, illustrations.

Bruff, Nancy. *The Manatee*. Bognor Regis, Sussex: John Crowther, 1946. A novel.

Carter, Isabel Hopestill. *Shipmates: A Tale of the Seafaring Women of New England*. New York: William R. Scott, 1934. Published in England in 1934 by Hodder & Stoughton under the title *All Sails Set*. Fiction, but closely based on the author's childhood experiences.

Chapelle, Howard I. *The History of American Sailing Ships*. New York: W. W. Norton, 1935.

Chapman, Angie H. *Windjammer Bride: The Journal of Angie H. Chapman's Voyages on the Maine-built Sailing Ship "Leading Wind."* Elizabeth Balmer, editor. Damariscotta, Maine: Chapman-Hall House, 1979. Angie Chapman's husband was Captain Francis M. Hinckley; the *Leading Wind* was a ship of 1,208 tons, and the voyage took place in 1885.

Child, Frank and Frances. *The Search for the Schooner "Palestine."* Port Jefferson, N.Y.: Port Jefferson Historical Society, 1989.

"Children on Blue Water." *New York Times*, December 22, 1889.

Clark, Arthur H. *The Clipper Ship Era: An Epitome of Famous American and British Clipper Ships, Their Owners, Builders, Commanders, and Crews, 1843–1869*. New York: G. P. Putnam's Sons, 1910.

Clinton, Audrey. "Clipper Ship Days." *Newsday*, March 2, 1961.

Cluff, John A. "A New England Seafaring Family." *American Neptune*, July 1959.

Coghill, Burgess (Sorensen). *When God Was an Atheist Sailor*. 1985. New York: W. W. Norton, 1990. Reminiscent account of a childhood aboard the *Snow & Burgess*. Illustrations, ship plans, appendix.

Colby, Barnard L. *For Oil and Buggy Whips: Whaling Captains of New London County, Connecticut.* Mystic, Ct.: Mystic Seaport Museum, 1990.

Colcord, Joanna. "Domestic Life in American Sailing Ships." *American Neptune* 2 (1942): 193–202.

Cooper, Diane E. "She Dressed Herself in Sailors' Clothes . . ." *Sea Letter* (National Maritime Museum Assn., San Francisco) 49 (Fall/Winter 1994): 2–11.

Cott, Nancy. *The Bonds of Womanhood: "Woman's Sphere" in New England, 1780–1935.* New Haven, Ct.: Yale University Press, 1977.

Crapo, Thomas. *Strange, but True: Life and Adventures of Capt. Thomas Crapo and Wife.* William J. Cowin, editor. New Bedford, Mass., 1893.

Cutler, Carl. *Greyhounds of the Sea.* Annapolis, Md.: Naval Institute Press, 1961.

Dana, Richard Henry. *Two Years Before the Mast.* New York: Harper & Brothers, 1840. Available in several reprint editions.

De Freycinet, Rose. *A Woman of Courage.* Marc Serge Riviere, editor and translator. Canberra: National Library of Australia, 1996. Journal and family correspondence.

De Pauw, Linda Grant. *Seafaring Women.* Boston: Houghton Mifflin Co., 1982.

"Distinguished Career of Captain J. F. Murphy Ends." *Bath* (Maine) *Daily Times,* April 15, 1912. Obituary.

Doane, Benjamin. *Following the Sea.* Heather M. Doane Atkinson, editor. Halifax: Nimbus Publishing and Nova Scotia Museum, 1987.

Druett, Joan. *Petticoat Whalers: Whaling Wives at Sea, 1820–1920.* Auckland: Collins, 1991.

———. "Petticoat Whalers," *Seaport* (South Street Seaport Museum, New York City) XXIX:1 (Spring 1995): 8–13.

———. "Those Female Journals." *The Log of Mystic Seaport* 40 (Winter 1988): 115–24.

———. *Captain's Daughter, Coasterman's Wife: Carrie Hubbard Davis of Orient.* Orient, N.Y.: Oysterponds Historical Society, 1995.

———, and Mary Anne Wallace. *The Sailing Circle: 19th Century Seafaring Women from New York.* Introduction by Lisa Norling. East Setauket, N.Y.: Three Village Historical Society/Cold Spring Harbor Whaling Museum, 1995. Illustrations, appendices, index.

Dulles, Foster Rhea. *America in the Pacific—A Century of Expansion.* Boston: Houghton Mifflin, 1938.

Duncan, Fred. *Deepwater Family.* Afterword by Karl Kortum. New York: Pantheon, 1969. Illustrations and glossary.

Engle, Eloise, and Arnold S. Lott. *America's Maritime Heritage*. Annapolis: Naval Institute Press, 1975. Foreword, illustrations, index.

Faragher, John Mack. *Women and Men on the Overland Trail*. New Haven, Ct.: Yale University Press, 1979. Many parallels to the seafaring experience.

Frank, Stuart M. *Dictionary of Scrimshaw Artists*. Mystic, Ct.: Mystic Seaport Museum, 1991.

FreeHand, Julianna. *A Seafaring Legacy. The Photographs, Diaries, Letters and Memorabilia of a Maine Sea Captain and His Wife 1859–1908*. New York: Random House, 1981.

Freeman, Hattie Atwood. *A Trip Around the World on Board the Merchantman Bark "Charles Stewart."* Bangor, Maine: On Furbrush, 1907.

Gattey, Charles Nelson. *The Bloomer Girls*. London: Femina Books, 1967.

Gordon, Linda. *Women's Body, Women's Right—A Social History of Birth Control in America*. New York: Grosman, 1976.

Greenhill, Basil, and Ann Giffard. *Women Under Sail. Letters and Journals Concerning Eight Women Travelling or Working in Sail Vessels Between 1829 and 1949*. New York: Great Albion Books, 1971.

Haffey, Joseph C. "The Metamorphosis of the Ship *Alert*, 1828–1862." *The Log of Mystic Seaport*, v. 46, no. 3 (Winter 1994): 66–75.

Hale, Sarah Josepha. *Women's Record, or, Sketches of all Distinguished Women, from the Creation to A.D. 1854* . . . New York: Harper & Brothers, 1855. The preface, beginning "The want of the world is moral power," is quite illuminating.

Harris, Max, ed. *1811 Dictionary of the Vulgar Tongue*. London: Bibliophile Books, 1984.

Hawkins, Clifford W. *Argosy of Sail. A Photographic History*. Auckland: William Collins, 1980.

Hay, Mary. *I Saw a Ship a Sailing*. London: H. M. Stationery Office, 1981. Account of author's mother's childhood at sea on the *Ladye Doris*, 1903–1909.

Hennessy, Mark W. "Master of Windjammers Rounded Horn 60 Times." *Portland* (Maine) *Sunday Telegram*, March 7, 1954.

"Heroic Conduct of a Woman" (story of Mary Ann Patten). *Whalemen's Shipping Paper & Merchants' Transcript* (New Bedford, Mass.), March 3, 1857.

Howe, Octavius T., and Frederick C. Matthews. *American Clipper Ships 1833–1858*. Two volumes. Salem, Mass.: Marine Research Society, 1926–27.

Humiston, Fred. *Blue Water Men—and Women*. Portland, Maine: Guy Gannett Publishing Co., 1965.

"An Intrepid Woman" (story of Mrs. Howe). *Whalemen's Shipping Paper & Merchants' Transcript* (New Bedford, Mass.), July 30, 1867.

Jernegan, M. W., ed. "A Child's Diary on a Whaling Voyage." *The New England Quarterly* 11:1 (1929).

Kugler, Elizabeth H. "Chasing the Bowhead: Letters from a New Bedford Whaling Captain's Wife." *Cape Cod Life,* vol. 13, no. 3 (July 1991): 41–47.

Langdon, Robert. *American Whalers and Traders in the Pacific: A Guide to Records on Microfilm.* Canberra: Pacific Manuscripts Bureau, Australian National University, 1978.

Lawrence, Mary Chipman. *The Captain's Best Mate: The Journal of Mary Chipman Lawrence on the Whaler "Addison," 1856–1860.* Edited and with introduction and appendices by Stanton Garner. Providence, R.I.: Brown University Press, 1966.

Lawson, Will. *Blue Gum Clippers and Whaleships of Tasmania.* Hobart: Shiplovers' Society of Tasmania, 1949. Illustrations, index, discursive list of wrecks.

Leavitt, John F. *Wake of the Coasters.* Mystic, Ct.: Mystic Seaport Museum, 1970.

Levesque, Rodrigue. "Canadian Whalers in Micronesia (1840–1850)." *Journal of Pacific History* 14 (October 2, 1989): 225–37.

Linklater, Elizabeth Young. *Child Under Sail.* London: Jonathan Cape/New York: Farrar & Rinehart, 1938.

Lowell, Joan. *The Cradle of the Deep.* Illustrated by Kurt Wiese. New York: Simon & Schuster, 1929.

MacGregor, David R. *The Tea Clippers: Their History and Development.* London: Conway Maritime Press, 1952.

"Maine Schooners Sought for Inter-American Trade." *Portland* (Maine) *Press Herald,* July 21, 1942.

Malley, Richard C. Graven by the Fishermen Themselves: Scrimshaw in Mystic Seaport Museum. Mystic, Ct.: Mystic Seaport Museum, 1983.

———. "On Shore in a Foreign Land: Mary Stark in the Kingdom of Hawaii." *The Log of Mystic Seaport* 37:3 (Fall 1985): 79–92.

Mathieson, P. John R. *Master of the Moving Sea.* Gladys M. O. Gowland, editor. Flagstaff, Ariz.: J. F. Colton & Co., 1959. Captain Mathieson's memoirs.

Meisel, Irene. "Nanny at Sea." *Seaport* (South Street Seaport Museum, New York City) XXIX:1 (Spring 1995): 14–17.

Morgan, Charles. "New England Coasting Schooners." *American Neptune,* January 1963.

Morrell, Abby Jane Wood (Mrs. Benjamin). *Narrative of a Voyage to the Ethiopic and South Atlantic Ocean, Indian Ocean . . .* New York: J. & J. Harper, 1833. Reprint: Saddle River, N.J.: The Gregg Press, 1970.

Morris, Paul C. *American Sailing Coasters of the North Atlantic.* Chardon, Ohio: Bloch and Osborn Publishing Co., 1973.

Mortland, Donald F. *Lincoln Colcord: At Sea and at Home.* Searsport, Maine: Penobscot Marine Museum, 1985.

Myers, Sandra L. *Westering Women and the Frontier Experience 1800–1915.* Albuquerque: University of New Mexico Press, 1982.

Noble, Richard B. "Captain 'Shotgun' Murphy and the 'SHENANDOAH.' " Unidentified magazine article. Hennessy Papers, coll. 53, Maine Maritime Museum, Bath, Maine.

Nordhoff, Charles. *Life on the Ocean.* First published in Cincinnati in 1874. Facsimile reprint. London: MacDonald and Jane's, 1974.

Norling, Lisa. "Contrary Dependencies. Whaling Agents and Whalemen's Families." *The Log of Mystic Seaport* 41 (1990): 3–12.

———. "How Fraught with Sorrow and Heartpangs: Mariners' Wives and the Ideology of Domesticity in New England, 1790–1880." *New England Quarterly* 65 (September 1992): 433–46.

Overton, Jacqueline. *Long Island's Story.* New York: Doubleday, 1929.

Page, Charlotte A. *Under Sail and In Port in the Glorious 1850's.* Alvin Page Johnson (the diarist's son), editor. Salem, Mass.: Peabody Museum, 1950.

Parker, Mary Anne. *A Voyage Around the World.* 1795. Facsimile reprint. Sydney: Hordern House for the Australian National Maritime Museum, 1994.

Parker, Lt. W. J. Lewis. *The Great Coal Schooners of New England 1870–1909.* Mystic, Ct.: Maritime History Association, 1948.

Petroski, Catherine. *A Bride's Passage: Susan Hathorn's Year Under Sail.* Boston: Northeastern University Press, 1997. Maps, illustrations, appendices, notes, index.

Pfeiffer, Ida Reyer. *A Woman's Journey Round the World: From Vienna to Brazil, Chili, Tahiti, China, Hindostan, Persia, and Asia Minor.* London: Office of the National Illustrated Library, 1852.

Pope-Hennessy, Una. *Three Englishwomen in America.* London: Ernest Benn, 1929.

Railton, Arthur. "Jared Jernegan's Second Family." *The Dukes County Intelligencer,* vol. 28, no. 2 (November 1986): 51–91. Includes the story of Helen Jernegan's passage from Martha's Vineyard to San Francisco to join her husband.

Ritter, Thomas. *A Medical Manual and Medical Chest Companion for Popular Use in Families and on Ship-Board.* Burt Printing House: New York, 1890.

Robinson, Edith Derby. "Mutiny on the Thayer." *Long Island Forum,* May 1941. Pp. 107–108.

Schwabel, Peg Connolly. "Yankee Women at Sea." *New Bedford* 4:3 (1984): 52–54.

Sharf, Frederic A. "Melville B. Cook: A Traveler in Meiji Japan." In *Meiji Japan, A Sailor's Visit.* Bath, Maine: Maine Maritime Museum, 1996. Exhibition catalogue.

Smith, Egbert Bull. *Voyage of the "Two Sisters."* New York: Albert B. Kind & Co., 1908.

Smythers, Ruth. *Instruction and Advice for the Young Bride on the Conduct and Procedure of the Intimate and Personal Relationships of the Marriage State for the Greater Spiritual Sanctity of this Blessed Sacrament and the Glory of God.* New York: Spiritual Guidance Press, 1894. Supplement to the *Madison Institute Newsletter.*

Springer, Haskell. "The Captain's Wife at Sea." In *Iron Men, Wooden Women: Gender and Seafaring in the Atlantic World, 1700–1920.* Margaret S. Creighton and Lisa Norling, editors. Baltimore: Johns Hopkins University Press, 1996. Pp. 92–117.

Starbuck, Alexander. *History of the American Whale-Fishery . . .* 1876. Secaucus, N.J.: Castle Books, 1989.

Stark, Suzanne J. "Mates at Sea: The Adventures of 19th-Century Captains' Wives." *Seaport* (South Street Seaport Museum, New York City) XX:1 (Spring 1986): 24–29.

Strong, Kate W. "Down to the Sea in Ships." *Long Island Forum,* October 1956: 187–88.

————. "The Bark Mary and Louise." *Long Island Forum,* December 1954: 235.

Tabili, Laura. "A Maritime Race: Masculinity and the Racial Division of Labor in British Merchant Ships, 1900–1939." In *Iron Men, Wooden Women: Gender and Seafaring in the Atlantic World, 1700–1920.* Margaret S. Creighton and Lisa Norling, editors. Baltimore: Johns Hopkins University Press, 1996. Pp. 169–88.

Vicinus, Martha. *Suffer and Be Still.* Bloomington: Indiana University Press, 1972.

Villiers, Alan, et al. *Men, Ships, and the Sea.* Washington, D.C.: National Geographic Society, 1962. Maps, illustrations, foreword, index.

[Wallis, Mary Davis Cook.] *Life in Feejee, or, Five Years Among the Cannibals.* By a Lady. Boston: William Heath, 1851.

Wallis, Mary Davis Cook. *The Fiji and New Caledonia Journals of Mary Wallis 1851–1853.* David Routledge, editor. Fiji: Institute of Pacific Studies/ Salem, Mass.: Peabody Essex Museum, 1994. Illustrations, maps, introduction by the editor, references, glossary, index. Wallis's journal on the *Maid of Orleans.*

Wasson, George S. *Sailing Days on the Penobscot.* New York: W. W. Norton, 1949.

Webb, Robert Lloyd. "Tinned Light: The Case-Oil Trade to Meiji Japan." In *Meiji Japan, A Sailor's Visit.* Bath, Maine: Maine Maritime Museum, 1996. Pp. 21–48.

Weinstein, Robert A. *Tall Ships on Puget Sound. The Marine Photographs of Wilhelm Hester.* Seattle: Washington University Press, 1978.

———. "Elegance Afloat. Captains' Quarters in Victorian Sailing Ships." *Seaport* (South Street Seaport Museum, New York City) XX:1 (Spring 1986): 20–23.

Welter, Barbara. "The Cult of True Womanhood 1820–1860." *American Quarterly* 18 (Summer 1966): 151–74.

Woodward, Helen. *The Lady Persuaders.* New York: Ivan Obolensky, 1960. See especially pp. 1–31.

Wooldridge, Emily. *The Wreck of the "Maid of Athens," Being the Journal of Emily Wooldridge, 1869–1870.* Laurence Irving, editor and illustrator. London: Macmillan, 1953.

Unpublished Research Papers

Brouwer, Norman. "Life in Deepwater Sailing Ships 1840–1940: A Bibliography and Cumulative Index of First-Person Accounts." Library, South Street Seaport Museum, New York City.

Girard, Susannah J. W. "Calista M. Stover Papers of Bucksport, Maine: 1859–1891." RF 169, G. W. Blunt White Library, Mystic Seaport Museum, Mystic, Connecticut.

Hand, Lindsley. "The Captain's Daughter." Paper on Emma Gray. RF 564, G. W. Blunt White Library, Mystic Seaport Museum, Mystic, Connecticut.

Jackson, Christie. "Exemplifying the Victorian Woman—Be It by Land or by Sea: Material Culture of Transposed Victorian Lifestyles Aboard Ships,

1850–1900." RF 629, G. W. Blunt White Library, Mystic Seaport Museum, Mystic, Connecticut.

Lund, Judith. Letter to author from the New Bedford Whaling Museum, dated May 5, 1995, detailing the experiences of the two wives of Captain Joshua Slocum.

Meisel, Irene. "Floating Parlors: An Examination of Several Long Island Seafaring Captains' Wives, 1855–1875." Commissioned by the Three Village Historical Society and Cold Spring Harbor Whaling Museum, August 1993.

Oaks, Amy. "The *Maid of Athens* in Historical and Social Perspective." A paper on Emily Wooldridge. RF 460, G. W. Blunt White Library, Mystic Seaport Museum, Mystic, Connecticut.

Peruti, Rita F. "Portrait of a Seafaring Lady." Paper on Calista Stover. RF 149, G. W. Blunt White Library, Mystic Seaport Museum, Mystic, Connecticut.

Wallace, Mary Anne. 1993. "Days of Joy and Fear: Nineteenth Century New England Family Life at Sea." Master's thesis, University of Southern Maine.

Worsfold, Louisa. "The Social History of Russell." Auckland Institute & Museum, Auckland, New Zealand.

INDEX

Page numbers in italics refer to illustrations.